INDIA AND THE UNITED STATES

The Cold Peace

TWAYNE'S INTERNATIONAL HISTORY SERIES

Akira Iriye, editor
Harvard University

INDIA AND THE UNITED STATES

The Cold Peace

H. W. Brands
Texas A & M University

TWAYNE PUBLISHERS • BOSTON
A DIVISION OF G. K. HALL & CO.

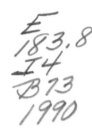

Copyright 1990 by H. W. Brands
All rights reserved
Published by Twayne Publishers
A division of G. K. Hall & Co.
70 Lincoln Street, Boston, Massachusetts 02111

Twayne's International History Series no. 6

Book design by Barbara Anderson
Book production by Gabrielle B. McDonald
Typeset by Huron Valley Graphics, Ann Arbor, Michigan

Printed on permanent/durable acid-free paper
and bound in the United States of America

Library of Congress Cataloging-in-Publication Data

Brands, H. W.
    India and the United States : the cold peace / H.W. Brands.
      p. cm.—(Twayne's international history series ; no. 6)
    Includes bibliographical references.
    1. United States—Foreign relations—India. 2. India—Foreign
relations—United States. 3. United States—Foreign
relations—1945–   4. India—Foreign relations—1947–1984. 5. India—
Foreign relations—1984–   I. Title. II. Series.
E183.8.I4B73 1990
327.73054—dc20   89-77296
                                                        CIP

0-8057-7915-9 (alk. paper) 10 9 8 7 6 5 4 3 2 1
0-8057-9207-4 (pbk. alk. paper) 10 9 8 7 6 5 4 3 2 1

CONTENTS

ILLUSTRATIONS

Illustrations are found between pages 93 and 94.

FOREWORD

Twayne's International History Series seeks to publish reliable and readable accounts of post–World War II international affairs. Today, nearly fifty years after the end of the war, the time seems opportune for a critical assessment of world affairs in the second half of the twentieth century. What themes and trends have characterized international relations since 1945? How have they evolved and changed? What connections have developed between international and domestic affairs? How have states and peoples defined and pursued their objectives, and what have they contributed to the world at large? How have conceptions of warfare and visions of peace changed?

These questions must be raised if one is to arrive at an understanding of the contemporary world that is both international—with an awareness of the linkages among different parts of the world—and historical—with a keen sense of what the immediate past has brought to civilization. Hence Twayne's *International History* Series. It is hoped that the volumes in this series will help the reader to explore important events and decisions since 1945 and develop the global awareness and historical sensitivity required for confronting today's problems.

The first volumes in the series examine the United States' relations with other countries, groups of countries, or regions. The stress on the United States is justified in part because of the nation's predominant position in postwar international relations, and also because far more extensive documentation is available on American foreign affairs than is the case with other countries. The series addresses not only those interested in international relations, but also those studying America's and other countries' histories, who will find here useful guides and fresh insights into the recent past. Now more than ever before, it is imperative to understand the linkages between national history and international history.

This volume offers a fascinating story of the love-hate relationship that has characterized America's and India's dealings with each other since the latter attained independence in 1947. By emphasizing personalities, many of them with strong and even idiosyncratic ideas, H. W. Brands enables the reader to understand why U.S.-Indian relations have so often been charged with emotion, sentiment, and idealism on both sides. But the author, who has written extensively on postwar American foreign policy, puts the bilateral relationship within the framework of U.S. dealings with Asia and with the Third World, for which India has frequently spoken. Thus the book is a good introduction to one of the crucial developments since 1945: the self-conscious emergence of the Third World and America's role in fostering, or frustrating, a stable relationship with it.

Akira Iriye

PREFACE

During the four decades since India achieved independence in 1947, the world's largest democracy and the world's oldest have suffered through a succession of disputes, misunderstandings, and near crises. Relations have never broken down completely, and apostles of harmony between the United States and India have periodically discovered grounds for hope that the situation will improve. But on the whole, and to a far greater degree than most observers expected at the beginning, tension rather than cooperation has characterized the relationship.

This tension followed in part from the disintegration of the antifascist coalition of World War II and the de facto division of the globe into superpower-dominated blocs in the subsequent decade. While the United States organized much of Asia into alliances against the Soviet Union and China, India attempted to remain outside the cold war. Through most of the 1950s, Indian leaders displayed an affinity for the communist countries that many Americans found deeply disturbing, especially when American soldiers engaged Chinese troops in battle between 1950 and 1953. For their part, Indians looked askance at U.S. support for Pakistan, considering Washington's 1954 weapons deal with Karachi a violation of the neutrality of the subcontinent and a threat to India's security. In analogous ways, conflict among the great powers during the next thirty years repeatedly spilled over into the U.S.–Indian arena. As a first approximation, one could often guess the state of relations between Washington and New Delhi from the state of relations among Washington, Moscow, and Beijing.

But considerations of global politics alone cannot explain the distrust that has permeated the U.S.–Indian relationship. Much—at times, most—of the tension and disappointment has arisen from the nature of the two societies involved. Each is culturally self-confident, often to the point of arrogance. Each sees itself in significant ways as a model for the rest of the world. In pressing its claims to international leadership, each has taken umbrage at the competing postulates of the other. Each practices a lively form of democracy, in which foreign policy is judged fair game by dissidents and demagogues. Too similar for outright hostility, too different for real understanding, India and the United States have followed paths that, while never leading quite to collision, have commonly placed the countries in each other's way.

The chapters below attempt to explain U.S.–Indian relations in terms of this interaction between power politics and culture. Because both countries have played a central role in the major events of the postwar period, illuminating relations between them requires explaining the global context in which both have operated. At times, the narrative comes close to being an international history of the cold war. At other times, the focus shifts to developments within the United States or India, to capture the equally important domestic influences—social, cultural, and political—that have shaped the foreign policies of each country.

As becomes evident in the first chapter, the story of American relations with India begins long before Indian independence—indeed, before American independence. The patterns that have characterized the relationship since World War II were already apparent in the early decades of this century. These patterns have persisted to the present, and one suspects that they will continue into the future. Understanding these patterns is vital to understanding where both countries—and with them, much of the world—are bound. For better and for worse, the United States and India are stuck with each other, as they have been for generations.

I am indebted to the numerous scholars on whose work I have relied in producing this volume. They are identified in the Notes and Bibliography. For special thanks I would like to mention Akira Iriye and Robert McMahon, who read the manuscript and offered valuable suggestions and encouragement.

H. W. Brands

Texas A & M University

chapter 1

THE ROOTS OF DISILLUSIONMENT: TO 1945

FIRST BRUSH

Columbus made the initial connection between India and America, although he erred in doing so. But despite his six-thousand-mile navigational mistake, which he went to his grave denying, the Admiral of the Ocean Sea set in motion a train of events that eventually linked the destinies of the two regions. Once the Spanish figured out that their hired Italian pilot had hit the wrong Indies, they bent to exploit the Western ones with energy and success that inflamed the cupidity of their European neighbors. The English, led by the pirate-princes Drake and Raleigh, and the French, whose monarch Francis I demanded to see the clause in Adam's will reserving America to the Iberians, entered the fray with special zeal. By the middle of the eighteenth century, the Anglo–French rivalry had spread around the globe, and the same Seven Years War that won North America for the British also gained for King George a far greater prize: India.

Aside from helping provoke the American colonists to rebellion, the conflict that ended in 1763 contributed to the Americans' knowledge of India. Some soldiers connected with the British imperial army found service in both the North American and the Indian theaters. One American trooper, William Duer, traveled to India and became aide-de-camp to Robert Clive; another, John Parker Boyd, landed a job as quartermaster to the Nizam of Hyderabad. Following the American Revolution, an enterprising trooper in the battle of ideas, William Duane, founded a newspaper in Calcutta in 1791, dedicated to the proposition that "all subjects whatever, ought, of right, to be publicly, openly, and undoubtedly discussed." By this time, the British had seen where such license led, and they deported the would-be Paine.

More enduring links between India and the United States developed in the footsteps of Yankee merchants, who began pursuing the profits of the India trade in the seventeenth century. In 1672, a Connecticutter named Elihu Yale sailed east to win his fortune. Within a decade and a half, he had become governor of the East India Company's fort at Madras. Later, when Connecticut's Collegiate School ran into financial difficulties, the illustrious divine Cotton Mather thought to write for assistance to Governor Yale, who responded by endowing the college with two large trunks of trade goods. Proceeds from the sale gave the college a new lease on life. The transaction also provided the college with a new name.

A subsequent generation of New Englanders had their differences with Yale's successors in the East India Company, to the point of dumping a cargo of the company's tea into Boston harbor. But the India trade remained a staple of American overseas commerce. Operating first out of Salem, Massachusetts (whose town seal bore the legend "*Divitiis Indiae usqua ad ultimum sinum*," or "To the farthest gulf for the wealth of India"), Yankee merchantmen established a traffic that in the early nineteenth century doubled the more noticed China trade.[1]

The Indian–American relationship took a new twist in the 1830s, when American missionaries began traveling to the subcontinent in significant numbers. Earlier, the Reverend Mather had attempted to repay India's favor to Yale College by writing a tract entitled *India Christiana,* in which he laid out a plan for propagating the gospel among India's heathen millions, but the spirit of proselytization did not really take hold until more than a hundred years later. Riding the same wave of reform and expansionism that produced the abolitionist movement and the culture of manifest destiny, and assisted by the insertion of the "pious clause" into the charter of the East India Company, Baptists, Presbyterians, and Congregationalists descended upon India. As missionaries usually do, these uninvited guests struck many of their reluctant hosts as morally arrogant and self-righteous. The impression would stick.

Those few Americans who looked beyond the basic non-Christianity of the subcontinent detected much worth studying. A British Indianist, William Jones, introduced Thomas Jefferson and other curious souls to the major works of Hindu literature and philosophy; later free-thinkers like Ralph Waldo Emerson (whose intellectual coming of age coincided, as one observer put it, "with the stirring of the literary mind of Boston by oriental breezes") built upon this foundation an intriguing, if not quite imposing, edifice. By 1850, Emerson was citing the *Vedas* and the *Bhagavad-Gita.* His 1856 poem *Brahma* attempted to assimilate oriental with occidental thought. Henry David Thoreau continued this effort, applying the results to his idiosyncratic life. Others—Melville, Whitman, Hawthorne, Poe—delved less deeply into the mysteries of the Orient, but by the last decades of the nineteenth century, most literate Americans possessed some notion of Indian ways of thinking.[2]

Of Indian politics, Americans knew far less—and what they did know commonly reflected the chauvinistic and racist ethos of the age. That the anti-British rising of 1857—the so-called Sepoy Mutiny—sent shudders down the spines of southern slave-masters occasions little surprise; that the British got the best of the press through the rest of the United States is more remarkable. In fact, despite their own anticolonial origins, Americans were growing increasingly entranced by the idea of empire. Mark Twain, in *Following the Equator,* applauded the courage of the redcoats in subduing the native masses. Ulysses Grant, on a postpresidential world tour, described himself as "very much pleased with English rule" in India.[3]

But it required the archimperialist Theodore Roosevelt to make the most blatantly apologetic case for the rule of whites in Asia. By Roosevelt's day, the United States had its own empire in the Philippines; not surprisingly, Americans were demonstrating less affinity than ever for the nationalist aspirations of Indians. As TR put it,

> In India we encounter the most colossal example history affords of the successful administration by men of European blood of a thickly populated region in another continent. . . . Indeed, it is a greater feat than was performed under the Roman Empire. . . . If the British control were withdrawn from India, the whole peninsula would become a chaos of bloodshed and violence; all the weaker peoples and the most industrious and law-abiding would be plundered and forced to submit to indescribable oppression and the only beneficiaries among the natives would be the lawless, the violent and the bloodthirsty.

Roosevelt concluded that the administration of India constituted "one of the most notable achievements of the white race during the past two centuries."[4]

The attitudes underlying Roosevelt's claims of superiority took form at a more popular level as well. The first group of Indian immigrants to the United States arrived in the late 1890s. Mostly Sikhs from Punjab, they aroused in their West Coast neighbors the same fear and hostility that the latter had vented on the Chinese for more than a generation. "We don't want these Hindus," a California senator declared, misidentifying the objects of his scorn; "and they should be barred out just as the Chinese are excluded." The senator added that when he returned to Washington, he would "do my best to protect the Pacific coast from the brown horde. . . . There is plenty of room for good citizens, but there is no room at all for fakirs and mendicants." In 1907, a mob of six hundred in Bellingham, Washington, assaulted a community of Indians, injuring many and running the rest out of town. During the next decade, American officials enacted a de facto policy of discouraging Indian immigration; in 1917 and 1924, legislative actions formally slammed the door. Indian poet Rabindranath Tagore, a Nobel laureate who had attracted wide attention during a 1916 visit, noted bitterly that not even Jesus would be able to get into the United States now, "because, first of all, He would not have the necessary money and secondly he would be an Asiatic." Attempting to return in 1929, Tagore encountered what he deemed "barbarous" treatment at the hands of U.S. immigration officials. Incensed, he turned around and left.[5]

Yet something of American idealism remained. A famine in India at the beginning of the century prompted an outpouring of support for an America–India Famine Relief Committee, whose sponsors embraced the notion of human solidarity across racial, religious, and cultural lines. The development in India of organized protest against British rule a few years later—coinciding with the Japanese victory over Russia in the battle of Tsushima Straits, which worked wonders for Asian self-confidence vis-à-vis Europeans—inspired William Jennings Bryan to visit the country for himself. Bryan, the most prominent opponent of American annexation of the Philippines and three-time standard-bearer for the Democratic party, remarked a growing "national spirit" in India that portended great changes. He went on to denounce the British presence in the country.

> Let no one cite India as an argument in defense of colonialism. On the Ganges and the Indus the Briton, in spite of his many notable qualities and his large contribution to the world's advancement, has demonstrated, as have many before, man's inability to exercise with wisdom and justice irresponsible power over helpless people. He has conferred some benefits upon India, but he has extorted a tremendous price for them. While he has boasted of bringing peace to the living, he has led millions to the peace of the grave; while he has dwelt upon order established between warring tribes, he has impoverished the country by legalized pillage.

Another veteran of the antiannexation struggle, capitalist-philanthropist Andrew Carnegie, predicted that good roads and English schools would not satisfy the longing of the Indian people for self-government, although he conceded the sizable material benefits British rule had brought India. Indians, Carnegie declared, knew "the long and glorious struggle of the people against absolute monarchs. . . . They have the story of Washington and the American Revolution." Progressive leader Robert La Follette contrasted the trappings of empire with the reality of Indian life under the British raj: "One hundred million dollars spent for glitter, two million fleshless bodies dead of starvation; one hundred million dollars paid for dazzling pageants, two hundred million hungry people."[6]

WILSONIANISM: PRINCIPLE AND PRACTICE

The election of Woodrow Wilson as president brought the most fluent of the idealists to the apex of American power (and Bryan to the State

Department). After the outbreak of war in Europe, renewed anticolonial agitation in India moved the president to speak in language inspiring to Indian nationalists. Avowing "the rights of nations great and small and the privilege of men everywhere to choose their way of life," Wilson pledged U.S. support for self-determination against colonial oppression. The president's ringing statement prompted the editor of the *Hindustan Ghadar*, the leading organ of Indian expatriates in the United States, to write Wilson that "your declaration to the effect that no people shall be compelled to submit to the yoke of a foreign government raises within us the hope that the time may be near at hand when the cry of India for freedom and self-government will receive sympathetic response by the great Nations of the World."[7]

Unfortunately for the nationalists—and for Indian–American understanding—a pattern that would recur throughout the next seventy years soon emerged in U.S. diplomacy: while sympathizing with Indian aspirations for independence, American leaders placed greater weight on what they considered their own country's security requirements. The remarks of British diplomat Harold Nicolson regarding Wilson's world audience applied particularly to Indians: "The public imagined that what was intended as a doctrine of perfectability was in fact a statement of American intentions." At the rhetorical level, the president spoke of self-determination and national independence; but in the operational sphere, he gave precedence to smooth relations with the allied (or "associated," as the finicky Wilson insisted) powers. When Indian leaders requested that Wilson intercede on behalf of the jailed Annie Besant, an Irish supporter of Indian independence, the State Department derailed the request. Bryan's successor at State, the pro-British Robert Lansing, advised a Wilson aide that the Indian message was "apparently an attempt to use the President to assist the propaganda" of Indian nationalism.[8]

Despite this rebuff, Indian nationalists recognized the advantages the relatively open atmosphere in the United States afforded their movement, and they mounted an anti-British campaign from a base in California. The *Ghadar* ("Revolt") appealed from San Francisco to freedom fighters everywhere:

- Wanted—Brave soldiers to stir up Ghadar in India;
- Pay—Death;
- Prize—Martyrdom;
- Pension—Liberty;
- Field of battle—India.

The message proved effective, and significant numbers of Indians heeded the call. "Hindus Go Home to Fight in Revolution," announced the *Portland Telegram* in August 1914, evincing relief as well as some concern that a source of cheap labor was drying up.[9]

Carrying their case further, a group of Indian nationalists joined what became known as the "Hindu conspiracy"—an unsuccessful attempt to parlay

German financial and political support into a revolutionary uprising against the British in India. The operation was aborted when British agents provided U.S. Justice Department officials with evidence that the group (which included, according to the indictment, fifty-six Indians, twenty-six Germans, and thirteen Americans) had violated U.S. neutrality laws.

The conviction of most of the defendants, combined with the assassination of one of the group's leaders by a codefendant, did considerable harm to the nationalist movement in the United States. The war brought out all the latent insecurities in the American psyche, pitting as it did the ancestral lands of various ethnic groups in the United States against each other. The national unease manifested itself in one direction in the nearly hysterical campaign for "100 percent Americanism." In another direction, it took form in the passage of the grossly unconstitutional Sedition Act. In yet another, it produced the postwar "red scare." As it related to India, the psychological turmoil of the war years, combined with undeniable evidence that Indians in the United States were indeed working with Germany, created an anti-Indian backlash that tended to neutralize American support for India's nationalist goals.

Distracted by these fears and concerns, Americans generally overlooked the Amritsar massacre of April 1919, a seminal event in the development of Indian nationalism. A few die-hard progressives and Anglophobes protested the killing of nearly four hundred demonstrators by British troops: Senator George Norris of Nebraska denounced it as "the bloodiest slaying in late Western history," while Senator Joseph France of Maryland mourned the "unarmed helpless protesting people" who were "ruthlessly mowed down" by the British machine guns. Illinois Representative William Mason went so far as to introduce a resolution encouraging the Wilson administration "to give such recognition without intervention to the people of India who are struggling for self-determination, as will assist them in their efforts." But Mason's bill sank without a bubble, and the American press and public, fascinated by the big story of the day—developments at the Paris peace conference—paid little heed to India's distress.[10]

In Paris, Wilson demonstrated that his concept of self-determination did not necessarily apply to the world war's winners. Revolutions in Mexico, Russia, and Central Europe caused him to rethink the readiness of humanity at large to assume responsibility for its own fate. Equally important, the British and French held Wilson's cherished League of Nations hostage to a more complaisant American attitude on colonial questions.

For all his compromises at Paris, Wilson returned home only to see the Senate reject his handiwork—lock, stock, and League. The war and its aftermath, in terms of U.S.–Indian relations, left a sour taste all around. For Americans, it was difficult to forget that Indians had taken advantage of American hospitality to collaborate with the enemy. Indians could not forget that the United States had failed to live up to its fine rhetoric on behalf of oppressed peoples.

NONVIOLENCE, NONCOOPERATION, AND NONSENSE

The emergence of Mohandas Gandhi at the head of a nonviolent noncooperation movement in the early 1920s attracted some attention in the United States, although the interest centered as much on Gandhi's unorthodox style and tactics—especially his fasts—as on the issues he represented. Americans did not know quite what to make of this man who—unarmed, and nearly unclothed—was taking on the most powerful empire in the world. Yet most who followed his activities wished him well. They knew little enough about India, but baiting the British lion remained a favorite autumn sport among Americans, especially politicians in Irish districts.

Gandhi's jailing in 1922 removed him from the news, as British authorities had intended, and Americans turned back to their own affairs. Katherine Mayo's 1927 *Mother India* portrayed what she described as India's "inertia, helplessness, lack of initiative and originality, lack of staying power and sustained loyalties, sterility of enthusiasm, weakness of life vigor itself," convincing many Americans that India did not deserve their attention. The book verged on the preposterous, as any but the most gullible should have recognized. Describing child-bearing and rearing practices in the central provinces, Mayo wrote that when a woman went into labor, the local midwife, or *dhai*, commonly "takes two iron nails, and stretching out her victim's unresisting arms—for the poor creature knows and accepts her fate—drives a spike straight through each palm fast into the floor." Having done so, the *dhai* then "walks up and down her body, like one treading grapes." Should infant and mother survive the ordeal, the baby would probably receive for its first feedings "crude sugar mixed with the child's own urine."[11]

Astonishingly, Mayo's book received favorable notices in the United States and immediately became a best-seller. The *Nation* and the *New Republic* pointed out its deficiencies; the latter journal's British reviewer denounced the work as "profoundly untrue" and "a libel upon a unique civilization and a people of extraordinary virtue, patience and spiritual quality." But publications closer to the American mainstream, including the *New York Times* and the *New York Herald-Tribune*, found it deserving of praise rather than condemnation. The *Chicago Evening Post* declared that "with the facts of *Mother India* available, there will henceforth be no excuse for criticism of the British or even of their presence in India at all, in terms of doctrinaire idealism." The *Boston Independent* asserted that "India lacked independence because she is incapable of anything else."

Not surprisingly, Indians found this flagrant distortion intolerable. Many wondered what had inspired the author to such a malign caricature and suspected that it was a put-up job sponsored by the British government. Gandhi countered Mayo in an article entitled "The Drain Inspector's Report." Another rebutter began his book-length reply, *Father India,* by quoting Shakespeare:

> 'Tis slander whose edge is sharper than the sword;
> Whose tongue outvenoms all the worms of the Nile;
> Whose breath rides on the posting winds
> And doth belie all corners of the world.

The Indian nationalist press applied the Mayo treatment to the United States, featuring lurid depictions of sexual misconduct, lynchings of blacks in the South, and corruption at all levels of society. Typical of this treatment was a book entitled *Uncle Sham: Being the Strange Tale of a Civilization Run Amok.*[12]

Most portentously, the storm surrounding Mayo's book inspired many Indian nationalists to distrust the United States. Congress party leader Jawaharlal Nehru, already disposed by education in England to consider Americans uncultured, thought the Mayo affair just what one should expect from the United States. The future prime minister took his suspicions to the 1927 Brussels Congress of Oppressed Nationalities, where they received further support. Delegates from Latin American countries spoke bitterly of American domination. Commenting on his discussions with Mexicans and other Latin Americans, Nehru wrote: "Most of us, especially from Asia, were wholly ignorant of the problems of South America, and of how the rising imperialism of the United States, with its tremendous resources and immunity from outside attack, is gradually taking a stranglehold of central and south America. But we are not at liberty to remain ignorant much longer, for the great problem of the near future will be American imperialism, even more than British imperialism." Nehru predicted that England, "in order to save herself from extinction, will become a satellite of the United States and incite the imperialism and capitalism of America to fight by her side."[13]

Meanwhile, representatives of the communist movement impressed Nehru with the sincerity of their support for Asian nationalism. "We have felt the full weight of imperialism," Nehru told the Brussels gathering. "We know exactly what it means, and we are naturally interested in any movement which concerns imperialism." Visiting the Soviet Union on this same European tour, Nehru found the Russians' progress toward alleviating poverty and other social problems enormously impressive.[14]

Gandhi's inauguration of a civil disobedience movement in 1930, dramatized by his march to Dandi to break the salt law—a procession that would inspire American freedom marchers in the 1960s—helped redirect American attention from the Mayo controversy to the continuing fact of British rule. The *Baltimore Sun* wrote in wonder of Gandhi that "there is no other political leader in the world today who could dare so deliberately to put aside all traditional instruments of leadership and put his faith in a ceremony so simple that it appears almost trifling." The *Cleveland Plain Dealer* added, "He has no arms and wants none. He has none of the paraphernalia of militarism."[15]

Even so, an America reeling from the stock-market crash of 1929 and looking for the bottom of the Great Depression had little interest to spare for India. Gandhi himself recognized this when he declined an invitation to visit the United States. Explaining his decision later, he commented, "I had no faith that I would be able to do any good for India. Americans would not listen to others; they would lionise people, but they would go their own ways." In a statement that captured a predominant mood in India, the mahatma added, "It is difficult to wean the golden calf from the worshippers of Mammon."[16]

MORE WAR

The ominous world events of the mid-1930s, especially the rise of fascists and militarists in Germany and Japan, at first reinforced the United States' isolationist tendencies. But the outbreak of the Sino-Japanese war in 1937 and the multiple crises that followed strengthened the arguments of those who contended that head-burying simply encouraged aggression and deferred the day of reckoning.

The apparently imminent outbreak of another war drew the U.S. government closer to that of Britain. Yet Americans never quite forgot India. Indian nationalists, despite their misgivings about the hypocrisy of American politics and shallowness of American culture, took pains to ensure for themselves a continued hearing in Washington, recognizing the weight Washington could bring to bear upon London if it so chose. As Indians pointed out, the declaration of Indian independence, issued by the Congress party in 1930, drew heavily on the American declaration. Nehru suppressed his distrust of the United States long enough to explain the Congress party's position in a 1938 article in the prestigious American journal *Foreign Affairs* and again two years later in the more broadly circulated *Atlantic Monthly*. "India is far from America," he wrote in the latter periodical, "but more and more our thoughts go to this great democratic country, which seems almost alone to keep the torch of democratic freedom alight in a world given over to imperialism and fascism." Nehru asserted that Americans could not avoid a role in determining the fate of India: "They should seek to understand India's problem in relation to the world, for on them will fall the burden of the future, whether they will it or not. Their great material resources and dominating position in the world have cast this burden on them today, but even more so has the responsibility been cast upon them because of their leadership of the forces of democracy." In 1939, the John Day publishing house in New York produced a popular biography of Nehru, authorized by Anup Singh, editor of a monthly newsletter for the India League of America. Singh aptly titled his volume *The Rising Star of India.*[17]

Britain's declaration of war against Germany in September 1939 triggered a new wave of unrest among Indian nationalists, not least because the British viceroy, Lord Linlithgow, declared war on behalf of India without consulting Indian opinion. The leaders of the Congress party denied any interest in taking advantage of Britain's danger to negotiate concessions, but they contended that "only a free and consenting India" could make a maximum contribution to the fight against fascism. Linlithgow responded to demands for a statement of British war aims, as they related to India, by saying simply that when the fighting ended, His Majesty's government would listen to suggestions regarding modifications of present arrangements. The Congress party leaders began a new campaign of noncooperation.[18]

During the six months of the "phony war" in Europe, the noncooperation movement produced relatively little result. The most important event of the period—the Muslim League's call for the partition of India and the creation of a Pakistan—had implications that became fully apparent only later. But the fall of France in June 1940 and the accession of Winston Churchill to the premiership in London altered the situation drastically. Enjoying—indeed, reveling in—his well-deserved reputation for reaction in imperial matters, Churchill made clear that he would brook no interference from Indian nationalists in his conduct of the war. As an initial measure, Churchill slapped several thousand members of the Congress party into jail.

Americans greeted this development with ambivalence. Many pundits expressed disappointment that London had adopted such a hard line against the nationalists, if only because Britain appeared to need all the cooperation from India it could get. On the other hand, some observers criticized the Congress party for attempted extortion and sabotage of the war effort. Almost no one, however, thought the United States had much leverage in the matter.

American leverage increased somewhat during the first months of 1941, when Franklin Roosevelt proposed and the U.S. Congress approved the lend-lease program of aid to Britain. Liberals in the Roosevelt administration sought to use lend-lease to help the Indian nationalist cause. Assistant Secretary of State Adolph Berle recommended an initiative on behalf of India, or rather on behalf of the United States *and* India: he declared that "considerations of principle as well as of policy" converged to recommend an effort to get the British to compromise with the nationalists. India, Berle said, was the pivot of a strategically vital region, exerting a vast influence on the countries around. India's manpower and other resources could well prove crucial in the struggle ahead. But mobilizing these resources efficiently required the transformation of India into "an active, rather than a passive, partner." For this reason, Berle urged the administration to press the British to grant dominion status to India.

Berle's boss, Secretary of State Cordell Hull, raised the issue with the

British ambassador in Washington, Lord Halifax. Halifax, a former viceroy of India, had a reputation as the most enlightened of his class and easily fended off the American approach. He declared that the noisy nationalists represented but a small portion of educated opinion in India; that pro-British sentiment remained strong in the country; that Indians already enjoyed a large measure of self-government, especially at the provincial level; and that in any event the middle of war was hardly the best time to discuss fundamental changes in government policy. The administration accepted Halifax's response and shelved the Berle proposal. A State Department officer, describing the reaction of Undersecretary of State Sumner Welles to Halifax's response, summarized Washington's attitude: "Mr. Welles feels it would be undesirable to do anything which might upset the Indian apple cart at this critical juncture."[19]

The British did agree, however, to a State Department proposal to upgrade the official U.S. presence in India. Contending that the United States could not accurately follow developments in India without proper diplomatic representation there, the Roosevelt administration requested the right to send a minister to New Delhi. In exchange, it would allow the British embassy in Washington to add an agent-general for India to its staff. Reluctantly, London acquiesced to the basic idea, although it insisted on publicly denominating the American envoy a "commissioner" and keeping his true rank secret, lest other countries demand equivalent representation.

To fill the new post, the White House appointed Thomas Wilson, until then consul at Calcutta. Wilson became a thorn in Britain's side almost at once, since his sympathies clearly lay with the nationalists. For months, he had criticized British policy in India. He thought the British were underestimating the strength and staying power of the nationalist movement, and he argued that the longer London let the problem fester, the more vexing it would grow. He blasted the secretary of state for India, Leopold Amery, for refusing to accept "a realistic view of what is taking place." After Nehru's arrest in the Congress party roundup, he forwarded to Washington the party leader's long and eloquent address to the court.[20]

WILSONIANISM REDUX: THE ATLANTIC CHARTER

For all the liberals' protests, India slumbered as an issue in American politics and diplomacy until August 1941, when Roosevelt met with Churchill to discuss a joint policy toward the war. By then, the administration had committed itself in all but name to Britain's cause in the struggle with Germany. American dollars maintained Britain's economic equilibrium; American equipment outfitted British soldiers; American ships patrolled the North Atlantic. Yet the U.S. government had little say regarding the ends to which the British were putting American resources. Beating Hitler, yes; but beyond that? What would a post-Hitler world look like?

Isolationism in the United States had not disappeared. Many Americans, disillusioned a generation earlier by the outcome of the Paris peace conference, feared a repetition and looked askance at London. Senator Gerald Nye went further than most in declaring that "the greatest aggressor in all modern history has been the British Empire," but few doubted that Churchill and company were concerned more immediately with the future of the British empire than with the general welfare of humanity. Most opposed any American aid designed to further Britain's imperial ambitions.[21]

Roosevelt had broached the issue of war aims during the previous months, to the rapt attention of nationalists in India. In January 1941, flushed with his unprecedented third victory at the polls, the president enumerated "four freedoms" necessary to any peaceful postwar order: freedom of speech and expression, freedom of worship, freedom from want, and freedom from fear. Listeners in India, straining for a political handle, found little to grasp in this vague formulation. But in August, Roosevelt afforded them greater purchase with the Atlantic Charter.

The Atlantic Charter was the product of considerable negotiation between Washington and London. This communiqué of the conference between Roosevelt and Churchill reflected compromises made by both, couched in terms that each could interpret as his political exigencies required. The British had originally offered a five-point plan involving guarantees against future aggression, self-determination in territorial changes, respect for "the right of all peoples to choose the form of Government under which they will live," liberalization of economic policies, and support for an effective international organization. The Americans, most concerned about the fourth and fifth points, insisted on more specific commitments regarding freer access to postwar markets, lest the world repeat the disastrous experience of the Great Depression, and less specific mention of a successor to the League of Nations, lest American isolationists succeed in making it an issue against the administration.

Amid the negotiations, the third point, regarding self-government, underwent minor but not inconsequential modification. To Churchill's draft, Roosevelt appended the hope that "self-government would be restored to those from whom it has been forcefully removed." The prime minister accepted the change after adding a new phrase of his own regarding the restoration of "sovereign rights." In the final version, the third point asserted that the United States and Britain would "respect the right of all peoples to choose the form of government under which they will live" and that they wished "to see sovereign rights and self-government restored to those who have been forcibly deprived of them."[22]

The Atlantic conference took place in secret. When the fact of the conference and the joint statement burst on the world, most observers scanned the document for clues as to the Roosevelt administration's intentions toward Germany. Under the circumstances, article three appeared most obviously applicable to countries like Poland and Belgium, which had quite clearly been "forcibly deprived" of their "sovereign rights and self-government." Few American commentators made an immediate connection with India.

In Britain, however, the issue was soon raised, both by critics on the left, who attacked Churchill's heavy-handed policy toward Indian nationalism, and by conservatives, who wondered whether the government had hocked the empire's crown jewel for increased American aid. Rebuffing the left and reassuring the right, the prime minister told the House of Commons in September that he and President Roosevelt had had in mind primarily the countries of Europe. As for the empire, Churchill said that "the joint declaration does not qualify in any way the various statements of policy which have been made from time to time about the development of constitutional government in India."[23]

To Indian observers, Churchill's reversion to imperialist form came as a disappointment if as no particular surprise. But the failure of the Americans to contradict Churchill's narrow construction of the Atlantic Charter provoked considerable dismay. Two Indian historians, afterwards contrasting the elevated language of the charter with the absence of follow-up, summarized much feeling in their country when they dismissed the document as a propaganda hoax. In neighboring Burma, upon which the burden of Churchill's comments fell with equal weight, Prime Minister Maung Saw spoke for his own compatriots, for Indians, and for millions of other non-self-governing peoples in the British empire when he wrote to Roosevelt that he could not believe "that the generosity of the terms of Article 3 should have been intended by you to be qualified and altered in this way." He added,

> We claim that the Joint Declaration, promulgated to a waiting and anxious world and received with acclamation, cannot afterwards be declared to be not what it seems. . . .
> The right which you have pledged yourself to respect of all peoples to choose the form of government under which they will live is a right to which all peoples are entitled. It would be absurd if, in your aim to grant freedom to all peoples in the world, you exclude the peoples who were in the past forcibly brought into the British Empire. If force gives no moral right to nations now, force applied in the past lacks the same right. The British should grant freedom to the subject peoples within their own Empire first, if there is to be any truth in their professed war aim of restoring freedom to the peoples who have lost it in the present war.[24]

Some in the U.S. government thought that the president should distance himself from Churchill's reactionary statements. Wallace Murray, head of the State Department's Near Eastern division and a profound skeptic on all matters relating to the British, contended that in light of the prime minister's recent gloss, "there may be greater justification than there has been heretofore of an effort on behalf of this Government to assist in a solution of problems involved in the political status of India."

But Undersecretary Welles, who better than any other American diplomat knew the president's mind, vetoed all such initiatives. With the United States on the verge of war with Germany, and probably with Japan too, it could not afford to antagonize the British. Welles argued that the administration must view the Indian issue "from the standpoint of our own national policy and of our national defense." He did not deny the worthiness of the goal of Indian independence, but he said that the president's decision on the matter had to turn on the "question of expediency."[25]

Welles's position, which at once became Roosevelt's, was understandable in the autumn of 1941, but Indians expressed disappointment. To a certain degree, their disappointment was genuine. Hope that the United States would live up to its noble ideas had not died in the subcontinent. Equally, however, India was dismayed by design. Gandhi, Nehru, and other nationalists were realistic enough to know that American leaders would not risk the security of the United States for India's sake. Nonetheless, as would happen repeatedly during the war and in the years that followed, Indian leaders seized on American statements related to their cause and used them as clubs against the British and as goads to the American conscience. Indians perceived Britain's growing dependence on the United States, even as they recognized the moralistic element in American foreign policy. The Americans might not always practice their precepts, especially if practice entailed a strain on Anglo–American relations, but it could never hurt to be able to quote chapter and verse from America's high-sounding rhetoric.

Actually, it could hurt, and over the years it would. Playing the politics of conscience proved irresistible to Indians, and to Americans as well. Although the tactic sometimes produced favorable consequences at home, it usually exacted a cost to U.S.–Indian relations. By harping on the failure of American leaders to live up to their promises—an impossible task since Americans commonly couched their pledges in terms of universal applicability—Indian politicians could score domestic points. But America-bashing almost always produced a backlash in the United States, which, exacerbated by the open nature of each country's politics, reinforced the anti–American feelings in India. The problem only grew worse from the fact that Indian leaders, subject to the same kinds of political pressures that confronted the Americans, would allow a similar gap to develop between what they said and what they did. Denouncing the Indian "double standard" grew into a cottage industry among American conservatives by the mid-1950s. Each side eventually discovered, but neither really managed to learn, that words echo, and that no one can tell where the echoes will stop.

ANTIIMPERIALISM UNDER THE GUN

Only a few weeks after Welles announced that expediency would govern Washington, the Japanese attacked Pearl Harbor and Germany declared war on the United States. Although the Roosevelt administration had anticipated war in both theaters for some time, the grim fact of actual belligerency pushed collateral considerations to the rear while U.S. officials pondered their new situation.

Before long, they discovered that India counted more than ever. Singapore surrendered in February 1942, and with Germany winning in the Middle East, the specter of the major Axis powers joining forces in South Asia sent shudders through the Anglo–American combined military staff. To lose India could also mean losing contact with China, as transmontane supply routes closed. A linking of Germany and Japan would sever the Iranian connection with the Soviet Union. It might deprive the Allies of oil from the Persian Gulf. Most directly, India's fall or neutralization would eliminate the British empire's primary source of manpower, thereby emasculating the imperial army. Four days after the Singapore defeat, the assistant chief of the U.S. War Department's planning division, Dwight Eisenhower, summarized the two necessities confronting the Allies: "We've got to keep Russia in the war—and hold India!!!"[26]

London felt the strain most acutely. In fact, even before Pearl Harbor, Churchill's cabinet had decided that the security of the empire required a gesture to win the cooperation of the Indians—and appease pro–Indian Americans. Accordingly, the British announced the release of most of the jailed nationalists.

London's move yielded swift results in American public opinion. Typifying sentiment in the United States, the *New York Times* characterized the announcement as "good news for friends of Britain and bad news for the Axis." The *Times* expressed hope that the British action would "open up fresh opportunities for re-examining problems hitherto standing in the way of dominion status for India." The paper concluded that "an old-fashioned Empire is dying, but a cooperative federation is in the process of birth."[27]

Although Churchill rejected hesitant efforts by Roosevelt to raise the India issue at a meeting shortly after Pearl Harbor, the British continued to compromise with the nationalists through the first part of 1942. In January, London allowed the Indian agent-general in Washington, Girja Bajpai, to sign the declaration of the United Nations on behalf of India—in this instance, at least, making India the equal of the self-governing dominions. After prodding from Roosevelt, Churchill agreed in February to a visit to India by China's Chiang Kai-shek, who, as expected, stated his strong support for the nationalists' goals. In March, Whitehall unveiled a special committee that would travel to the subcontinent to reexamine the Indian question.

The British mission came at a time of unparalleled American interest in the fate of India, upon which, it seemed, hung the fate of much of the world. Americans generally applauded the selection as delegation head of Stafford Cripps, a leader of the Labour left with friendly ties to Nehru and others in the nationalist movement. When Cripps made an offer of dominion status, redeemable at the end of the war, under a constitution devised by representatives of British India and the princely states, American interest overwhelmingly turned into approval. The major organs of the American press deemed the offer an eminently reasonable compromise, granting full satisfaction neither to the Congress party, which insisted on immediate independence, nor to the hard-shell imperialists, who rejected any timetable for devolution, but that provided each side with enough of what it wanted to justify acceptance. The *Chicago Sun* asserted that the Cripps plan afforded India a choice between "delayed independence from Britain and perpetual slavery to Japan." The *New York Herald-Tribune* characterized the offer as a "momentous step in the evolution of the British Empire into the British Commonwealth." The *Los Angeles Times*, the *Christian Science Monitor, Time,* and *Newsweek* took similar positions, as did the *New York Times*, which, referring to the Congress party leaders, added a warning: "If they refuse this gift of freedom for petty, or personal, or spiteful reasons, they will lose the American sympathy and the offer of American comradeship that is now theirs for the asking." Should Nehru, Gandhi, and the others reject the plan and help produce a "world catastrophe," the *Times* continued, "they will not be remembered as friends of human freedom."[28]

But the nationalists did reject the Cripps plan. They wanted responsible, independent government immediately; Gandhi likened the offer of self-rule after the war to a "post-dated cheque." The nationalists also objected to a provision that Britain would retain control of the Indian army during the war and to a provision that allowed provinces not wishing to join the proposed Indian Union to remain outside. The Congress party considered the last point exceedingly important and unacceptable since it would only encourage groups, especially the Muslim League, that were bent on the partition of the country.[29]

The Roosevelt administration sought to break the impasse. Before the Cripps proposal, the president had written Churchill that in the United States there was a feeling "almost universally held" that the British were to blame for the deadlock with the nationalists. After the Cripps plan knocked the ball back to the Indians' side of the net, Roosevelt directed Louis Johnson, who was in India on a technical mission, to mediate between Cripps and Viceroy Linlithgow on the one hand and Nehru and the Congress party on the other. The appearance of Johnson as a deus ex machina threw a momentary scare into the British. Linlithgow worried that an unfavorable report by Johnson might lead to a curtailment of American lend-lease aid. But Johnson had no authority to force the British to bend, as Churchill discovered on questioning Roosevelt aide Harry Hopkins. "I told the Prime Minister," Hopkins noted in his diary, "that Johnson's original mission to India had nothing to do with the British proposals and that I was sure that he was not acting as the representative of the President in mediating the India business. . . . I told Mr. Churchill of the President's instructions to me that he would not be drawn into the Indian business except at the personal request of the Prime Minister." Delighted by this news, Churchill told Linlithgow to sit tight. The viceroy sat; Johnson's mediation efforts failed; and the Cripps mission died without issue.[30]

The Roosevelt administration viewed the Cripps negotiations chiefly in the context of the Allies' immediate struggle against the Axis; the American press and public did too. When the Congress party rejected the British offer on what seemed trivial grounds, observers tended to blame the nationalists. The normally sympathetic *New Republic* admitted that although the nationalists had cause for reservations, in the present crisis "it should be clear even to the Indians that the British cannot be stripped of all their military control in India." The *Chicago Daily News* wondered editorially whether India's "two and seventy warring sects" could ever agree on a devolution plan. The *Philadelphia Bulletin* carried things a bit far when it asserted that the British had displayed "a tact, patience, tolerance and understanding that has few parallels in history," but most agreed with the *New York Times'* judgment that the fault lay with the Indians. "Indian leaders who have had no experience or training whatever in the matter insist that they be placed in immediate charge of defense," the *Times* wrote. "They talk of 'freedom of India' when unless they cooperate fully with England and the United Nations, this may mean today nothing more than freedom to be conquered. They have been trained in the habits of protest and seem unable to change quickly enough to the habits of responsibility."[31]

Nehru recognized Roosevelt's sensitivity to the winds of American public opinion and attempted to disarm this criticism by a direct appeal to the president. Few world leaders in the twentieth century had charm that could match Nehru's, when he chose to deploy it. He did so now. Although he distrusted the United States as much as ever, he understood that American pressure afforded the only hope of getting Britain to compromise. In a letter sent to Washington via Louis Johnson, Nehru explained the Congress party position. He declared that he and his associates, no less than Americans, appreciated the danger posed by the Japanese. Indeed, he said, this very appreciation lay behind the party's rejection of the British offer. "The peril of today made us desire above everything else that an opportunity should be given to us to organize a real national and popular resistance to the aggressor and invader. We were convinced that the right way to do this would have been to give freedom and independence to our people and ask them to defend it. That would have lighted a spark in millions of hearts which would have developed into a blazing fire of resistance which no aggressor could have faced successfully." By way of reassurance, Nehru promised that although the British had blocked the most effective means of mobilizing the country for defense, "still we shall do our utmost not to submit to Japanese or to any other aggression and invasion." He concluded, "Our sympathies, as we have so often declared, are with the forces fighting against fascism and for democracy and freedom. With freedom in our own country those sympathies could have been translated into dynamic action."[32]

WHOSE SIDE IS INDIA ON?

During the next few months, Americans had occasion to question the sincerity of Nehru's assertions. From half a world away, it was easy to confuse the opinions of an unabashed Axis sympathizer like Subhas Chandra Bose, who declared that it would be "an honor and privilege for India to co-operate intimately with Japan in the noble task of creating a great Asia," with those of the nationalist majority. Such confusion became all the easier when the Congress party rejected the idea of armed resistance to a Japanese invasion. Gandhi asserted that "if the British left India to her fate as they had to leave Singapore . . . probably the Japanese would leave India alone." Gandhi initially intended to propose a resolution to an important party conference at Allahabad, to the effect that "India bears no enmity with Japan" and that "if India were free her first act would probably be to negotiate with Japan." Recognizing that such language would produce an uproar in the United States, Nehru persuaded Gandhi to modify his resolution, but even the "non-violent non-cooperation" the Allahabad meeting approved sounded uncomfortably akin to appeasement.[33]

With Japan expanding in the Pacific and Southeast Asia, with Rommel rolling through North Africa, and with the Russians retreating across the steppe, American opinion reacted predictably. The *New York Times* branded Gandhi a "pseudo-pacifist who is willing to have other men fight his battles"; the *Christian Science Monitor* denounced "the confusion whose name is India"; the *Philadelphia Inquirer* declared that "Gandhi must make Tojo happy."[34]

Gandhi lost India even more friends when he roundly criticized the American presence in the subcontinent. Americans admitted that the GIs in India served American purposes, but they believed the troops and American aid also safeguarded India. So what could they think when the old man decried the "never-ending stream of soldiers from America"? He went on to say, "We know what American aid means. It amounts in the end to American influence, if not American rule added to British. It is a tremendous price to pay for possible success of allied arms." Gandhi attacked the United States for participating in the war. "America could have remained out, and even now she can do so if she divests herself of the intoxication that her immense wealth has produced." He tarred Americans with the brush he used for the British: "Both America and Britain lack the moral basis for engaging in this war, unless they put their own houses in order, while making a fixed determination to withdraw their influence and power both from Africa and Asia, and remove the color bar. They have no right to talk about protecting democracies and protecting civilization and human freedom until the canker of white supremacy is destroyed in its entirety." How would India deal with the Japanese if the Americans and British followed his advice and withdrew? "Leave India to God," the mahatma replied.[35]

Naturally, after the trauma of Pearl Harbor Americans reacted indignantly to the charge that they lacked a "moral basis" for their fight against Japan. Under the best of circumstances, they would not have taken kindly to a lecture about the "color bar" from the spokesman of a country known for its caste system. As for leaving India—with all India implied for Allied security—"in God's hands," most Americans adhered to the belief that God helps those who help themselves.

Belatedly recognizing the bad impression he was creating in the United States, Gandhi wrote to Roosevelt explaining his views. "Dear Friend," he began, and he added that he felt "nothing but good wishes" for America. "I twice missed coming to your great country. I have the privilege of having numerous friends there both known and unknown to me. Many of my country-men have received and are still receiving higher education in America. I know too that several have taken shelter there. I have profited greatly by the writings of Thoreau and Emerson. I say this to tell you how much I am connected with your country." Yet Gandhi refused to temper his convictions. "The Allied declaration that the Allies are fighting to make the world safe for freedom of the individual and for democracy sounds hollow, so long as India and, for that matter, Africa are exploited by Great Britain, and America has the Negro problem in her own home." He repeated his demand that the British immediately transfer power to Indians, although he allowed that the Allies might maintain troops in India for the purpose of preventing Japanese aggression and assisting China.[36]

Gandhi's steadfastness became even more evident a short while later, when he threatened to bolt the Congress party and mount a separate struggle for independence unless the party leaders accepted a resolution calling on Britain to relinquish power at once or face a massive outbreak of civil disobedience. Since the British had made clear they were not leaving, Gandhi's measure amounted to a declaration of political war.

The "Quit India" campaign was directed at the United States no less than at Britain. Churchill would not yield willingly; his continuing statements left no room for doubt. The British still possessed the force to silence dissent if they so chose. But should the Americans speak boldly on the India question, even Churchill would have to listen. Naturally, the Congress leadership could not supplicate Washington—India had its pride. Gandhi himself had said that India must gain freedom by its own efforts. Yet as the more diplomatic Nehru remarked, "If America took the initiative, it would be another mat-ter." Congress party president Maulana Azad went so far as to acknowledge that the Congress party had aimed the Quit India campaign implicitly at the United States.[37]

The United States once again proved a disappointment. For Americans, defeating Japan and Germany took priority over Indian independence. During the summer of 1942, the outcome of the war remained very much in the balance. Even those confident of an Allied victory understood that the longer the conflict lasted, the greater destruction it would wreak and the more lives it would cost. Under such conditions, a few years' patience did not seem an excessive favor to ask of the Indians. Nor did the Americans, despite their suspicions of British imperialism, think London would—or could—welsh on its pledges at war's end.

The Indian perspective was entirely different. Having suffered through the Amritsar massacre and other less spectacular manifestations of white rule for two centuries, Indians had no confidence in London. Neither, should the worst come, did they think a Japanese victory would bring the end of the world. After all, despite Japan's arrogance, it could hardly treat India worse than the British had. In any event, the need for independence justified taking the risk. Finally, over the whole matter hung the question of partition. Most Congress leaders considered the Muslim League a British stalking horse. Even if the British did not use Muslim demands for a Pakistan as a device to delay withdrawal, their encouragement of the Muslims might leave the Hindu majority with nothing more than a truncated state. On the whole, prudence dictated applying pressure—through the Americans, if necessary—while the exigencies of war rendered the British susceptible to pressure. The end of the war would ease the pressure—and the Americans would probably lose interest.

As a result of these differing priorities, the Quit India campaign in the summer of 1942 marked the low point of U.S.–Indian relations during the war years. Churchill responded to the Congress party declaration by jailing the party's leadership and some 100,000 of their supporters. Despite pleas from George Merrell, the ranking American diplomat in New Delhi; from Chiang Kai-shek, from members of the U.S. Congress, and from assorted friends of Indian nationalism in the United States; and despite his own misgivings about Churchill's ham-fisted handling of the whole affair, Roosevelt refused to intervene in any serious way. The United States needed Britain at the moment far more than it needed India, he reasoned. To please the Indians would anger the British, and given Churchill's obsession with empire, an American initiative would fail in any event.

The British noted American criticism of their India policies, but they did not expect anything to come from the complaints and held to their course. Halifax remarked from Washington that "there is always a good deal of loose talk floating about both in and outside the administration about India and on the general problem of backward peoples." In a September speech, Churchill denounced the Congress party as unrepresentative of the Indian people, even of the Hindu majority. "It is a political organization," he told the House of Commons, "built around a party machine and sustained by certain manufacturing and financial interests." The Congress party, he continued, certainly did not speak for the 90 million Muslims, who looked instead to the Muslim

League; it ignored the 95 million residents of the princely states; it left out some 50 million untouchables and denizens of the lowest classes. Fortunately—as Churchill interpreted matters—"the Congress party has no influence whatever with the martial races on whom the defence of India, apart from the British forces, depends." "Unbridgeable religious gulfs" separated much of the Indian population from the Hindu Congress party. The recent rebellion had given the lie to the peaceful claims of the nationalists. The Congress party had followed "criminal courses" and made plain its real nature as "a revolutionary movement."[38]

Churchill's inflammatory speech, coming as it did in the wake of widespread violence that accompanied the mass arrests, increased pressure on the Roosevelt administration to take action on the Indian question, if only to distance the United States from Britain's excesses. Indians certainly looked to America. The nationalist *Hindu* of Madras wondered at the "mysterious silence" gripping Washington and the rest of the United States: "Who can forget the ballyhoo that was raised in the American press, ranging from the most obscure state journals to the national newspapers, when Sir Stafford Cripps made his offer to India? What has happened to all those newspapers who roundly lectured India on the folly of rejecting Britain's generous gesture. Why are they tongue-tied now?"

American papers and magazines in fact were *not* tongue-tied. Many editors pressed the administration to respond. Freda Kirchwey of the *Nation* castigated Churchill's address as the diatribe of an "unreconstructed, unrepentant imperialist." The *New Republic* declared that the prime minister was "gambling not only his own future but that of the British Empire and the United Nations on the assumption that his old emotional attitude is the right one and carries the key to victory." The *New York Times* condemned Churchill's attitude, predicting that British rule in India "would be symbolized by the whipping post." The *Times* also carried a full-page petition signed by more than fifty prominent American authors, publishers, academics, and labor and civil rights leaders, calling on the president to demand that the British reopen negotiations with the nationalists. Most tellingly, the Republican party began to make a political issue out of the Indian situation. The GOP's recent presidential candidate, Wendell Willkie, took to the stump to decry the administration's refusal to act on the principles it professed: "By our silence on India we have already drawn heavily on our reservoir of good will in the East. People of the East who would like to count on us are doubtful. They cannot ascertain from our government's wishy-washy attitude toward the problem of India what we are likely to feel at the end of the war about all the other hundreds of millions of Eastern peoples. They cannot tell from our vague and vacillating talk whether we really do stand for freedom, or what we mean by freedom."[39]

Halifax, hearing the uproar and reading the denunciations, revised his earlier estimate that nothing would come of the Quit India fallout in the

United States. "The Cabinet should realise how strongly public opinion is moving on these lines," the ambassador wrote, "and I hope it may be possible to say or do something to counteract it. Otherwise I fear the American press, which on the whole has stood by us remarkably well in the recent Indian crisis, will rapidly and perhaps completely change its attitude, much to the detriment of Anglo–American relations."[40]

At the end of October, less than a week after Willkie's attack and just before the midterm elections in the United States, Roosevelt bowed to the pressure and appointed the distinguished career diplomat William Phillips as his personal representative to India. The appointment owed more to Roosevelt's need to buy time than to a presidential commitment to an Indian solution, as Phillips himself recognized. Phillips indicated that he understood the near impossibility of producing a settlement under the conditions then obtaining in India. "I have no delusions with regard to the difficulties and complications, and the ease with which one can make a false step and ruin one's usefulness," he wrote. "I shall maneuver carefully and will not attempt anything at first except gaining the confidence of the Indians themselves. . . . The divisions throughout India between the social and political groups are so deep-seated and of such historical significance that the problem of a free and independent India, able to stand on its own feet, is certainly a terrific one."

Phillips also took pains not to raise false expectations in India. But the mere fact of his presence at a crucial moment for the independence movement inevitably did. Why, Indians asked themselves, would the American president send a personal representative to meet with and discuss the concerns of a broad spectrum of Indian leaders unless Washington intended to take positive action? And despite his diplomatically correct approach, Phillips contributed to the heightened hopes by a warm manner with those he met. As a correspondent for the Delhi *National Call* remarked, two William Phillipses coexisted in the same person.

> It is one thing seeing Mr. Phillips wearing his mask of diplomatic reserve, the eye muscles carefully distended, the lips puckered, the lower jaw in solemn control, wearing a pincenez, starch collar, a diamond tie-pin and clothes that are a tribute to the best tailors in Paris.
>
> Quite a different thing to meet Mr. Phillips without his pincenez, in a palm beach summer suit with eyes glittering with human understanding and a vivacious smile playing on his lips.

The latter Phillips won the confidence of many to whom he spoke; they interpreted his sympathy as reflecting the views of the president he represented.[41]

Roosevelt was sympathetic, all right, but not sufficiently to change his mind about the inadvisability and likely inefficacy of intervening in the affairs of the British empire. Phillips made a plea for decisive action, urging the president to call for a meeting of British representatives and leaders of the various groups in India, to set a timetable for devolution and to determine the makeup of a provisional government. Roosevelt refused this plea, but he did allow Phillips to present his arguments to Churchill—and the prime minister reacted as Roosevelt expected he would. "Take India if that is what you want!" Churchill thundered. "Take it by all means! But I warn you that if I open the door there will be the greatest blood-bath in all history; yes, blood-bath in all history. Mark my words. I prophesied the present war, and I prophesy the blood-bath." Phillips withdrew. "It was hopeless to argue," he commented afterward.[42]

Although Phillips failed to deliver what the nationalists wanted, he deflected much of the responsibility for his failure back onto the British. He asked Linlithgow for permission to speak with Gandhi and Nehru in prison. As Phillips had anticipated, Linlithgow refused. Just before he left India, Phillips hosted a reception for the press at which he revealed the request he had made and the viceroy's rejection of it. "I should like to have met and talked with Gandhi and Nehru," Phillips said. "I asked permission and was told by the proper authorities that they were unable to grant the necessary facilities." As a result of Phillips's maneuver, most of the news stories surrounding his departure focused on the intransigence of the British rather than on the diffidence of the United States. The *Hindustan Times* summarized a common feeling when it declared that "the refusal may be an exhibition of strength of sorts, but it is equally an exhibition before the world of the ineptitude of the men controlling our destiny at a critical period in our history."[43]

Another event further distracted Indians and Americans from the failure of the Phillips mission. In February 1943, Gandhi declared that the British had provoked the Indian people beyond endurance and commenced a fast. Although the mahatma specified a time limit of twenty-one days for the fast, many observers doubted that his frail constitution could survive a three-week ordeal. Linlithgow refused to compromise, believing that if Gandhi starved, the fault would be his own. Churchill backed the viceroy.

At first, the prospect of Gandhi's death brought demands on Washington to prevent it. Gandhi's followers in India called on Phillips to intercede with the viceroy; nationalist supporters in the United States made similar appeals to the White House. One group of U.S. activists joined the hunger strike to underscore their concern. But to the surprise of many, Gandhi survived the fast, and the crisis atmosphere eased. In India, relief that he lived replaced much of the dismay at the United States for not demanding a British compromise. In the United States, meanwhile, matters more directly related to the war, especially the success of the North African campaign, pushed India off the front pages.

Through the remainder of 1943 and all of the following year, the situation changed little. The Allied invasion and defeat of Italy, the island-hopping counteroffensive in the Pacific, the landing at Normandy and the liberation of France and the Low Countries, the aerial bombardment of Germany and Japan, the Battle of the Bulge—not to mention the 1944 presidential election—commanded the attention of Americans. In India, the policy of repression had succeeded for the time being. With the most important Congress party leaders in jail and the press muzzled, a sullen silence covered India. Gandhi was released in May 1944, bringing some hope of concessions to nationalist sentiment, but Linlithgow's replacement by General Archibald Wavell indicated that the military and strategic importance of India to the Allies and to the empire overshadowed political considerations.

FIRST SHOTS OF THE PEACE

Amid the general distraction, supporters of Indian independence in the United States continued to argue their case. The indefatigable president of the India League of America, J. J. Singh, became a regular caller at the State Department, impressing the India desk officer as "an extremely sincere and convincing protagonist of the cause of Indian freedom." Wisely, Singh presented India's case in terms of American self-interest. At this time Subhas Bose was organizing fifth columnists in India into the so-called Indian National Army, which fought on the side of the Japanese. Singh asserted that Bose's success in this treasonous venture indicated the depth of Indian animosity toward the British and the danger the Allies faced in the subcontinent. Gandhi and Nehru, he explained, embodied the best hope for a moderate settlement; absent American support, the moderates might continue to lose ground.[44]

Singh buttonholed senators, representatives, and other political figures, and he organized rallies and lectures on behalf of the nationalist cause. On each anniversary of the Congress party's declaration of independence, he orchestrated marches and parades, as he did periodically to commemorate the jailing of the Congress party leaders. In October 1944, the India League celebrated Gandhi's seventy-fifth birthday with speeches by noted clergy and pronationalist journalists and politicians.

If these and other consciousness-raising efforts did not convince the Roosevelt administration to attempt to break the deadlock between the British and the nationalists, they did keep India at least on the edge of the U.S. public's field of vision. Singh did well enough, in fact, that London felt obliged to respond with a public-relations offensive of its own. A representative of London asserted on returning from the United States, "To Americans, Congress is the champion, the voice of the whole of India," and recommended a campaign of reeducation. The British propaganda blitz took as its theme a statement that Churchill had made to Harry Hopkins that "we are fighting to defend this vast mass of helpless Indians from imminent invasion." Consciousness-raising efforts included speeches by Halifax to a variety of audiences, articles by imperial officials and friends in influential journals, and an assortment of books and miscellanea such as the Information Ministry's monthly *Bulletins from Britain*. This last outlet reminded American readers that Hindus constituted scarcely two-thirds of the inhabitants of India, that the subcontinent resounded with two dozen major languages, that the political patchwork of the raj embraced some five hundred states, and that as a result of this variegation the Congress party leaders could hardly claim to represent the voice of a united India.[45]

Neither side won the struggle for the American mind, and neither lost. The outcome, like that of most pressing political and diplomatic controversies, awaited the end of the fighting.

Notes

1. R. K. Gupta, *The Great Encounter: A Study of Indo–American Literature and Cultural Relations* (New Delhi: Abhinav, 1986), 3–6.

2. Ibid., 29.

3. Ibid., 110.

4. Md. Abul Khair, *United States Foreign Policy in the Indo–Pakistan Subcontinent, 1939–1947*, vol. 1 (Dacca: Asiatic Society of Pakistan, 1968), 3–4; Norman D. Palmer, *The United States and India: The Dimensions of Influence* (New York: Praeger, 1984), 14.

5. Joan M. Jensen, *Passage from India: Asian Indian Immigrants in North America* (New Haven: Yale University Press, 1988), 140–41; T. V. Kunhi Krishnan, *The Unfriendly Friends: India and America* (New Delhi: Indian Book, 1974), 121; S. C. Tewari, *Indo–U.S. Relations, 1947–1976* (New Delhi: Radiant, 1977), 7.

6. M. S. Venkataramani and B. K. Shrivastava, *Quit India: The American Response to the 1942 Struggle* (New Delhi: Vikas, 1979), 9; Diwakar Prasad Singh, *American Attitude towards the Indian Nationalist Movement* (New Delhi: Munshiram Manoharlal, 1974), 104–6.

7. Singh, *American Attitude*, 197–98.

8. A. Guy Hope, *America and Swaraj: The U.S. Role in Indian Independence* (Washington: Public Affairs, 1968), 7; Singh, *American Attitude*, 203–4.

9. Jensen, *Passage from India*, 183–90.

10. Singh, *American Attitude*, pp. 235–37.

11. Katherine Mayo, *Mother India* (New York: Harcourt, Brace, 1927), 16, 94–104.

12. Gupta, *Great Encounter*, 140–42; C. S. Ranga Iyer, *Father India: A Reply to Mother India* (New York: Carrier, 1928), 9.

13. Sarvepalli Gopal, *Jawaharlal Nehru: A Biography*, vol. 1 (London: Jonathan Cape, 1975), 103–4.

14. Sarvepalli Gopal, ed., *Jawaharlal Nehru: An Anthology* (Delhi: Oxford University, 1980), 12.

15. Tewari, *Indo–U.S. Relations*, 11.

16. P. K. Goswami, *Ups and Downs of Indo–U.S. Relations* (Calcutta: Firma, 1983), 8.

17. Jawaharlal Nehru, "India's Demand and England's Answer," *Atlantic Monthly*, April 1940: 449–55; Anup Singh, *Nehru: The Rising Star of India* (New York: John Day, 1939).

18. Venkataramani and Shrivastava, *Quit India*, 25.

19. Ibid., 37–38.

20. Gary R. Hess, *America Encounters India, 1941–1947* (Baltimore: Johns Hopkins University Press, 1971), 21.

21. Venkataramani and Shrivastava, *Quit India*, 28.

22. Hess, *America Encounters India*, 24–27; Venkataramani and Shrivastava, *Quit India*, pp. 39–44.

23. V. P. Menon, *The Transfer of Power in India* (Princeton, N.J.: Princeton University Press, 1957), 111.

24. M. S. Venkataramani and B. K. Shrivastava, *Roosevelt, Gandhi, Churchill: America and the Last Phase of India's Freedom Struggle* (New Delhi: Radiant, 1983), 11; Venkataramani and Shrivastava, *Quit India*, 45–46.

25. Venkataramani and Shrivastava, *Quit India*, 45.

26. Louis Galambos, ed., *The Papers of Dwight David Eisenhower*, vol. 1 (Baltimore: Johns Hopkins University Press, 1970), 126.

27. Venkataramani and Shrivastava, *Quit India*, 53–57.

28. Ibid., 88–89.

29. Menon, *Transfer of Power*, 126.

30. R. J. Moore, *Churchill, Cripps, and India, 1939–1945* (Oxford: Clarendon, 1979), 130; Robert E. Sherwood, *Roosevelt and Hopkins: An Intimate History* (New York: Harper, 1950), 524.

31. Venkataramani and Shrivastava, *Quit India*, 132.

32. Nehru to Roosevelt, 13 April 1942, *Foreign Relations of the United States 1942* (Washington: U.S. Government Printing Office, 1960), 635–37.

33. Venkataramani and Shrivastava, *Quit India*, 152–53; Menon, *Transfer of Power*, 139–41; Venkataramani and Shrivastava, *Roosevelt, Gandhi, Churchill*, 40–42.

34. Venkataramani and Shrivastava, *Quit India*, 153–54.

35. Hess, *America Encounters India*, 65–66.

36. Gandhi to Roosevelt, 1 July 1942, *Foreign Relations 1942*, vol. 1, 677–78.

37. Venkataramani and Shrivastava, *Quit India*, 185; Hess, *America Encounters India*, 70.

38. Nicholas Mansergh, ed., *The Transfer of Power, 1942–7: Constitutional Relations between Britain and India*, vol. 2 (London: Her Majesty's Stationery Office, 1971), 249; *Parliamentary Debates: House of Commons*, 5th series, vol. 383, cols. 302–5.

39. Venkataramani and Shrivastava, *Quit India*, 283–84, 324.

40. Mansergh, ed., *Transfer of Power*, vol. 2, 969–70.

41. Venkataramani and Shrivastava, *Roosevelt, Gandhi, Churchill*, 74–75, 88–89.

42. William Phillips, *Ventures in Diplomacy* (Boston: Beacon, 1952), 390.

43. Hess, *America Encounters India*, 109.

44. Hope, *America and Swaraj*, 20.

45. Mansergh, ed., *Transfer of Power*, vol. 2, 471–73.

chapter 2

INDEPENDENCE AND THE COLD WAR: 1945–1948

AN END AND A BEGINNING

In the summer of 1942, Graham Spry, a member of the British Cripps delegation, assessed American reaction to the failure of the mission. Spry pointed out that American attitudes toward Indian affairs largely reflected American feelings toward Britain. "The interest of the American public in India is enduring and widespread," he wrote. "It varies with the stimulus of events, but it is persistent; there is almost everywhere and at almost any period an audience for speakers or writers on India." He continued:

> That interest is not primarily founded in India as India, but in British relations with India. If the accidents of history had made India part of the Portuguese instead of the British empire, there would be no comparable interest.
>
> British relations with India appeal to and stir American nationalism. The interest in India arises from the seeming similarity between the relations of Britain to Indian independence and of Britain to the independence of the Thirteen Colonies. The superficial pattern of the relations of Britain to India neatly dovetails into the pattern of the American Revolution—of colonies struggling to unite into a nation, to free themselves from the commercial restrictions, political interference and control by Britain.
>
> The American readiness to adopt a critical attitude towards British relations with India derives not from India herself, but from the very pattern of American nationalism.[1]

27

Spry's assessment remained valid in 1945. It had captured a fundamental ambivalence in American attitudes toward India. At the deepest levels of their culture and history, India and the United States had little to say to each other. Geopolitically, India occupied a position of minor importance in the American world scheme. Other countries usually counted more than India did in the designs of American policymakers, with the result that Washington often gave short shrift to Indian concerns. Not surprisingly, Indians took offense at this neglect. It might have mattered little—plenty of countries object to their treatment at American hands. But the Indian experience, especially India's struggle for freedom and its aspirations to democracy, struck a chord in the American psyche. Americans, having suffered similarly at the hands of the British, could identify with India's efforts toward freedom. Feeling a certain bond, Americans cared about what Indians thought of them. If considerations of material and strategic interest prevented Americans from embracing India unreservedly, considerations of sentiment precluded a complete rejection.

For their part, Indians believed that they deserved better treatment than as a geopolitical pawn in the contests of the great powers. And they objected to Americans' penchant for reading Indian history in light of their own. Indian leaders recognized the parallels between the American experience and the Indian, and they did not hesitate to play on the feelings of kinship when it served their purposes to do so. But they saw no compelling reason to follow in American footsteps. The world had changed since the eighteenth century, and in any case India had its own legacy to draw upon. India preferred socialism to the capitalism the Americans promoted, and it chose neutralism over alignment with the West. Indians found American culture insipid, and American preachments of human equality, coming from a country with a long and continuing history of oppression of the nonwhite races, seemed the height of hypocrisy. Most Indians doubted the United States had anything to teach them.

The end of the war cast into bold relief the disparity between the American and Indian views of each other and of the world. To the United States, the surrender of Germany and Japan closed the last chapter of a book Americans rejoiced to put down. Americans would never again retreat into their prewar shell. Pearl Harbor had killed American isolationism. But having set the world right, for the time being, at least, they had no desire to continue such intensive intervention as they had engaged in for four years. They had won their battle. Now they wanted to go home and get rich and fat.

To Indians, the Axis surrender marked less an end than a beginning. It was a new time to press forward to independence—which could now be done without the stigma of disloyalty and sabotage—and to call in the loans London had floated during the war. The replacement of Churchill's Conservatives by Clement Attlee's Labour party in July 1945 raised the nationalists' expectations and further increased their momentum. Remembering the interest Americans had given their plight during the war and recalling especially American claims that the United States would gladly do more for India if not for the prior demands of the war, Indians prepared to hold Washington to its promises—but only discovered American interest ebbing. Predictably, more disenchantment followed.

POTHOLES ON THE ROAD TO SWARAJ

The end of the war began in February 1945 at Yalta. With Germany in an Allied vise, the leaders of the Big Three met to divide the spoils of Europe and agreed on the Elbe as the line of demarcation between the eastern and western zones of occupation. Victory in the Pacific appeared no less certain if considerably more distant. The atom bomb remained untested, and while American B-29s were already pounding Japan's home islands, an Allied invasion seemed a prerequisite to Tokyo's surrender.

Roosevelt, Churchill, and Stalin had little to say at Yalta about India, but they did set final arrangements for the inaugural session of the United Nations, at which the Indian question immediately came up. The British carefully excluded fire-eating nationalists from the accredited Indian delegation to the San Francisco conference, although some in London questioned the reliability of K.P.S. Menon, the delegation's principal adviser and for years after a distinguished Indian diplomat. The big powers had agreed to keep colonial questions off the San Francisco agenda, but the Indian nationalists managed to raise the question of independence anyway. Vijaya Lakshmi Pandit, Nehru's sister and a veteran of the struggle against the British, showed up to contest the credentials of the official delegates.

Pandit had arrived in the United States some months earlier, ostensibly to visit her daughters, who were students at Wellesley College. Yet as the only major Congress party figure allowed to travel to the United States during the war, she put her access to the American media to good use. Eleanor Roosevelt, ever supportive of liberal causes (and in Franklin's absence at Yalta) hosted a luncheon for her. The Chinese consul-general gave a large reception in her honor, as did Henry Luce, founder of *Time* and *Life* magazines. Luce, born to missionary parents in China, had a consuming interest in Asian affairs and took an immediate liking to Pandit. (Unfortunately for Pandit and India, Luce's fierce opposition to Communist China later cast a cloud over his perceptions of Indian foreign policy, and he came to consider Nehru little more than an apologist for Beijing.)

At the beginning of 1945, Pandit traveled to Hot Springs, Virginia, to attend a conference on the future of Asia. As her first encounter with the American system of segregation, the experience came as a shock. Recalling her feelings later, she wrote, "The notices 'For Whites' and 'For Colored' on different doors took me back through the years to the time in my own country when benches marked 'For Europeans Only' had been a familiar sight. I could hardly believe my eyes."[2]

The Hot Springs conference increased Pandit's visibility, and she soon arranged a lecture tour. Promoters booked her opposite spokesmen for the British government, anticipating a rousing debate; topics typically bore on the question, "Is India ready for independence?" Playing to generally friendly audiences, Pandit more than held her own, prompting one British reader of accounts of her progress to remark acidly, "If the British had not been in India, that woman would have been burnt on her husband's funeral pyre."

By the time Pandit reached San Francisco for the U.N. conference, she was a celebrity. The unofficial Indian delegation, which had no difficulty raising funds for publicity, met outside the official chamber, and Pandit received representatives of many world powers, including the chief Soviet delegate, V. M. Molotov. Pandit was polite to her American hosts, but she expressed regret that the United States had lost interest in Indian independence. This provoked the State Department, as she had no doubt hoped it would, to respond that the United States remained as committed as ever to that worthy goal.

After the adjournment of the U.N. conference, Pandit traveled east again before leaving the United States. In Washington, the new president, Harry Truman, greeted her cordially but noncommittally. In New York, Mayor Fiorello La Guardia expressed puzzlement regarding the tactics of the Indian nationalists. "It doesn't make sense to me," said La Guardia, a scarred veteran of New York's political wars. "You come here to ask the Americans for their moral support. How far will anybody's *moral* support take you toward your freedom? Now if you had asked me for *arms* I could have understood and I would have tried to help you. But I begin to doubt India's ability to become an independent nation if she fights with abstract weapons. Of course you have my sympathy but it's of little value."[3]

When Pandit left New York in the summer of 1945, even the least prescient observers were beginning to suspect that genuine peace might not follow the war. After a meeting of the Allied foreign ministers broke down in September, the nature of the postwar confrontation became clearer. Americans accused the Soviet Union of violating its Yalta pledges regarding Eastern Europe and of generally obstructing the peace. In the American mind, communism replaced fascism as the epitome of aggressive totalitarianism. Many American leaders had sincerely hoped that the war's end would free them from having to collaborate with colonialists, but they found the necessity still there—this time in the name of anticommunism rather than antifascism. After a brief fling with Ho Chi Minh in Vietnam, Washington acquiesced to France's reoccupation of Indochina. Likewise, it tacitly supported Dutch efforts to put down a revolution in Indonesia.

Indian nationalists sympathized not at all with America's anticommunist worries. They interpreted this continuing denial of the Atlantic Charter as moral treachery. "We are in the midst of the aftermath of war," Nehru de-clared, "and inevitably all the assurances given and promises made during the war demand fulfillment. Yet we see the attempt to crush with armed forces the freedom movement in Indonesia and Indo-China. . . . The American government has declared that lend-lease goods used against the Indonesians should have their labels torn off. That is poor consolation for the Indone-sians. They will be shot down by guns whether the guns bear this label or that."

Nehru went on to assess the situation with respect to India.

> In India, the U.S.A. has kept itself clear from all entanglements. We cannot blame it for this attitude especially in wartime, but there has been something much more than this during the past few years—a passive and sometimes even an active support of British propaganda. We realize fully that India's freedom will be won by India's strength and we cannot rely on any foreign power. Nevertheless it is obvious that India's reactions to other powers will be gov-erned by their policy to India. . . . So far as one can see American policy in regard to India has been been strongly subservient to British policy.[4]

Indian frustration with the United States' failure to follow through on its wartime promises gave rise to anti-American violence. In November 1945, a student-led demonstration in Calcutta to protest Britain's decision to try officers of the Indian National Army for treason turned into a general anti-Western riot that led to the injury of two dozen American soldiers and the death of one American ambulance driver. The rioters damaged or destroyed more than fifty American army vehicles and besieged an American hospital for a day. Two months later, renewed rioting in Calcutta, sparked by the conviction of one of the INA officers, claimed three dozen more injuries, while a mob in Bombay attacked the office of the U.S. Information Service and burned the American flag.

By this time—the beginning of 1946—the antennae of American officials were quivering to the stirrings of communist agitation throughout the world. Naturally, Washington wanted to know how much of the anti-Americanism in India had been the work of communist agents. Reports from the field indicated a complex situation in which communists played upon a variety of popular impulses. The consul at Madras explained:

> Anti-White feelings were exploited, certainly, but the emphasis was on labor solidarity against employers of any race. It was all permeated with anti-British and anti-White feelings, but there was ample evidence that the prime movers were ready to attack fellow Indians. . . .
>
> One notes an intermingling of anti-British and anti-class impulses. While the former is more obvious, the evidence points to premeditated Communist exploitation of it for their special ends, that is, to promote class friction as a means of influencing the masses.

In New Delhi, George Merrell essentially concurred, asserting that while the communists exacerbated the troubles, they had not instigated the riots.[5]

During the next few months, communists continued to stoke the fires of discontent in India. In June the *People's Age*—the mouthpiece of the Indian Communist party, seized the opportunity of an approaching harvest shortfall to run an article entitled "100 Million Indians Threatened with Starvation—Where Anglo–American Food Politics Has Brought Our Country." The article attributed to President Truman the statement, "The world is a bitch with too big a litter. We have to decide which of the puppies to drown." It went on to assert that the Truman administration, "tied hand and foot to the big banks which control American farming interests," had elected to starve India in order to feed Japan, its new "colony." The Americans intended "to let the British burn their fingers in an Indian famine and then rush in to the rescue on their own terms—cut-throat profits and a share in the political and economic domination of India."[6]

Although the Communist paper put the argument more stridently than most Indian papers, anti-Americanism continued to characterize publications across the spectrum of Indian politics. Merrell in New Delhi summarized the situation in June 1946 by saying that virtually all the papers—pro-Hindu, pro-Muslim, pro-British—exhibited "a remarkably anti-American bias in their editorials and in their handling of news stories on the subject of food." Even journals normally friendly to the United States had rallied to the attack, giving readers the impression "that the average American is not only a glutton, but a racketeer, or at best a candidate for an institution for the feeble-minded."

Merrell laid much of the blame for this outpouring of disaffection upon the United States itself.

> It has become obvious that during the early part of our participation in the recent war, our Government—through various official channels—"oversold" itself to Indians. Rightly or wrongly many of them gained the impression that the United States was going to "liberate" them from British rule. When this hope was not realized, Indians were bitterly disappointed and in many cases not only decided to question the United States' "sincerity" as a democratic nation, but began to class the United States with Britain as an imperialistic power.

Local politics, Merrell continued, subsequently entered the picture, and Indian editors found it easy to use the United States as a whipping boy for the ills of the moment. (When Muslim leader Mohammed Ali Jinnah was asked about the Muslim League *Dawn*'s constant complaints of American economic imperialism and dollar diplomacy, he commented that the editors had to make a living, confirming Merrell's point.) American support for the French in Indochina and the Dutch in Indonesia gave new ammunition to the critics. Under the circumstances, Merrell concluded, "it is perhaps not surprising that the Indian press in general is hypercritical of the United States' efforts to avert famine."[7]

Congress party leaders expressed similar dissatisfaction, sometimes more diplomatically, in private conversations with Americans. Party wheelhorse Sardar Vallabhbhai Patel told Merrell that the British still influenced American policy unduly, largely by giving Washington only the information London wanted the Americans to know. Patel deeply distrusted the British and did not believe that they would transfer power without a contest. Patel reminded Merrell that in the course of America's struggle for independence, a time had come when fighting was necessary, and he suggested that if the British wanted a scrap with India, they would get one. Indians, he said, were a peace-loving people, and the Congress party had always preferred nonviolence to violence. But if the Labour government reneged on Britain's promises, there would be trouble. In any event, the United States should reconsider its policy of acquiescence in British actions. Once Washington had "full possession of the facts," Patel believed it would.[8]

Patel erred in this prediction. To the increasing dismay of the Congress party, the Truman administration insisted on acting as a politically disinterested outsider. American hesitancy to get involved was in part a reflection of its continuing desire to avoid treading on British toes in a part of the world in which Americans had little experience and hardly more interest. To a degree that grew daily, Americans believed that the subcontinent's troubles would only increase with independence.

Through the end of 1946, the administration publicly supported a unified India. Undersecretary of State Dean Acheson, speaking for the president, called on the various parties to the Indian dispute to show "the magnanimous spirit the occasion demands" and "to forge an Indian federal union in which all elements of the population have ample scope to achieve their legitimate political and economic aspirations." But as the rift between the Congress party and the Muslim League deepened and the prospect of communal violence increased, Washington distanced itself from the matter. "Indian problems," Acheson remarked to Morrell, "must in the last analysis be solved by Indians themselves."[9]

While American leaders encouraged Nehru, Jinnah, and others on both sides of the Hindu–Muslim divide to compromise, Washington declined to back this verbal encouragement with diplomatic pressure. Following Attlee's announcement on 20 February 1947 that his government intended to transfer power to Indian hands not later than June 1948, the Truman administration persisted in its preference for a single successor state. Acheson, writing to the American embassy in London in April, acknowledged the "serious obstacles in the path of Indian unity," but he asserted that the political and economic interests of the United States in southern Asia would "best be served by the continued integrity of India." Yet Washington confined itself to words; it knew it possessed little leverage in the matter and it did not wish to alienate any party in the affair. In June, as partition became an inevitable accompaniment to *swaraj*, or self-government, the administration declared that "the future constitutional pattern is a matter to be determined by the Indian people themselves." The State Department went on to say that "the United States Government looks forward to the continuance of the friendliest relations with Indians of all communities and creeds."[10]

CONFLICTING CLAIMS, COMPETING VISIONS

Arriving just as the battle lines of the cold war were hardening, India's independence threw into still sharper contrast the differing world views of Americans and Indians. Indian leaders remained as wary of the United States as ever. Several months before the transfer of power, a visitor asked Gandhi if he had any message for the United States. "Dislodge the money God called Mammon," the mahatma replied. "Find a corner for poor God." America, he said, had "a dismal future if it swears by Mammon." At about the same time, Nehru congratulated the people of the Philippines on receiving independence from the United States, but he indicated skepticism as to what this portended. "We hope that this really signifies independence, for this word has become rather hackneyed and outworn and has been made to mean many things. Some countries that are called independent are far from free and are under the economic or military domination of some great power."[11]

Few Americans appreciated either India's preoccupation with independence or its insistence on sundering all the ties that bound them to the will of other countries. Nearly two centuries of American independence, more than anything else, explained this failure of comprehension: not feeling a necessity to vindicate their own autonomy, Americans found it difficult to perceive the need of Indians to do so. India's principal task consisted of proving to the world and to themselves that after decades of struggle and generations under a foreign yoke, they had become their own masters. Americans of the mid-twentieth century, taking autonomy as a birthright, viewed India much as possessors of inherited wealth observe nouveaux riches and wondered at all the fuss.

Americans' misunderstanding of India's national priorities led directly to their failure to discern the depth of India's insistence on nonalignment. To Nehru and other Indian leaders, the essence of independence was a country's ability to shape its own foreign policy. "What does independence consist of?" the prime minister asked. "It consists fundamentally and basically of foreign relations. That is the test of independence. All else is local autonomy. Once foreign relations go out of your hand, into the charge of someone else, to that extent and in that measure you are not independent." To this thinking, alliances limited a country's freedom of action and thereby diminished its independence. In extreme cases, alliances might even lead a country into wars bearing slightly or not at all on its own security. Having been dragged by the British into two world wars, Indian leaders refused to put themselves in the way of anything similar.[12]

From India's perspective, independence and nonalignment connected closely with the larger question of world peace. "Peace and freedom have become indivisible," Nehru told an American audience on a visit to the United States. "The preservation of peace forms the central aim of India's foreign policy. It is in the pursuit of this policy that we have chosen the path of nonalignment." Nonalignment did not imply "passivity of mind or action, lack of faith or conviction." Nor did it mean "submission to what we consider evil." Instead, it was "a positive and dynamic approach" to the problems confronting India and the world. Nonalignment, Nehru explained, reflected India's belief in the necessity for all peoples to choose their destinies, free from the coercion of the great powers. It also followed from India's conviction that truth would triumph over force, if given a chance.

> We believe that each country has not only the right to freedom, but also to decide its own policy and way of life. Only thus can true freedom flourish and a people grow according to their own genius. We believe, therefore, in non-aggression and non-interference by one country in the affairs of another, and the growth of tolerance between them and the capacity for peaceful coexistence.
>
> We think that, by the free exchange of ideas and trade and other contacts between nations, each will learn from the other, and truth will prevail. We, therefore, endeavor to maintain friendly relations with all countries—even though we may disagree with them in their policies or structure of government. We think that, by this approach, we can serve not only our country, but also the larger causes of peace and good fellowship in the world.[13]

In reflecting on alliances, Indian officials took their cue from the events that led to World War I. After the assassination of the Austrian archduke at Sarajevo, the intricate network of alliances the powers had constructed during the previous two decades acted like a spider's web, dragging one country after another toward the vortex, until nearly all Europe was at war. In the Indian view, alliances amplified mistakes, which even the most careful diplomats could not avoid, and they raised the level of international tension and fear.

Nehru and most of his associates did not fully adhere to the pacifist philosophy of Gandhi, but they generally accepted the mahatma's teaching that fear, not anger or acquisitiveness or megalomania, lay at the root of most wars. Alliances and preparations for war, by focusing on countries' fear of each other, simply made wars more likely. "These pacts and alliances," Nehru once said, "do not add to the strength of any nation. They only create hostility, leading to a piling up of armaments." He asked, "This constant wrestling, this cold war, this piling up of armaments, this search for a more powerful weapon, the ultimate weapon—where does it all lead to? Nowhere except destruction."[14]

Americans, in marked contrast, viewed alliances and military readiness in an entirely different light: not as causes of war but as guarantors of peace. If Sarajevo informed the alliance-phobic neutralism of the Indian government, Munich, the site of the 1938 Anglo–French capitulation to Hitler, motivated the makers of American foreign policy. Had the anti-Nazi front held firm, the American reasoning went, Germany almost certainly would have backed down. Like generals refighting their last battle, American diplomats constructed cold war policies on a foundation designed to prevent another Munich. Communism—"red fascism," in American parlance—represented the latest manifestation of aggression. By avoiding the mistakes of the 1930s, the Western countries might avert a replay of World War II. "Collective security" became the American shibboleth. At first, American leaders hoped to pursue the collective approach through the United Nations. But when superpower disagreements brought paralysis to that body—further confirming Americans' conviction of Soviet intransigence—Washington settled for less comprehensive alliances. Characteristically considering their interpretation of history the sole legitimate one, Americans found nearly incomprehensible India's inability—or unwillingness—to learn what seemed to them the transparent lessons of the recent past.

If Americans failed to appreciate the political arguments behind India's nonaligned policy, they also gave insufficient weight to that policy's economic justification. To Nehru and other Indian leaders, peace deserved to be sought not simply for its own sake, worthy though that was, but for the sake of India's economic development as well. Painfully aware of his country's pervasive poverty, Nehru realized that war and preparation for war would steal the resources his government required to raise the living standard of the Indian people. In the same speech in which Nehru laid out the basis for Indian nonalignment, the prime minister also described his plans for India's development. "We are now engaged in a gigantic and exciting task of achieving rapid and large-scale economic development of our country." Such an ambitious project would require all of India's energy and resources. To divert that energy and those resources to military preparations would condemn India to endless poverty. Rich countries like the United States could afford both guns and butter, but India could not.[15]

A final divergence of views between India and the United States involved the dangers they perceived themselves as facing. Geographically isolated, demographically unwieldy, and economically underdeveloped, India was relatively unthreatened by foreign invasion. The nearby great powers, Russia and China, would have to cross some of the roughest terrain in the world to attack India. Should they do so, they could never effectively occupy the country, not least because of its enormous and diverse population. The British had ultimately given up on the task, and they had had more help from the locals than attacking Russians or Chinese could expect. Nor did Moscow or Beijing have any great incentive to attack in the first place, since India, poor and out of the way as it was, had little to offer even a successful invader. The only country India considered a likely threat was Pakistan, but Pakistan would pose no serious danger unless sponsored by some outside power. Lastly, India did not possess large overseas investments or require extensive foreign markets, and hence its security interests did not extend much beyond its frontiers.

With a tendency to universalism that matched the Americans', Indians thought that since they did not feel threatened, neither should anyone else. But Americans *did* feel threatened—severely so. As the leading practitioners of democratic capitalism, they took communism's revolutionary challenge quite seriously, and in 1946, when Stalin declared the incompatibility of communism and capitalism, they knew the Soviet dictator was talking to them. In the dawning nuclear age, they could no longer count on two oceans and weak neighbors for security. Moreover, in the postwar period, their worldwide economic interests required a forward defense, just as they had during the two world wars. Ideologically, communism struck at the heart of everything Americans held dear. Should the communists prevail, the three-hundred-year American experiment would prove for naught. To Indians, the cold war—the struggle between capitalist democracy and communism—seemed a sideshow, a distraction from the more immediate tasks of nation building and economic development. To Americans it involved their raison d'être and their mission to the world.

THE PRICE OF PARTITION

At the moment of India's independence, Nehru had addressed a massive throng from the balcony of the parliament building in New Delhi. India, he said, had fulfilled its "tryst with destiny." But he added significantly that the fulfillment had not been "in full measure." He was referring to the separation of Pakistan from India, which many Indians considered (and still do) one of modern history's great crimes. The partition entailed wholesale pillage and slaughter, as millions of Hindus fled to India and Muslims to Pakistan. In the longer term, the rivalry between the two countries led to an arms race, a series of wars, and incalculable hardship for countless persons on both sides.[16]

Even if the United States had had to deal with only one successor government, its leaders would have found the task challenging enough; confronting two proved more than a match for American wisdom, ingenuity, and patience. At first, Washington attempted to maintain a strict neutrality between India and Pakistan. Sometimes the Truman administration carried evenhandedness to almost absurd lengths. In the late summer of 1947, the Indian government requested the loan of ten American transport planes to ferry refugees from Pakistan's portion of Punjab to Indian territory. Henry Grady, who had replaced Merrell in New Delhi as ambassador, urged the administration to approve the request. "It means much," Grady wrote, "not only from the humane standpoint but from the standpoint of the whole future of India." The United States, he continued, must support Nehru "in every way possible." Grady knew enough of Nehru's past not to expect any favors for the United States in return, but he claimed that if the new prime minister's government fell from power, "disintegration could easily follow."[17]

Despite Grady's vigorous brief, Washington rejected the airplane request. Truman insisted on receiving the approval of the Pakistanis before releasing the planes, and when Karachi refused, the relief mission failed to materialize.

Washington also adhered to a laissez-faire policy toward the larger and more permanent issue of Kashmir. As a princely state, Kashmir had had the option of joining either India or Pakistan. Trouble arose when Kashmir's Hindu maharaja sought to cede control of the state to India, despite the fact that Muslims constituted four-fifths of the population and favored attachment to Pakistan. Pakistan, represented initially by Pathan tribesmen, contested the cession, producing conflict between Indian and Pakistani troops that quickly claimed some twenty-five thousand lives and threatened to flare into full-scale war.

To Indians, especially to Nehru, Kashmir symbolized far more than real estate (although few places on earth could match the storied vale, the prime minister's ancestral home, for physical beauty). The largest bone of contention between India and Pakistan, the Kashmir dispute highlighted their differing conceptions of nationhood. Pakistan self-consciously defined itself as a religious state; without Islam, Pakistan had no reason for existence. India, by contrast, followed the path of secularism. To some degree, India's secularism reflected the diversity of faiths the country embraced. Even if all the Muslims had gone to Pakistan, which they had not, the Hindu majority would still have had to deal with Sikhs, Christians, Buddhists, and a variety of smaller sects. Maintaining civil order required removing religion from the realm of politics. India's secularism also reflected the tolerance inherent in Hinduism, which in important respects is as much a culture as a religion. Nehru himself made no attempt to disguise his agnosticism. "I find myself incapable of thinking of a deity or of any unknown supreme power in anthropomorphic terms," he said, "and the fact that many people think so is continually a source of surprise to me." Lacking any desire to establish the Indian polity on a religious footing, Nehru looked down on the Pakistanis, who did. He also feared that Pakistan's insistence that religion formed the basis of nationhood would have disruptive effects on India. Each repetition of the doctrine made the harmonization of communal groups in India less likely.[18]

Moreover, many Indian leaders could not reconcile themselves to the permanence of partition. As late as March 1947 Gandhi said that "if the Congress wishes to accept partition, it will be over my dead body." The

Congress party did accept partition, but only (as Nehru later admitted) as a tactical maneuver to get rid of Britain before the British changed their minds. "The picture of India we have learnt to cherish," a Congress resolution declared, "will remain in our minds and hearts. The All-India Congress Committee earnestly trusts that, when present passions have subsided, India's problems will be viewed in their proper perspective and the false doctrine of two nations in India will be discredited and discarded by all."

After independence, the Indian government publicly disavowed designs on Pakistan, but less from acquiescence to the principle of partition than from a desire to avoid inflaming the Muslims who remained in India. At the beginning of 1948, Nehru went so far as to declare to a Muslim audience, "If today by any chance I were offered the reunion of India and Pakistan, I would decline it. . . . I do not want to carry the burden of Pakistan's great problems. I have enough of my own."

Yet hopes for reunification refused to die. Nehru, commenting on what he saw as the essential unity of the subcontinent despite its present division into two countries, declared, "Nothing can overcome the basic urges, historical, cultural and economic, that tend to bring us nearer to each other. . . . Even though Pakistan is a separate and independent country and we must treat it as such, I find it a little difficult to think of it as alien to India and its people as anything but Indians." Privately, the prime minister predicted that in one form or another, "integration will inevitably come."[19]

Denying the legitimacy of Pakistan's very existence, Indians naturally rejected Pakistani control over Kashmir. They perceived Pakistan in much the same way that Arabs have usually perceived Israel, and they considered Pakistan's occupation of part of Kashmir as akin to Israel's post-1967 control of the West Bank and Gaza. To India, the Kashmir affair seemed an open-and-shut case of Muslim aggression; to compromise would be to surrender.

In significant ways, the Kashmir question was the mirror image of the cold war in U.S.–Indian relations. American leaders, deeming Kashmir a distraction better left alone, took a neutral line between India and Pakistan on Kashmir, just as Indian officials hewed to a middle course between the superpowers—and for much the same reason. Regardless of the merits of the Kashmir case, Washington had to live with both sides. Not surprisingly, American neutrality on Kashmir played in India about as well as Indian neutralism played in America.

As soon as fighting broke out between Indian and Pakistani forces in 1947, the Truman administration embargoed military supplies to both sides. During the months that followed, Washington resolutely resisted involvement in what was evidently a no-win situation. At the beginning of 1948, Britain—also hoping to avoid alienating India and Pakistan—sent its Commonwealth relations secretary, Philip Noel-Baker, to Washington in an effort to persuade the Americans to take a lead position on the Kashmir dispute. Warning of impending and possibly immense violence in the subcontinent, Noel-Baker explained that London's intervention would look like an attempt to reimpose the British raj less than a year after the transfer of power and would be roundly rejected. But the United States, enjoying great prestige in both countries—he said—might play a decisive role in achieving a settlement. The State Department turned Noel-Baker down flat. Without belaboring the obvious reason—that an American initiative would make Washington the target of vituperation from both sides—Undersecretary of State Robert Lovett told Noel-Baker that the American Congress would never go along with a commitment to South Asia. Besides, he said, an American initiative would attract "undesirable Russian attention."[20]

THE COMMONWEALTH CONNECTION

The Truman administration's refusal to get involved in the Kashmir dispute fit into a more general American policy of leaving the security of South Asia to the British. Loy Henderson, chief of the State Department's Near Eastern division and soon to replace Henry Grady as ambassador in New Delhi, explained the reasoning behind the policy. Henderson spoke specifically about discussions of Kashmir at the United Nations, but his words had broader application. "The problem," he said, "is one in which British initiative is clearly indicated, not only in view of the strength of the British delegation and the familiarity which the British have with the problems of the area, but also because in essence the present situation is a further development in the evolution of the political problems connected with the British withdrawal from India." Henderson asserted that an American initiative "would not only carry with it the danger of extending our already heavy commitments in various parts of the world but might also involve an American formula which would require making a choice between giving support to the interests of India or of Pakistan." The United States, he pointed out, had assiduously avoided making such a choice so far. It should continue to do so.[21]

In retrospect, especially in light of the enormous expansion of American commitments during the 1950s, the Truman administration's reluctance to get involved in South Asia may appear to have been a ploy, a case of diplomatic posturing. In fact, through the end of the 1940s, the United States remained a reluctant neoimperialist. The first major redefinition of American interests, the 1947 Truman Doctrine, resulted less from aggressive U.S. expansionism than from an inability to think of any other response to Britain's decision to discontinue funding for anticommunist forces in Greece and Turkey. The sweeping language of the president's declaration of support for "free peoples who are resisting attempted subjugation by armed minorities or by outside pressures" reflected not globalist hubris but a political calculation of the shock necessary to jolt the U.S. Congress into accepting the administration's $400 million Greece–Turkey aid request. When London, at about the same time, tried to persuade Washington to accept a role in settling the

Palestine dispute, the Truman administration refused the invitation. Even the Atlantic alliance, the centerpiece of the postwar U.S. defensive network, had to wait until 1949, and then it provoked considerable debate throughout the country.[22]

Toward South Asia, the Truman administration adopted a policy of indirect influence, of working through the British and through Britain's Commonwealth connection to India to maintain a pro-Western balance of power in the region. The policy had much to recommend it. Although the British had handed over political control to the Indians and the Pakistanis, Britain still possessed considerable economic leverage in the region as a result of long-standing commercial and financial ties. The British had military connections as well, through weapons sales to the two countries and advisers in the Indian and Pakistani armies. Politically, both India and Pakistan remained within the Commonwealth, which granted London a certain, albeit unquantifiable, pull with the governments of the two dominions. Culturally, Britain retained a power of attraction, especially among Indian elites. To some degree, this attractiveness came about from the relative ease with which London had finally accepted the inevitability of devolution; Mountbatten, the last viceroy, had made a particularly good impression in India. Equally, it arose from the indoctrination that many Indian leaders underwent during schooling in England. Not even the years Nehru spent in British jails overturned his high opinion of British practices and institutions. And because India lacked the unifying focus Islam, for example, afforded Pakistan, the English language and other aspects of English culture helped supply the cement keeping heterogeneous India from flying apart.

To Washington's thinking, the Commonwealth strategy had the additional advantage of letting the British take the heat already arising, and certain to continue, from the Kashmir dispute. Moreover, the Commonwealth promised to provide agents of Western influence in Asia more credible than the United States could furnish. At a moment when American domestic racial policies constituted a diplomatic embarrassment, the transformation of the Commonwealth into a multiracial organization gave Commonwealth representatives a standing in the Third World American officials could only envy. As a policy paper written for Truman's National Security Council explained, "The cooperation of the white nations of the Commonwealth will arrest any potential dangers of the growth of a white-colored polarization." Further, the Truman administration was already finding itself under fire from Anglophobes who charged that the United States was being suckered into salvage operations for Britain in Greece and Turkey, and administration officials wished to avoid similar blame regarding South Asia.[23]

Finally, the British were growing increasingly touchy about the decline of their world influence. An American hands-off policy toward the subcontinent would provide reassurance to Britain that the United States did not intend to elbow Britain aside in the region that once constituted the core of its empire. To be sure, London encouraged the Americans to assume thankless chores like mediation on Kashmir, but the British had no desire to see the United States take over the more remunerative aspects of their relationship with India—arms sales, for instance. "The fact is," Ambassador Grady remarked, "that His Majesty's Government feels competitive toward the USA in India and does not look with favor on American cooperation with the Government of India and the Government of Pakistan." The year of Indian independence marked the birth of the Marshall Plan and other American efforts on behalf of European security, in all of which the British took a major part. Washington had no desire to jeopardize Britain's cooperation. Staying out of London's way in South Asia seemed as prudent a policy for Europe as for India.[24]

For this constellation of reasons, the Truman administration initially adopted a low-profile approach to the problems of the subcontinent. An April 1949 report, produced as a collaborative effort of the State and Defense departments, outlined the policy. Before India's independence, the paper explained, Britain had served as the primary guarantor of the security of South Asia. After the transfer of power, direct British control had disappeared, leaving the West with the problem of filling the consequent vacuum before the Soviets or their agents moved in. Fortunately, Britain's "manifold economic and cultural contacts," established in the region over several generations, would enable the British to hold India and its environs as a "Western salient on the Asian continent." At a moment when American resources were already stretching thin, the United States should explore with the British the means by which "they can continue to assume responsibility for meeting the military requirements of the South Asian area," and American leaders should endeavor to persuade the British "to bear as great a share of this burden as they possibly can."[25]

In a separate report, the American joint chiefs of staff added their endorsement of the Commonwealth strategy. The chiefs argued that although India possessed relatively little positive value for the West, the loss of the country to communism would strike a serious blow at Western security in that it would give the Soviets easy access to the Indian Ocean and an opportunity for endless mischief in the Middle East and Southeast Asia. The military brass noted that Pakistan had more to offer. The air force had its eyes on Karachi and Lahore as potential bases for operations against the central Soviet Union and in defense of the oil fields of the Persian Gulf; the CIA hoped to develop Pakistan as a launching pad for "ideological and intelligence penetration" of Russia. The joint chiefs argued that the principal threat to the security of the subcontinent arose not from invasion but from subversion by dissident groups already active in India and Pakisan, and they asserted that the British, with their long experience in the area and their familiarity with the intricacies of regional problems, could provide signal service in bolstering internal security. Consequently, the chiefs declared that the Truman administration should provide for "collaboration and consultation" with London to determine the security requirements of the subcontinent, and that Washington should energetically explore "the extent to which the British can meet such requirements."[26]

Not all American officials accepted the wisdom of the Commonwealth approach. Henry Grady contended from New Delhi that if the United States continued to take a backseat to Britain in India, it would incur the same animosity it had encountered during the war. Grady had forwarded India's request for the loan of the ten planes, and he had been dismayed that Washington deemed it necessary to consult London before replying. That the administration's negative response was just what the British advised made matters worse. Grady noted that the American policy of deference to London rested on the premise that Britain and the United States were pursuing similar objectives with respect to India. This premise he considered specious. He contended that behind the facade of Anglo–American friendliness, the British were attempting to shift blame onto the United States for the troubles their own failures had caused. Mountbatten, Grady declared, continually warned Nehru and other Indian leaders to beware "dollar imperialism," as if to distract them from the problems that partition—Britain's most important legacy to the subcontinent—had provoked. Grady added that while British officials in India maintained cordial relations with the American embassy, they made "no attempt to consult with us on common problems or to ask our advice."[27]

Grady advocated a more active American policy toward India, although he recognized the hazards a higher profile would entail. While the ambassador managed to see the bright side of most diplomatic situations, he confessed that optimism came hard amid the turmoil India was experiencing. "My disappointment is principally with respect to Nehru," Grady said. He granted Nehru's idealism but worried at the prime minister's failure to translate his ideals into action. Speaking from a background as a business executive and economist who had led a technical mission to India in 1942, Grady remarked of Nehru, "He is rather letting administrative matters drift. He does not seem to have much direction. . . . His leadership in the fight for independence was based on qualities which are not particularly adaptive to the responsibilities of Government. He seems to have little interest in the vast economic problems facing the Dominion or those involved particularly with the division of the country." Grady found Nehru's failures in the economic realm especially troubling. "I have tried to talk with him several times on some of the economic problems facing the country and have become quickly aware that his mind was somewhere else."[28]

On a visit to Washington at the end of 1947, Grady explained that sooner or later the prime minister would have to pay attention. India's economic troubles were crowding ever closer upon the government. When they could no longer be avoided, Nehru would have to turn to the United States for help, and American influence would greatly increase. Grady, a firm believer in the efficacy of American technical and financial aid in raising the standard of living in Third World countries, contended that American assistance would be a boon both to India and to the United States. "It is the most effective channel for keeping India on our side and under our influence," he asserted. Grady contended that the Truman administration must play its aid card carefully, lest it give substance to charges of neoimperialism. He said he himself had responded to tentative approaches from Indian officials by "appearing indifferent to whether or not they take our capital." This policy had had "a good effect," and he urged its continuance.

Others in the State Department wanted to know whether the economic lever would suffice to bring India into line with American policies in the cold war. "We have conceived of India as a possible stabilizing influence in Asia, taking the place of the Western powers," Ray Thurston of the Near Eastern division commented. "Is this overly optimistic?" Grady did not think so. India desired to exercise substantial influence in South and Southeast Asia, and although partition and the continuing conflict with Pakistan had set this goal back, Nehru and other Indian officials still considered their country the region's natural leader. A large role for India, Grady said, need not jeopardize American goals in the area, so long as the Indians did not get too ambitious.

Raymond Hare, chief of the department's South Asian bureau, wanted to know more about India's attitude regarding Pakistan. Did the Indians continue to hope for reunification? Grady replied that irredentism ran highest among the Indian people at large; government officials took a less fervent, though hardly detached, view. He did not see how any reasonable person could expect a return to the status quo ante independence, but he suggested that some form of cooperation in economics and defense might develop. All the same, he would not hold his breath.

Grady looked to the future with ambivalence. Between the Truman Doctrine and the incipient Marshall Plan, the United States had gone far toward containing communism in Western Europe. Grady expected a Soviet thrust in another direction, probably south. He said he did not fear that this thrust would take the form of military aggression; rather, the Russians would aim for "ideological penetration." The Truman administration must prepare to counter this effort. "India is worth a lot to us," Grady asserted. "We must realize its importance ideologically." The ambassador advocated an intensified propaganda campaign, claiming that behind the animus of certain editors and the provocations of rabble-rousing politicians, little hard-core anti-Americanism existed in India. If the administration avoided diplomatic minefields like Kashmir, it might establish a reasonably fruitful modus vivendi with the Indians.

But Washington would have to get out from under Britain's shadow. The British, despite their cooperation against communism in Europe, were not up to the challenge in South Asia. Nehru required more prodding than London was willing to provide, especially on the need for unity in the face of the communist challenge. "I have told Nehru that this is a question that cannot be straddled," Grady said. "India should get on the democratic side immediately."[29]

Notes

1. Nicholas Mansergh, ed., *The Transfer of Power, 1942–7: Constitutional Relations between Britain and India*, vol. 2 (London: Her Majesty's Stationery Office, 1971), 471–73.

2. Vijaya Lakshmi Pandit, *The Scope of Happiness: A Personal Memoir* (New York: Crown, 1979), 191.

3. Ibid., 192–94.

4. Gary R. Hess, *America Encounters India, 1941–1947* (Baltimore: Johns Hopkins University Press, 1971), 164.

5. Berry to Henderson, *Foreign Relations of the United States 1946*, vol. 5 (Washington: U.S. Government Printing Office, 1969), 85–86.

6. Merrell to Byrnes, 10 June 1946, ibid., 88–92.

7. Ibid.; Merrell to Marshall, 2 May 1947, *Foreign Relations 1947*, vol. 3 (Washington: U.S. Government Printing Office, 1972), 154.

8. Merrell to Byrnes, 11 December 1946, *Foreign Relations 1946*, vol. 5, 101–103.

9. Acheson to Gallman, 3 December 1946, ibid., 99–100; Acheson to Merrell, 11 December 1946, ibid., 103–4.

10. Acheson to Douglas, 4 April 1947, *Foreign Relations 1947*, vol. 3, 151; *Department of State Bulletin*, 22 June 1947, 1249–50.

11. P. C. Roy Chaudhury, ed., *Gandhiji and International Politics* (Ahmedabad: Navajivan, 1970), 73; Hess, *America Encounters India*, 172.

12. Sarvepalli Gopal, ed., *Jawaharlal Nehru: An Anthology* (Delhi: Oxford University Press, 1980), 366–67.

13. Ibid., 377–79.

14. Ved Vati Chaturshreni, *Indo–U.S. Relations* (New Delhi: National, 1980), 83.

15. Gopal, ed., *Nehru: Anthology*, 378.

16. Ibid., 76.

17. Grady to Marshall, 5 October 1947, file 845.00, State Department records (record group 59), National Archives, Washington.

18. Michael Brecher, *Nehru: A Political Biography* (London: Oxford University Press, 1959), 600.

19. S. M. Burke, *Mainsprings of Indian and Pakistani Foreign Policies* (Minneapolis: University of Minnesota Press, 1974), 57, 88–90.

20. Memorandum of conversation, 10 January 1948, file 501.BC, State Department records.

21. Henderson to Lovett, 9 January 1948, ibid.

22. *Public Papers of the Presidents of the United States: Harry S. Truman, 1947* (Washington: U.S. Government Printing Office, 1963), 176–80.

23. NSC 48.1, 23 December 1949, National Security Council records (record group 273), National Archives.

24. Grady to Marshall, 25 October 1947, file 845.00, State Department records.

25. SANACC (State-Army-Navy-Air Force Coordinating Committee) 360/14, 30 March 1949, State-War-Navy Coordinating Commitee records (record group 353), National Archives.

26. Memorandum from Joint Chiefs of Staff, 24 March 1949, ibid.

27. Grady to Marshall, 25 October 1947, file 845.00, State Department records.

28. Grady to Henderson, 9 August 1947, ibid.

29. Memorandum of conversation, 26 December 1947, ibid.

chapter 3

THE EAST IS RED: 1949–1952

INDIA APPRECIATES

Nehru, however, made it clear that he had no intention of getting on "the democratic side"—by which Grady, of course, had meant the American side. Even before the transfer of power, Nehru had announced India's insistence on eschewing the politics of combination. "We propose, as far as possible, to keep away from the power politics of groups, aligned against one another, which have led in the past to world wars and which may again lead to disasters on an even vaster scale." Speaking at the Asian Relations Conference in March 1947, Nehru explained that India's, and Asia's, past militated against future alliances: "The countries of Asia can no longer be used as pawns by others; they are bound to have their own policies in world affairs. . . . We propose to stand on our own legs. . . . We do not intend to be the playthings of others."[1]

But nonalignment did not imply inactivity. In Nehru's view, India could not avoid a central role in Asian affairs. Surveying the situation in the autumn of 1949, the prime minister expounded,

> Look at the map. If you have to consider any question affecting the Middle East, India inevitably comes into the picture. If you have to consider any question regarding South-East Asia, you cannot do so without India. So also with the Far East. While the Middle East may not be directly connected with South-East Asia, both are connected with India. Even if you think in terms of regional organizations in Asia, you have to keep in touch with the

other regions. And whatever regions you may have in mind, the importance of India cannot be ignored.[2]

Contemporary events lent weight to Nehru's remarks. Even as he spoke, China's Communist party was celebrating its hard-won victory over Chiang Kai-shek's Nationalists. After two years of declining fortunes, the Nationalists had fled the Chinese mainland for Taiwan, where they entrenched themselves against the day of final battle or, more optimistically but far less realistically, the launching of a back-to-the-mainland counteroffensive. Meanwhile, Mao Zedong, Zhou Enlai, and their associates inaugurated the latest dynasty in the long history of the Middle Kingdom, proclaiming the People's Republic of China, which in true Leninist fashion had little to do with the people and less with being a republic.

The Communist victory in China set off a wave of recriminations in the United States. The Republican party, which included more than its share of Asia-firsters, had been searching for a stick to beat the Democrats with since Truman's stunning upset of Thomas Dewey in the 1948 presidential race. China fit the need perfectly. Charging a sellout of America's best friend and protégé in Asia, Republicans lambasted the Truman administration for incompetence at best, treason more likely. Allegations that the administration had "lost" China soon merged with the sweeping assertions of the McCarthyites, poisoning the atmosphere and rendering a reasonable and measured policy toward the new regime nearly impossible.

Indians, for their part, viewed developments across the Himalayas in a different light. Having concluded that the Nationalists were, in the words of diplomat K.P.S. Menon, "beyond salvation," Indians generally perceived the Communist victory, if not as a triumph of democracy and liberalism, at least as inevitable, and in any event as an improvement over four decades of war and revolution. A certain satisfaction that China, like India itself, had bested the Westerners—represented in this case by America's client, Chiang—colored Indian attitudes as well. Nehru's first ambassador to Beijing, K. M. Panikkar, described the feeling:

> All my training has been in the liberal radicalism of the West and consequently, though I was in some measure familiar with the economic doctrines of Marx, I had no sympathy for a political system in which individual liberty did not find a prominent place. But as against all this, I had a deep feeling of sympathy for the Chinese people, a desire to see them united, strong and powerful, able to stand up against the nations which had oppressed them for a hundred years, a psychological appreciation of their desire to wipe out the humiliations which followed the western domination of their country and to proclaim the message of Asia Resurgent. In these matters the attitudes of India and China were similar.[3]

As both Indians and Americans recognized immediately, China's entry into the socialist camp, formalized by a treaty with Moscow in 1950, increased the value of India to the West. Geopolitically, the subcontinent comprised the greatest concentration of Asians still outside communist control. As such, it represented a line that must be held at almost any cost. A paper written for Truman's National Security Council assessed the situation: "Should India and Pakistan fall to communism, the United States and its allies might find themselves denied any foothold on the Asian mainland."[4]

Ideologically, India's value to the United States appreciated even more. Since China had chosen the communist path to political and cultural regeneration, India's ability to match or outstrip China's progress became an acid test of the viability of democracy in Asia. Although Indian leaders hoped to strengthen their ties with Beijing and chose to play down their country's competition with China, to Americans it seemed the vital issue. The *Washington Post* characterized India as "an island in a continent of turmoil." The *Nation* described Nehru as "a figure of immense significance to the whole world." *Time* dubbed the prime minister "Asia's key man" and editorially hoped India would act as "a new anchor" for democracy in Asia. *Newsweek* delineated for its readers "the great Indian experiment in democracy," predicting that if the Indian experiment failed, "all Asia will fall to Communism or into chaos." The *New Republic,* peering through the "gathering twilight" in Asia, pronounced India the new "heartland" of the continent and, extending the metaphor, concluded that "its future involves the future of the whole body." *This Week* labeled Nehru the "spokesman of a troubled continent," not to mention "the world's most popular individual."[5]

PERSONAL DIPLOMACY ON THE ROCKS

Consequently, Americans were breathless with anticipation when Washington and New Delhi announced that a state visit by Nehru had been scheduled for October 1949. The U.S. Congress invited the prime minister to address a joint session and reverberated with speeches of welcome and near-adulation. Representative Emanuel Celler of New York described Nehru to his colleagues: "There is a transcendental quality about this great man; an aura of the spiritual seems to hover over him. Yet his words are those of a man who understands the meaning and significance of the practical needs of day to day living." John Kee, the chairman of the House Foreign Relations Committee, assured Nehru that "this American Republic is marching forward upon the same road with you and toward the same goal. . . . We do not expect nor ask your country to fall in behind us. No, we are inviting you to take your place at our side and keep step with us as we march into the dawn of a new day." Hubert Humphrey, who once told Assistant Secretary of State George McGhee that he wanted "to be for India what Walter Judd is for China," reminded his fellow senators that "we need friends in Asia." (Humphrey had a knack for belaboring the obvious.) India's millions were just waiting to link hands with Americans, he said. "There already exist many bonds which bind us in friendship with India. The traditional love of freedom and democracy held by the Indian people strikes a similar chord in us. We likewise believe that this democratic freedom can only flourish in a world at peace."[6]

The inflated rhetoric raised expectations, which had considerably less to do with the realities of Asian politics than with the emotional needs of Americans at a moment of psychological crisis. The country's long love affair with China had come to a crashing halt, leaving Americans stunned and bewildered. Like many a jilted suitor, the American public sought to erase its bad memories of China by embracing India.

Not surprisingly, the India the pundits and politicians now extolled bore only a passing resemblance to the genuine article. Although the personal praise appealed to Nehru's considerable vanity, the prime minister had no desire to make his country into America's "new anchor" for Asia, nor did he intend to walk arm in arm with American leaders into the "dawn of a new day." On the contrary, it was India's self-interest that he aimed to pursue, not America's, and he certainly planned to keep his distance from the United States.

The visit proved a disaster. The State Department's George McGhee blamed the prime minister: "Nehru came to America with an apparent chip on his shoulder toward high American officials, who he appeared to believe could not possibly understand someone with his background. . . . Nehru and Truman didn't hit it off at all. Rumor has it that, in his first informal meeting with the President, he was offended by Truman's extended discussion of bourbon whiskey with Vice President Alben Barkley." Dean Acheson attempted to enliven a formal reception and demonstrate respect for Nehru by comparing the prime minister to great Americans of the past: Washington as father of his country, Jefferson as theorist of democracy, Jackson as political organizer, Lincoln as savior amid fratricidal conflict. The secretary of state's effort failed utterly. "The result," Acheson recalled, "was very definitely a change from the routine and caught our distinguished Visitor unprepared, like a student who had not done his homework for what should have been a 'gut course.' He was not pleased." Acheson conceded that Nehru would play a crucial role in world affairs; the secretary wrote: "He was so important to India and India's survival so important to all of us, that if he did not exist—as Voltaire said of God—he would have to be invented." Nonetheless, to Acheson Nehru would remain "one of the most difficult men with whom I have ever had to deal."[7]

Nehru had considered Americans philistines before he arrived, and his visit gave him no reason to change his view. A CIA informant who had sources close to the prime minister reported Nehru's reactions. Truman, the Indian leader thought, was a "mediocre man" whom luck—the world's bad luck, in Nehru's view—had placed in circumstances "far superior to his capacities."

Acheson was "equally mediocre." Other American officials were "uncertain, confused, superficial, too much inclined to improvisation and at the same time pretentious and arrogant." The American people were "elementary and material," lacking "cultural drives" and desiring only to "eat and drink and to live comfortably."[8]

Substantively, Nehru's trip yielded hardly better results, although in explaining the differences between India's approach to international affairs and the United States', the prime minister helped dispel misconceptions that had been clouding the matter. Nehru castigated the French for shortsightedness and incompetence in dealing with Ho Chi Minh's nationalist movement in Indochina—and implicitly criticized American officials for supporting the French misadventure. He presented India's side of the Kashmir dispute, depicting his government's behavior as purely reactive and defensive and declaring that the blame lay entirely with Pakistan's feudal and intolerant theocracy. He told the Americans that they were taking quite the wrong line in dealing with the Russians. Since the United States could not expect to match the Kremlin in "name-calling, deprecation and verbal belligerency," American officials should not even try. Instead, the United States should practice "mental jiujitsu" and employ the Soviets' clumsiness against them. It should make every gesture of cooperation, leaving to the Russians the burden of rejectionism and warmongering. Regarding China, Nehru commented that communism held obvious attractions for the country's millions of poor—as it did for many in India. For the moment, necessity had forced China into reliance on Russia. But a prouder people than the Chinese did not exist, and they would not suffer Soviet tutelage for long. The noncommunist countries should encourage Chinese "Titoism" by demonstrating a more tolerant attitude than most had yet displayed. So long as the West rebuffed and isolated China, hard-liners in Beijing could credibly blame the "foreign devils" for their problems.[9]

THUNDER AT THE THIRTY-EIGHTH

If the Communist victory in China increased the perceived importance of India to the West, it did not immediately alter U.S. policy toward the subcontinent. At the end of 1949, Truman's National Security Council reviewed the situation and advocated a steady-as-she-goes approach. An NSC policy paper commented that although Nehru remained wedded to neutralism, this need cause no particular alarm. Even a nonaligned India could serve as a "bulwark against communist expansion." Consequently, the administration should continue to rely on Britain and its Commonwealth partners to hold India for the West, seeking the means by which "all members of the British Commonwealth may be induced to play a more active role" in assuring the security of the subcontinent.[10]

Within six months, however, this complacency had vanished. In the last week of June 1950, communist troops from North Korea stormed across the

38th parallel into South Korea. Before long, they had the South Koreans—
America's last clients in that part of mainland Asia—on the run. Following so
soon after Mao Zedong's victory in China, and at a time when the Viet Minh
were increasing their pressure on the French in Indochina, the North Korean
invasion appeared part of an orchestrated communist offensive. Should Korea
fall, as it gave every indication of doing in the final days of June, the communists would reign supreme in East Asia. They would acquire confidence for a
takeover of Indochina; they might even place the U.S. position with Japan at
risk.

Better than any single event in the first half-decade of Indian independence, the outbreak of the Korean war revealed the divergent perspectives of
the United States and India. Americans, recalling the events that led to
World War II, saw Korea as a test of collective security. Korea became Czecho-
slovakia; June 1950 stood for September 1938; New York, home of the United
Nations, represented Munich. The democratic countries had quavered before
Hitler, and world war had followed. The free world must make no similar
mistake now. The noncommunist states must band together to halt aggression, lest the past repeat itself. Atomic weapons, since 1949 no longer an
American monopoly, would bring additional horror.

Indians interpreted the Korean affair in markedly different fashion. Unbe-
guiled by the Munich analogy, they doubted that Hitler and the Germans had
much to teach the world about Kim Il Sung and the Koreans. Without
denying a Soviet and Chinese connection to events in Korea, Indian officials
correctly saw the fighting there as primarily an indigenous dispute. Indian
leaders warned against overreaction. They contended that the United States,
by treating the North Korean assault as the opening round of World War III,
might succeed in making it just that.

The divergence of the American and Indian positions became evident at
an exchange between Ambassador Henderson and Nehru. Henderson had
been warning against Soviet expansionism for nearly two decades. Like most
Americans of his day, the U.S. ambassador firmly believed that the highest
ideals motivated his country's actions. President Truman's decision to send
troops to Korea to repel the communist invasion summarized for Henderson
all the fine and noble elements in American policy—and he told Nehru as
much. He said he had never felt prouder of serving the American government
than at present. Only a few years after World War II, and despite the "ardent
desire" of the American people to remain at peace, his country had taken the
selfless step of mobilizing, not in defense of American territory, but with the
objective of "showing aggressors and the world at large that it took its UN
obligations seriously." He hoped India did also. At this moment, Nehru was
wavering regarding a U.N. resolution calling for aid to South Korea. Henderson characterized the issue as one of "moral courage," and he asked whether
future generations of Indians would look proudly on a government that had
failed to stand up against aggression.

Nehru replied calmly that the Korean matter involved complications for India that rendered a simple yes-or-no decision difficult. In particular, the prime minister objected to Washington's announcement, in the context of the North Korean invasion, that the United States would step up military aid to the French in Indochina and that the American Seventh Fleet would begin patrolling the Taiwan Strait. Nehru told Henderson that the U.S. government was making a serious mistake by tying the defense of South Korea to intervention in Indochina and involvement in the Chinese civil war. Most Asians, the prime minister said, looked upon American actions regarding Indochina and Taiwan as irrefutable evidence of American imperialism. Under these circumstances, for his government to associate itself with the United States—however admirable American intentions in respect of Korea might be—would damage India's credibility. Most especially such an association would prevent improved relations with Beijing, which India considered necessary for its own welfare and for the peace of Asia. Nehru frankly added that domestic critics were already blasting him and his ministers as "tools of the Anglo–American imperialists." Any move that could be interpreted as deference to Washington would raise serious political problems for him. He must ponder the matter with care.[11]

Eventually, New Delhi came out in favor of the U.N. resolution, but Indian support for the U.N. effort in Korea never warmed beyond the tepid. Nehru continued to fear the fighting would spread, and he invested most of his energy trying to end the conflict by negotiation. In July, he wrote to Moscow and Washington urging the superpowers to seek a settlement before the dispute broadened into a larger war. The Russians were boycotting the Security Council over the exclusion of Beijing (only Moscow's absence had allowed the passage of the resolution to aid South Korea), and Nehru strongly recommended their return. To Washington, he suggested allowing Beijing to replace Taibei on the council, both to enable talks on Korea to begin and to reflect more accurately the power situation in East Asia. "My honest belief," he explained to Dean Acheson, "is that Moscow is seeking a way out of the present entanglement without loss of prestige and that there is a real chance of solving the Korean problem peacefully."[12]

The Truman administration summarily rejected Nehru's advice. Under the duress of war and the political pressure of Joseph McCarthy's wild but widely credited charges, the administration could hardly abandon the Chinese Nationalists in favor of the Communist regime. Acheson replied to Nehru that allowing Beijing a seat on the council would give the impression that "the United States had made a deal with the U.S.S.R. to buy off Communist aggression in Korea." The communists had started the fighting, Acheson said. The burden of concessions lay with them. In the meantime, the U.N. must resist stoutly.[13]

The tension between Washington and New Delhi engendered by their different approaches to the Korean conflict eased somewhat in September, when amphibious forces led by General Douglas MacArthur scored a spectacular victory at Inchon. With one blow, MacArthur reversed the fortunes of the war and seized for the U.N. the military initiative. In a matter of days, the general accomplished the U.N.'s original objective: the repulsion of the North Korean invaders.

Before Nehru had a chance to sigh with relief that the war had ended without becoming a big-power contest, American officials got greedy. Had Washington been offered a restoration of the status quo ante June 25 in August, the Americans would have snatched it without a second's hesitation. But with MacArthur on a roll and the communists on the ropes, Truman could not resist the opportunity to smash the North Korean regime—and spike the guns of his Republican critics. Without difficulty, the American delegation persuaded the U.N. to order a crossing of the 38th parallel, to the end of reunifying Korea under U.N.—that is, South Korean—control.

Indians shuddered at the Americans' recklessness. Their alarm increased when the Indian ambassador to Beijing, K. M. Panikkar, passed along a warning from Premier Zhou Enlai that an American crossing of the 38th parallel would bring China into the war.

American officials discounted the message. They distrusted Panikkar, who, in Truman's description, had "played the game of the Chinese Communists fairly regularly." They thought that even if the Indian ambassador had reported Zhou's remarks accurately, the Chinese premier was bluffing. Acheson did suggest that Henderson attempt to establish direct contact with the Chinese ambassador in New Delhi, in order to assure the Chinese that the United States harbored no designs on their territory. But China nixed the arrangement on the grounds that if Washington would not recognize Beijing, Beijing would not talk to Washington.[14]

At the end of November, the collision the Indians had feared occurred. Three hundred thousand Chinese troops crossed the Yalu River into Korea and launched a massive counteroffensive. American forces reeled from the blow, and Truman set warning bells ringing all around the globe by suggesting at a press conference that the United States might use atomic weapons against the Chinese.

The White House hurriedly corrected Truman's statement—Washington was not planning nuclear escalation. But the affair nonetheless heightened Indian feelings that the United States was bent on the destruction of humanity. "We are on the very verge of world war," Nehru told the Indian parliament. If the United States resorted to the atom bomb, the prime minister said, it would almost guarantee Soviet intervention—besides confirming the widespread belief that the West had designed nuclear weapons for use "only against Asiatics." Hoping to defuse the crisis, Nehru advocated an immediate cease-fire, the establishment of a demilitarized zone between the opposing armies, and the convening of a conference of the great powers, including China.[15]

The Truman administration ignored India's advice. The State Department also rebuffed an effort by Nehru to wangle an invitation to Washington to meet with the president and Prime Minister Attlee of Britain. In the administration's opinion, Nehru's peacemongering at this crucial stage of the conflict constituted appeasement; bringing him to the United States would merely amplify his voice.

For several weeks, through the beginning of 1951, the level of U.S.– Indian distrust remained high. It began to ease after the U.N. forces stemmed their retreat, taking pressure off Washington to escalate. In April, Truman sacked MacArthur for expressing too freely his dissatisfaction at not being able to bomb China, which indicated to New Delhi a heartening trend toward temperance.

But differences between India and the United States did not disappear entirely. India rejected a proposal to brand China an aggressor. Nehru also objected to the Americans' use of the "Uniting for Peace" resolution, which allowed the General Assembly to override Soviet vetoes in the Security Council. In Nehru's opinion, this circumvention of the U.N. charter succeeded only in "converting the UN into a larger edition of the Atlantic Pact and making it into a war organization more than one devoted to international peace."[16]

NOT BY BREAD ALONE

Americans hardly noticed the restraint, but India's criticism of American policy in Korea might have been more severe had not a domestic crisis forced Nehru's government into a corner from which only American assistance appeared to afford an exit. The partition of 1947 had not only provoked mass mayhem and instigated chronic conflict between India and Pakistan; it had separated India from much of the subcontinent's most fertile farmland. Economic warfare with Pakistan exacerbated the food problem. In 1950, a coincidence of natural calamities raised the distress level to emergency. By December, in the middle of the Korean panic, New Delhi's experts were forecasting a deficit of two million tons in India's grain crop. Ambassador Pandit visited the State Department to request assistance to prevent a famine that might claim as many as ten million lives.

Even beyond the humanitarian considerations, Truman administration officials recognized at once the political necessity of a favorable response. The U.S. government, through the Marshall Plan, was spending billions to put Europeans back on their feet, and it could hardly let Indians starve without convincing Asians of American racism. Moreover, as much as Nehru annoyed them, administration leaders understood that far more dangerous characters waited in India's wings. A State Department memo asserted that already "the political opposition, particularly the Communists, are exploiting the situation." In the opinion of Assistant Secretary George McGhee, "a quick response to the Indian Government's request for food grains is the most effective means, immediately available to our Government, of counteracting Communist subversion in India." Should the United States reject aid and the predicted famine occur, "the present government will be weakened and India may be threatened with anarchy, a dictatorship of the extreme left, or a dictatorship of the extreme right. The possibility of Communist subversion of the country and utilization of Indian manpower and other resources against us will be increased." The fact that the United States and India differed on matters of foreign policy intensified the need for a favorable reply, McGhee continued. If the administration refused the request and large numbers of Indians began to die, Indians would conclude that "we denied this request because we did not like the political attitude Mr. Nehru expressed."[17]

Acheson and Truman agreed with this reasoning, and early in 1951, the administration raised the matter with Congress. In certain respects, the timing of the Indian request presented problems for the administration. The Senate had just taken up the historic question of stationing American troops in Europe; this "great debate" lasted until April. Then the Truman–MacArthur controversy burst into the open, prompting another round of hearings and further debate. On the other hand, the pervasive sense of crisis worked in favor of passage of an India-aid bill—although not, paradoxically, to the advantage of smooth U.S.–Indian relations.

The paradox resulted from the ambivalence of Americans toward foreign aid. Americans like to think they provide help to countries in need as a selfless gesture, a sharing of their bounty. They like the recipients to think so too. At the same time, Americans hate the idea that some country might take advantage of them and exploit their generosity. Consequently, they usually insist on a demonstration that American aid will produce benefits for the United States. Congress, in particular, responsible for reconciling competing claims on taxpayers' patience and paychecks, often demands that the executive branch elicit a quid pro quo, tangible or otherwise. But to the degree that the executive delivers a quid pro quo, it undercuts the appearance of selflessness, rendering aid nearly useless as an instrument to display American goodwill.

In a period of bipartisan tranquillity, the Truman administration might have finessed the issue. But tranquillity had fled many months before, at about the time of Dewey's defeat. After two decades in the wilderness, the Republicans were almost as hungry for the White House as Indian peasants were for American grain. Finesse—not Truman's strong suit anyway—was impossible.

Early soundings on Capitol Hill indicated the direction the debate would take. The chairman of the Senate Foreign Relations Committee, Tom Connally, thought India was inflating the number of persons at risk in hopes of taking Uncle Sam for a ride. "Of course they are going to say there are a lot of people that are going to starve if you don't hurry up and give them some wheat," Connally told George McGhee. "If you are going to sit down and accept what they say and what they ask, we won't have anything to eat ourselves in a little while." The Texas Democrat also complained about Nehru's lack of helpfulness in international affairs, and he did not think an aid bill would improve matters. "Our relations with India now are not very good, are they? Nehru is out giving us hell all the time, working against us and voting against us. Is this a proposition to buy him? He won't stay bought, if you buy him."

Massachusetts Republican Henry Cabot Lodge—who, interestingly, would later become almost a lobbyist for India in the Eisenhower administration—asked bluntly, "What are the Indians going to do for us?" Wisconsin's Alexander Wiley, another Republican, wondered if the administration had thought to ask Nehru for "a quid pro quo, a little collaboration on the world stage." Speaking to the self-interested aspect of foreign aid, Wiley proposed a general principle: "Hereafter we are going to be practical realists. We are going to do charity where charity is done, but when there is no need for charity, when our own people have to pay the bill, we owe our people some responsibility." When McGhee answered that the administration had not asked for a quid pro quo and did not plan to, since Nehru would certainly refuse, Democrat Guy Gillette of Iowa declared that "if thirteen million people are dying and he is willing to let them die," the United States ought to make the prime minister bear the onus for the deaths.[18]

While Congress debated the aid measure, focusing primarily on whether the resolution would serve American interests in the cold war, liberal activists in the country at large mounted a campaign premised on humanitarianism. Dorothy Norman, writer and well-known political organizer, set up an emergency food committee for India, enlisting the support of Eleanor Roosevelt, author Pearl Buck, civil rights leader Walter White, and assorted other notables and dignitaries. The Young Men's Christian Association, the National Association for the Advancement of Colored People, the National Council of Churches, and the American Friends Service Committee rallied to the cause.

Editorial opinion generally favored the aid measure, usually emphasizing the humanitarian argument. "There should be no question of politics and no conditions of any sort," the New York Times asserted. "We are privileged to be in a position to help and there should be no hesitation about it in Washington." The Christian Science Monitor opposed the idea of using aid as a political tool, predicting that "the result in world opinion could be very unfortunate." The Washington Post said, "Hunger and politics do not mix," adding that "any attempt to associate them would do this country incalculable harm in Asia."[19]

Eventually, the administration got its aid bill and India its wheat. But congressional approval owed less to the humanitarian arguments of liberals than to conservatives' appeals to American self-interest, especially to the notion that the U.S. government, having entertained the request in the first place, could not now turn it down. Henry Cabot Lodge summarized the prevailing view on Capitol Hill when he said, "I can perfectly well see that if we don't do this we incur a lot of ill will. I am not so sure that if we do do th[i]. we get a lot of good will. Having observed Mr. Nehru and the Ambassador here, I just haven't got any faith at all that there is going to be any gratitude or appreciation or anything else."[20]

ASIA FOR ASIANS

The Indian reaction proved Lodge correct. While Congress debated the wheat legislation, Nehru declared that India was "not so down and out" as to accept conditions on aid, and he added that his government "would be unworthy of the high responsibilities with which we have been charged if we bartered away in the slightest degree our country's self-respect or freedom of action." Even before the grain ships reached their destination, Nehru made it clear that he would not let his country's reliance on American aid temper his independent foreign policy, by rejecting the recently completed peace treaty with Japan. The Truman administration had intended to make the Japan treaty a centerpiece of its Asia policy. For many months, the principal American negotiator, John Foster Dulles, had traversed the globe trying to produce a document that Japan's numerous former antagonists could all sign. Consequently, Nehru's rebuff, which the prime minister justified on grounds that the treaty granted the United States an inordinate role in Japanese affairs and slighted China and the Soviet Union, came as a particular blow.[21]

Many U.S. observers found Nehru's action intolerable. Even some who had backed the aid resolution considered his concern for China and the Soviet Union a shameless effort to cultivate the East while depending on the West. The *New York Times* declared Nehru one of the "great disappointments" of world affairs. "Instead of seizing the leadership of Asia for its good," the *Times* commented, with a shake of the editorial head, "Nehru turned aside from the responsibilities." History would not forgive Nehru's "abnegation of greatness." His statesmanship no longer inspired positive action; it only encouraged people and nations to leave things undone. "How the mighty have fallen!"[22]

Ambassador Henderson detected a deeper significance in Nehru's rejection of the peace treaty. In Henderson's interpretation, Nehru was aiming to increase India's influence in Asia at the expense of the United States and of the West generally. The prime minister desired, as Henderson put it, nothing less than "the eventual exclusion from the mainland and waters of Asia of all Western military power and what he would consider as Western political and economic pressure." Taking the side of China and the Soviet Union presumably would produce benefits for India in the short run. It required no particular insight to understand this part of the policy. But Nehru's objectives, vis-à-vis Japan, in opposing a treaty backed by the Japanese government, required more explaining. Here, Henderson contended, Nehru was engaged in a longer game. Henderson argued that Nehru counted on the resurgence of "nationalistic and

anti-white elements in Japan." These groups, chafing under American hegemony, would eventually regain power. When they did, they would throw out
the Americans. At that point, they would demonstrate their gratitude to India
for Nehru's prescient support.

Henderson gave the prime minister credit for subtlety.

> Nehru is not likely to move too openly or rapidly. He will not wish to arouse
> too much hostility or indignation in the United States. He realizes that, for
> some time to come, India will sorely need certain capital and consumption
> goods which only the United States can furnish.
>
> He is not likely to disclose his real objectives. He will probably try to
> appear as a democratic idealist primarily interested in the welfare of the
> downtrodden masses of Asia, of David who regretfully faces the materialistic
> and clumsy Goliath of militarism and imperialism. . . .
>
> He will continue to make minor concessions and friendly gestures from
> time to time to the United States in order to keep down the tide of resent-
> ment and make U.S. officials think, "He will come to our side eventually if
> we are patient and handle him properly."

But the United States would err in such reasoning. Nehru had no intention of
coming to the American side, and the sooner American officials dropped
such hopes the better. Henderson conceded that perhaps Nehru had not
consciously laid his plans so far in advance, but the ambassador argued that
they followed naturally, almost inevitably, from what the prime minister had
done to date.[23]

On one point, Henderson's analysis hit the mark. Nehru certainly did
intend to reduce American influence in Asia. The prime minister believed
that allowing the Americans an Asian sphere endangered the peace of the
continent and therefore the security of India. And he doubtless hoped to
increase India's influence. The Americans thought they had something to
teach the world; so did he. They pushed alliances and collective security; he
hawked neutralism. The allure of prestige, of being the leader of the "free
world," motivated American presidents; analogous ambitions inspired Nehru
to promote "Asia for Asians."

Nehru's behavior would hardly have occasioned comment had it been the
behavior of a general secretary of the Soviet Communist party or a prime
minister of France's Fourth Republic. The actions Henderson was describing
were simply those of a chief executive of an important country pursuing
reasonable and basically legitimate national goals. But Nehru—like his
American counterparts—so often spoke of higher aims and broader ideals that
evidence suggesting more mundane objectives came as welcome ammunition
in the battle for the moral high ground. Not that American leaders would use
it publicly: responsible American officials almost never attacked Nehru by
name. Yet they rarely objected, and no doubt felt a certain satisfaction, when

commentators in the press and critics in Congress assailed Nehru for professing one set of values and practicing another.

FIRST TILTINGS

As Washington, in the aftermath of the Chinese intervention in Korea, sorted through the rubble of its Asia policy to determine what might be salvaged, it looked upon the Indian subcontinent with greater interest than ever. India and its near neighbors seemed Asia's hinge of fate. The destabilization of South Asia, according to a fresh NSC estimate, would constitute "a catastrophe of major proportions" for the West.[24]

Until this time, the United States had relied on Britain and the Commonwealth to guarantee the security of the region. But the deficiencies of the Commonwealth strategy were becoming increasingly apparent. London was retrenching in South Asia as elsewhere; in the midst of the fighting in Korea, the British had announced a cutback in military aid to India and Pakistan. In addition, for all the enlightened policies that the British had followed in transferring power, and despite American hopes that the Commonwealth would provide more credible agents of Western influence than Americans, there remained throughout Asia considerable suspicion of European imperialism. To the degree that the United States worked with and through the British, some of the suspicion rubbed off.

Consequently, the Truman administration decided to reconsider the Commonwealth strategy. Neither the State Department nor the White House possessed any great desire to extend the American writ to South Asia, and the Pentagon positively rebelled at the idea. Truman and Acheson did not have to ask Congress to know the legislature would never countenance such a commitment. The Indians, of course, would also do their best to prevent any increase in the American role in the region. But despite all these drawbacks, the heightened importance of the subcontinent convinced the administration to adopt a higher profile. The United States, according to an administration policy paper, should undertake "more intimate consultation" with friendly countries in the region regarding political, military, and economic matters of common concern; it should increase economic aid to the area; it should explore opportunities for acquiring military base rights, particularly in Pakistan; and—most portentous—it should prepare to provide military assistance to countries desiring it.[25]

A month later, the State Department sent Assistant Secretary McGhee to South Asia to explain the change in policy to American diplomats stationed there. The Ceylon (later Sri Lanka) conference took place at a hill-country resort outside Colombo. In surroundings that reeked of the British raj—tea plantations, manicured golf course, wide verandas—American officials plotted what many Indians would later interpret as an assumption of Britain's remaining responsibilities.

McGhee set the tone for the conference in his opening remarks. Some persons, he said, thought the continuing war in Korea should have caused the cancellation of the meeting. He disagreed heartily. He considered a gathering of American officials involved in South Asian relations "more essential than ever." The last such meeting had taken place in 1949; the world had changed enormously since then: "The loss of China, the immediate threat to Indochina and the balance of Southeast Asia, the invasion of Tibet and the reverses in Korea have greatly increased the significance to the U.S. of the political, strategic, and resource potential of the countries in this region." The United States must undertake a "serious examination of where we stand in South Asia." In particular, Washington must ask, "Who are our friends? On whom can we rely in a crisis?"

McGhee explained that the administration's policy of relying on Britain to supply the defense needs of the subcontinent was running up against the harsh facts of imperial decline. Economically enervated at home, London could no longer carry the free world's burden overseas. Equally important, now that the voluntaristic Commonwealth was replacing the coercive empire and members had the option of resigning, British and American objectives increasingly diverged. The British needed to keep India in the Common-wealth if they hoped to retain even a shadow of their former world influence; therefore, they had to pay close heed to Indian preferences and prejudices. As McGhee told the conference, "The primary objective of the United King-dom, to which other objectives are subordinate, is to obtain the permanent adherence of India to the Commonwealth." American leaders, by contrast, while wishing the Commonwealth prosperity and long life, had other priori-ties. Washington sought "the orientation of India in particular and South Asia in general toward the United States and away from the Soviet Union."

McGhee conceded the difficulty of the task. Economic and political consid-erations limited the resources the administration could bring to bear in South Asia. India and Pakistan remained unable to settle their Kashmir quarrel. Lingering anticolonial sentiment, compounded by a "lack of understanding, especially by India, of the aggressive intentions of the Communists" and by "the emotional anti-U.S. attitude of Nehru," inclined the region toward neutralism. In a vicious circle, this neutralist attitude alienated the U.S. Congress and further limited the administration's economic and political options. "Even the small effort which is potentially possible is greatly endan-gered as far as Congressional action is concerned by the attitudes and activi-ties of the countries involved, especially India."

McGhee held such a low opinion of India and Nehru that he directly asked Loy Henderson whether "India might as well be written off as a friend or as a potential ally." Henderson held no brief for Nehru, but he replied in the negative. The administration, the ambassador said, would commit a "grave blunder" if it considered friendship with India out of the question. "I am convinced," he declared, "that in India underneath the crust of criticism of the United States and of constantly expressed distrust of American policies there is a hard core of basic friendliness for the United States and confidence in the motives which animate the American people."

Henderson recommended that Washington, rather than write India off, pursue a patient policy of educating Indians to the objectives of American diplomacy.

> We should quietly and consistently prove by acts that we are friends of India and that we really would like to cooperate with India and to assist India to the extent of our ability in case India should desire economic and cultural assistance for its development.
>
> We should take every occasion to help Indians to understand that American friendship and cooperation are just as advantageous to India as India's friendship and cooperation are to the United States. We should consult in a friendly way with India with regard to international problems in which India might have special interest, and we should explain to India, whenever we find that we cannot follow India's advice, the reasons for our actions.

Yet the United States should never adopt "a cringing or flattering attitude" toward Nehru. Such would serve only to encourage the prime minister to think "he has the whip hand over us." Nor ought Americans to acquiesce in Nehru's claims to the leadership of noncommunist Asia. "We must not appear to other Asian nations to have accepted the thesis that India is the dominant power in free Asia or that we consider that free Asia is in any sense an Indian sphere of influence." Finally: "We should always bear in mind that Nehru is not India; even now he cannot entirely ignore Indian public opinion. Events beyond his control may force him to decide to change his present tactics and methods."

After Henderson spoke, Avra Warren, the ambassador to Pakistan, described the situation there. Warren characterized Pakistan's overriding political and diplomatic policy determinant as being its "obsession with India." Because of this and its sincere Muslim antipathy to atheistic communism, he said, Pakistan would probably reject neutralism in favor of cooperation with the West.

Before the conference adjourned, the diplomats compiled a list of recommendations. Reflecting Henderson's advice, these included a statement that Washington should adopt toward India "a policy of patience built on firmness." Where Indian neutralism undermined American initiatives on behalf of collective security, the United States should "challenge it vigorously." In particular, U.S. officials should engage in "most active opposition to Nehru's efforts to create a neutral bloc among Asian and Arab states." At the same time, "India should be considered as a worthwhile long-term risk," and U.S. officials should endeavor through "non-pressure methods to insure India's friendship and ultimate support."

More significant, the conferees declared that the defense of South Asia required "strong flanks." These flanks included Indochina to the east and Turkey, Iran, and—most to the point of the present discussion—Pakistan to the west. Consequently, the United States "should consider on an urgent basis the desirability of entering into an early understanding with Pakistan which would provide for equipping and building up Pakistan's military force and insure the availability of its ground forces on the western flank at the outbreak of war."[26]

After adjourning the Ceylon conference, McGhee traveled to India and Pakistan. In New Delhi, he presented the American argument for collective security against communist aggression. The assistant secretary assured Nehru that the United States opposed not communism per se but only the aggressive actions of communist countries, as in Korea. Should the Soviets and the Chinese content themselves with implementing their ideology within their own borders, the U.S. government would not object. Moscow and Beijing, however, insisted on exporting their revolution, on forcing their system on other countries by subversion and military power.

Nehru replied with what struck McGhee as "a rather involved, and to me irrelevant, discourse." The prime minister declared that "Russia is what she is today largely because of the way the nations of the world isolated her when she was young," and he warned that the Americans were making the same mistake with China. To ostracize China was to risk war, as the Americans had discovered in Korea. Should the conflict in Korea escalate further and draw in the Soviet Union, no one would win. Even if the West gained a military victory—which was exceedingly unlikely, considering the size and population of the communist powers—"social and economic chaos" would engulf the world. Humanity would be worse off and more susceptible than ever to communist blandishments.

McGhee, in response, recited the great sacrifices the United States had made to vindicate the principle of collective security in Korea—to the measure of fifty thousand American casualties—and expressed disappointment at India's refusal to condemn China's invasion of the country. The prime minister objected and suggested that the United States and the United Nations had only themselves to blame for their troubles. He argued that by treating China as an outcast, they had convinced Beijing that it had nothing to lose by acting as an outcast. He also rejected the American notion of China's aggressiveness. He asserted that the Chinese faced too many problems at home to engage in foreign adventures. Once again, he warned that by preparing for war the Western powers made war more likely, if not inevitable.[27]

McGhee had not expected to convert Nehru to the collective security policy, and he didn't. Rather, on his way to Karachi to investigate the possibility of a closer relationship with Pakistan, the assistant secretary desired to give Nehru the right of first refusal on American friendship. Anticipating—correctly—that Nehru *would* refuse, Washington wished to deny the prime minister grounds for complaining that the United States was offering Pakistan something it withheld from India.

FROM MADISON AVENUE TO NEW DELHI

Even as the Truman administration embarked on a course guaranteed to antagonize Nehru, it sought to cushion the blow by changing its representation in India. No one in the administration denied Loy Henderson's gifts, but few would have argued that they included an ingratiating style. After the strains the developments of the preceding three years had placed on U.S.–Indian relations, Henderson and Nehru had run out of patience with each other. Journalist C. L. Sulzberger, a frequent visitor to India, summarized the situation: "Henderson detested Nehru and Nehru knew it." Truman decided to appoint a replacement.[28]

In certain respects, Chester Bowles seemed a throwback to 1949, the apogee of American enthrallment with Nehru. A liberal Democrat of the Hubert Humphrey mold, a former advertising executive, recently governor of Connecticut, and a tireless advocate of Third World causes, Bowles brought to the ambassadorship the enthusiasm for things Indian that Henderson lacked. "India really is a miracle," Bowles told the Senate Foreign Relations Committee, which had gathered to consider his appointment. Where Henderson viewed Nehru's motives with profound skepticism, Bowles proved the proverb that no one falls for a sales pitch faster than a salesman. He took Nehru at the prime minister's most charming word. Upon his arrival in New Delhi, Bowles embraced India with both arms—and with those of his family as well. He made a point of engaging Indians of all classes in conversation. He patronized Indian arts. His wife adopted Indian dress. His children attended Indian schools. Indian food graced the Bowles dinner table—to the dismay of Indian guests who came to the embassy hoping for a break from curry and rice.

Bowles's enthusiasm had created problems at his confirmation hearings. Many conservatives in the Senate considered Nehru a closet communist or a fellow-traveling equivalent and found trouble between Washington and New Delhi reassuring. They had no particular desire to see the relationship improve. They objected to Bowles's penchant for taking India's side of arguments and feared that he would become an advocate for Indian policy in the United States rather than a defender of American policy in New Delhi. For the Republicans among Bowles's opponents, an inclination to make problems for the administration provided further cause for complaints. The fact that the nominee had been baptized a Republican and later apostasized to the party of Franklin Roosevelt heightened their opposition.

Bowles's interrogators on the Foreign Relations Committee did not directly call him a socialist, but they came close, forcing Bowles explicitly to disavow any such unorthodoxy. "I have never run away from the word 'capitalist'," he said. "I am a capitalist. That is my economic belief." Some Republicans on the committee objected to the fact that the Truman administration had not nominated a career professional instead of a political creditor of the president. Maine Republican Owen Brewster declared that a position of such "extreme delicacy" as the ambassadorship to India required expertise that only a lifetime in the foreign service could provide. "If there is any point in the world," Brewster declared, "where there should be a career man, I think it should be India." Conservative Democrat Walter George questioned the nominee's defense of Indian policies. Did Bowles conceive it the duty of the U.S. ambassador "to proselyte in behalf of India"? Brewster shared this concern: "It would be particularly dangerous to have a man there who was too sympathetic with the Nehru approach." New Jersey Republican H. Alexander Smith agreed, deftly mixing metaphors in asserting that the U.S. ambassador in New Delhi should be "a strong anchor to windward to keep Nehru from going off the rails."

The importance of Bowles's appointment lay in the new approach it suggested in American treatment of India. Bowles openly advocated large increases in American aid. He contended that while American actions had stabilized Europe, Asia remained at grave risk. The loss of Asia might moot the European success. "We can succeed in Europe, and if we are not doing the right things in the East, if we are not building foundations out there that are solid, we can lose the world in the East in the next five years and the whole free world can crumble." Describing the poverty and backwardness of India, Bowles declared that if the United States did not pay attention to India's plight, the communists would, to both India's and America's detriment. "The Communists didn't invent poverty, but they have certainly taken advantage of it." The United States must therefore address the fundamental problem of economic development: "The answer to communism is an attack on world poverty."

Such notions did not sit well with Bowles's interlocutors on the Foreign Relations Committee. Smith heaped scorn on the ambassador-designate's "save the world" philosophy. Brewster asserted that Bowles's loose talk would cause Indians to believe that "manna is going to fall from heaven." When it didn't—and it wouldn't, if Brewster had anything to say in the matter— Indians would vent their displeasure on the United States. Iowa's Bourke Hickenlooper thought that if it sent aid to India, the United States would be repeating its past error of assisting countries that "take our bounty" while "behind their hands they laugh at the stupid Americans who have so much money."[29]

Bowles's critics delayed his confirmation, thereby registering their opposition to the policies he recommended. But they lacked the votes to veto Bowles, and off he went to India.

Nehru promptly fell asleep at their first meeting. Yet Bowles's admiration for the great leader survived the snooze. He wrote later,

In a personal conversation, Nehru was the most articulate man I have ever met. He always seemed to talk fully and freely, to say just what he thought, to make every effort to see that his listener understood his viewpoint, regardless of what he might think of its merits. Nehru never painted the world in harshly contrasting blacks and whites, but in subtle intermediate shades. He seemed sometimes to reach a conclusion almost reluctantly, as though hesitant to give up the good that lay along other paths. His conversation often consisted of literally thinking aloud, and he explored all sides of a problem until its full complexity was felt.

Two weeks after the new ambassador's arrival, Nehru employed his charm in explaining India's foreign policies. The prime minister warned that Americans missed the point in worrying so much about communism, when nationalism posed the real challenge to world order. The Soviet–Chinese alliance could not last. The Chinese looked down on the Russians as semibarbarians and resisted Soviet control of territory that was traditionally Chinese. The Russians felt culturally inferior to the Chinese and worried about the pressure of China's expanding population. Internal problems plagued both countries. The Chinese had to reconstruct a society torn by four decades of war. The Soviets, having reached the point where economic development required investment in education, had to figure out how to keep a more aware population under control.

Bowles was captivated. "Never have I listened to a more articulate survey of world affairs," he remarked. He considered the conversation further evidence of the importance of furnishing aid to Nehru's government. Bowles believed that the prime minister represented the best hope for Indian progress along moderate, noncommunist lines. Therefore, the United States should back him. The U.S. Congress had previously provided India with assistance as a stopgap in emergencies; Bowles wanted to establish an aid program on a permanent basis.[30]

He set out to persuade the State Department first. He wrote Acheson explaining that India was moving closer to the United States by the day: "I have talked to scores of peasants and working people and I have yet to see anyone whose face did not light up when he heard I was from America. I have drunk many cups of tea in the homes of peasants who have been eager for every snatch of information about our country." He granted that Indian foreign policy diverged from American on a number of issues, but he reminded Acheson that as recently as the 1930s, the United States had followed a neutralist path. "The Indians are one up on us," he added. "We turned down the League of Nations while they are active in the U.N." Meanwhile, the Indian people and government were souring on Moscow and the methods of the communists: "Every top Indian official with whom I talked has gone out of his way to condemn the Soviet Union and the Communist approach to economic, social and political problems." Nehru himself had criticized the communists in "most emphatic" terms. Washington must take advantage of this favorable trend. Rather than begrudge Nehru his neutralism, the United States should turn it to American advantage, since a neutral India would have a better chance "to wean China away from the U.S.S.R." than would an India identified with the capitalist camp. More substantially, the United States should underwrite India's economic development, to the amount of some $1 billion.[31]

The State Department bought Bowles's idea in principle, at least the part having to do with Indian economic development. The Indian Communist party had exploited food shortages and other causes of discontent in elections at the end of 1951 and the beginning of 1952 and had scored worrisome gains. As annoying as administration officials found Nehru, they increasingly feared that his successor would only be worse. For all his deficiencies, they came to consider him the best guarantee against a communist takeover of India.

But Congress remained unconvinced. On a visit to Washington in January 1952, Bowles explained to the Senate Foreign Relations Committee the importance of making India a "going concern." American assistance, he said, was the means to this end. Democrat Theodore Green suggested skeptically that aid to India would yield no greater returns than aid to China had. Owen Brewster asked the ambassador to explain recent speeches by Nehru indicating a policy of "pure unadulterated national socialism." The committee's ranking Republican, Alexander Wiley, wanted to know what the Indian government was doing about birth control. (This led Republican Charles Tobey to inquire about marital fidelity in India. Brewster responded that Indian husbands were "too loyal to their wives"; he reasoned, "That is the difficulty. That is where the kids come from.") Democratic chairman Tom Connally declared, "We cannot finance the whole world, and we cannot finance India. You know good and well that the more money we give them the more they want."[32]

Bowles did not change many minds in Congress, and the White House declined to help. Truman, entering his final months in office, refused to make aid for India a priority. Acheson predicted that a request for funds would provoke a "massacre" on Capitol Hill. The president preferred to leave any massacres to his successor.[33]

Notes

1. Sarvepalli Gopal, ed., *Jawarharlal Nehru: An Anthology* (Delhi: Oxford University Press, 1980), 360–64.

2. *Jawaharlal Nehru's Speeches*, vol. 1 (New Delhi: Ministry of Information and Broadcasting, 1961), 235.

3. K.P.S. Menon, *Many Worlds: An Autobiography* (London: Oxford University Press, 1965), 241; K. M. Panikkar, *In Two Chinas: Memoirs of a Diplomat* (London: Allen & Unwin, 1955), 72.

4. NSC 48/1, 23 December 1949, National Security Council records (record group 273), National Archives.

5. *Washington Post*, 11 October 1949; *Nation*, 22 October 1949; *Time*, 17 October 1949; *Newsweek*, 17 October 1949; *New Republic*, 10 October 1949; *This Week*, 9 October 1949.

6. *Congressional Record*, 1949, 14230, A2374, A5445–46, A6409, A6463, A6581; George McGhee, *Envoy to the Middle World: Adventures in Diplomacy* (New York: Harper & Row, 1983), 52.

7. McGhee, *Envoy*, 47; Dean Acheson, *Present at the Creation: My Years at the State Department* (New York: Norton, 1969), 334–36.

8. Report attached to memorandum by Hillenkoetter, 20 December 1949, Harry S. Truman papers, Truman Library, Independence, Missouri.

9. Memorandum of conversation, 12 October 1949, Dean Acheson papers, Truman Library; memorandum of conversation, 19 October 1949, file 845.002, State Department records (record group 59), National Archives.

10. NSC 48/2, 30 December 1949, NSC records, National Archives.

11. Henderson to Acheson, 27 and 28 June 1950, *Foreign Relations 1950*, vol. 7, pp. 204–6, 218–20; Henderson to Acheson, 29 June 1950, file 795.00, State Department records.

12. Nehru to Acheson, 17 July 1950, file 330, State Department records.

13. Acheson to Nehru, 25 July 1950, file 795.00, ibid.

14. Harry S. Truman, *Memoirs: Years of Trial and Hope* (Garden City, N.Y.: Doubleday, 1956), 362.

15. Jawaharlal Nehru, *Jawaharlal Nehru's Speeches, 1949–1953* (New Delhi: Ministry of Information, 1961), 418.

16. Charles H. Heimsath and Surjit Mansingh, *A Diplomatic History of Modern India* (Bombay: Allied, 1971), 68–69.

17. Memorandum by Fluker, 15 January 1951, *Foreign Relations 1951*, vol. 6, 2085; memorandum by McGhee, 24 January 1951, ibid., 2103; United States Senate, *Executive Sessions of the Senate Foreign Relations Committee* (historical series) (Washington: U.S. Government Printing Office, 1976), vol. 3, 43.

18. *Executive Sessions*, vol. 3, 27–46.

19. Robert J. McMahon, "Food as a Diplomatic Weapon: The India Wheat Loan of 1951," *Pacific Historical Review* 56 (1987): 349–77.

20. *Executive Sessions*, vol. 3, 369.

26. McMahon, "Food as a Diplomatic Weapon," 373.

22. *New York Times*, 28 August 1951.

23. Henderson to Acheson, 6 September 1951, *Foreign Relations 1951*, vol. 6, 2179–81.

24. NSC 98, 5 January 1951, NSC records.

25. NSC 98/1, 22 January 1951, *Foreign Relations 1951*, vol. 6, 1165–1652.

26. Report of South Asian conference, 26 February–3 March 1951, George McGhee papers, Truman Library; notes on Ceylon conference (undated), Loy W. Henderson papers, Library of Congress, Washington.

27. Memorandum of conversation, 8 March 1951, McGhee papers.

28. C. L. Sulzberger, *A Long Row of Candles: Memoirs and Diaries, 1934–1954* (New York: Macmillan, 1969), 791.

29. *Executive Sessions,* vol. 3, 409ff.

30. Chester Bowles, *Promises to Keep: My Years in Public Life, 1941–1969* (New York: Harper & Row), 488–89.

31. Bowles to Acheson, 6 December 1951, *Foreign Relations 1951,* vol. 6, 2191–2201.

32. *Executive Sessions,* vol. 4, 62ff.

33. Memorandum of conversation, 9 June 1952, Dean Acheson papers, Truman Library.

chapter 4

BOTTOMING OUT: 1953–1956

SEMISTRANGE BEDFELLOWS

Dean Acheson had a well-deserved reputation as an Atlanticist. The Democratic secretary of state struck many observers as more British than the British, and he tended to think of Asia as merely an unfortunate distraction from the pressing affairs of U.S. relations with Europe. But his Republican successor, John Foster Dulles, entered office determined to pay greater attention to the world's largest and most populous continent.

The Republican emphasis on Asia followed in some measure from the logic of American party politics. The Democrats' handling of China and Korea had afforded the GOP an opening it could not resist. Most commentators agreed that Dwight Eisenhower had clinched the November 1952 election when he pledged to "go to Korea" to find a solution to the war there. In addition, by the beginning of 1953, the affairs of Europe had settled into the pattern they would retain for the next three decades: the armies of East and West glared at each other across the Elbe, but neither side was much inclined to challenge the other's sphere of influence. Meanwhile, Asia seethed with civil wars, revolutions, and sundry further challenges to the status quo. Even if Dulles and Eisenhower had wanted to concentrate their efforts elsewhere, Asia would have demanded their attention.

While the 1952 elections transformed the political landscape in America, with Republicans taking control of the presidency and capturing both houses of Congress, in India Nehru reigned and ruled essentially unchallenged. Gandhi's assassination in 1948 had left Nehru as the principal surviving

70

symbol of the freedom struggle; the 1950 death of Vallabhbhai Patel removed his only real political rival. The first general elections since independence, in 1951–52, produced gains for parties of the left, but the country confirmed its support for the prime minister. As one Indian newspaper commented, "Nehru and not Congress has been voted to power."[1]

In the world at large, Nehru's voice carried loud and far. In 1953, no one credibly competed with him in speaking for what French journalists were just about to call *le tiers monde*. Yugoslavia's Tito and Nasser of Egypt, who would join Nehru by mid-decade to form the big three of the neutralist movement, stood head and shoulders below the Indian prime minister. Tito's European background limited his constituency; Nasser would represent the Arabs, but not all of them and in any event not yet. Indonesia's Sukarno aspired to a large role among the nonaligned countries, but the uniqueness of Indonesian society circumscribed his appeal and the restiveness of those he governed distracted his energies. China, as Nehru had predicted, remained absorbed in affairs close to home, including its war with the United States. Stalin's death in March 1953 removed the longtime leader of the communist movement. Another world figure, Winston Churchill, had returned to power in 1951, but the years were taking their toll and the old imperialist was growing more anachronistic by the day. Nehru, having forced the Commonwealth in 1949 to accept India on India's republican terms, represented what the British empire was becoming—a multiracial organization with a minority of Europeans—better than Churchill ever could. (With the victor's grace, Nehru went so far as to comment that he had "great sympathy for England in her present plight.") Remarking the trend in the early summer of 1953, Nehru declared that "facts are compelling the world to give a new status and position to India in the larger scheme of things." He might fairly have said the same about himself.[2]

As the new U.S. administration was turning toward Asia, Nehru was thus emerging as Asia's spokesman. Cooperation in resolving Asia's most pressing problem—the war in Korea—appealed to both. Truce talks had begun in July 1951, but negotiations had stalled on the issue of prisoner-of-war repatriation. The United States demanded that POWs have the opportunity to choose freely between South and North Korea, while the Chinese and North Koreans insisted on what they called "international practice"—forcible repatriation, regardless of prisoners' wishes. For more than a year, the talks had stuck on this point.

At the end of 1952, Nehru launched a new initiative. His special delegate to the United Nations, V. K. Krishna Menon, offered a resolution calling for the establishment of a neutral repatriation commission to examine the prisoner issue on a case-by-case basis and to determine the disposition of those who did not wish to return home. Nehru urged China to accept the proposal, declaring that "a moment comes in the life of a nation, and sometimes of the world, when the future hangs on a decision that might be taken." Beijing, on the advice of Moscow, initially rejected the overture, prompting Nehru to exclaim in disgust that "the world is determined to commit suicide." But in March 1953, after Stalin's death, the Kremlin shifted toward a more conciliatory line, and China's leaders reconsidered. They made a counteroffer considerably closer to the Indian plan than anything the communists had accepted to date.[3]

At this point, Washington used India's contacts with Beijing to try to push China the final step to an agreement. John Foster Dulles visited New Delhi in May and explained—for Chinese ears more than for Indian—that if the armistice talks failed, "hostilities might become more intense." What this would mean, Dulles left to the Chinese imagination.[4]

Whether or not this message figured in their calculations, the Chinese presented a new offer that differed from the Indian plan primarily by specifying that there would be five neutral nations, rather than four, on the repatriation commission. After Indian lobbying, Washington accepted the offer.

Unfortunately the South Koreans did not. President Syngman Rhee, whose nationalist roots went as deep into Korea's history as Nehru's into India's, violently resisted the notion that the war might end with Korea divided. Characterizing an armistice as a "death sentence for Korea," Rhee implored Eisenhower to resume the battle. When Eisenhower declined, Rhee attempted to sabotage the cease-fire by allowing the "escape" of twenty-five thousand North Korean and Chinese prisoners awaiting repatriation hearings.[5]

Rhee's action infuriated Nehru. Having listened to endless American protestations that the conflict in Korea involved all the United Nations and not simply South Korea and the United States, Nehru thought the time had come for the U.N. to put up or shut up. Writing to former viceroy Mountbatten, who agreed, Nehru fumed, "Who commands in South Korea? Are there two different commands—the United Nations and Syngman Rhee? Either the United Nations Command has full control over Syngman Rhee and South Koreans or it has not. If the former, then they should do something about it and, as you suggest, should smack him down. If they do not wish to do so, then they are equally incapable of signing the armistice with effect." Beyond the potentially damaging impact of Rhee's action on the cease-fire, Nehru considered it a gross insult to India, which had staked its prestige on a settlement. The prime minister threatened to pull out of the repatriation commission, informing the U.S. State Department that the government of India "cannot be expected to accept a position which is not in keeping with their self-respect."[6]

Eisenhower, too, thought Rhee needed smacking down, although the president obviously did not say so in public. Having just approved a CIA operation to topple the leftist prime minister of Iran, Mohamed Mosaddeg, Eisenhower considered switch-hitting and taking out Rhee on the right. But the likely successors appeared no more reliable than Rhee, and the president dropped the idea. He did, however, threaten to withdraw American support and cancel plans for a U.S.–Korean defense pact. Rhee gave in and accepted the cease-fire.

The truce eliminated most—but not quite all—of the distrust the Korean conflict had engendered in U.S.–Indian relations. When the interested parties gathered at Geneva to convert the cease-fire into a definitive peace settlement, a squabble arose regarding who counted as interested. Nehru, deeming India interested in anything Asian and believing India's intermediary role entitled it to a voice, angled for an invitation. American leaders, not wishing to grant Nehru a wider forum for his neutralist views and distrusting his sympathy for the Chinese, aimed to restrict participation to those countries directly involved in the fighting. The American view prevailed, largely on account of Washington's weight in the U.N.

Nehru was exasperated. "It really has been an extraordinary experience to see how a great Power behaves," he wrote.[7]

SELECTIVE SECURITY

More exasperation awaited. With the fighting in Korea ended, the Eisenhower administration turned its attention to southwestern Asia—specifically, to the region stretching from the Turkish Straits to the Hindu Kush. American strategy in the Middle East, as in the Indian subcontinent, had originally envisioned Britain as prime guarantor of Western interests. But U.S. officials, again as in South Asia, were discovering that Britain was not up to the job. Deciding they must take action themselves, they looked for allies in the region. Their eyes fell on Pakistan.

Immediately after partition, Pakistan's viability had appeared doubtful. Facing a sullen if officially unstated Indian irredentism and the logistical nightmare of communications across a thousand miles of hostile territory, Pakistan lived in a condition of perpetual crisis. Yet the country survived, in no small part as a result of the brashness of its leadership. In 1947, Governor-General Jinnah requested $2 billion in U.S. military and economic aid. In exchange, Jinnah offered to align Pakistan with the United States in the cold war. Although Jinnah believed—and Washington recognized—that India, not the Soviet Union, posed the greatest threat to Pakistan's security, he and his associates stressed the anticommunist qualities of their country and regime. A Pakistani diplomat assured his American counterpart, "Pakistan will fight to the last man against Communism."[8]

Filling Jinnah's request, of course, was out of the question. Two billion dollars was more than the U.S. Congress had ever dreamed of giving anyone in peacetime. (It had yet to see the bill for the Marshall Plan.) Besides, arming Pakistan would alienate India, which the Truman administration wanted to avoid. Moreover, South Asia remained Britain's sphere. Finally, in 1947, Pakistan was not exactly at the center of postwar geopolitics.

But by 1953, the situation had changed. Congress was getting used to the idea of alliances and to the fact that allies cost money. Nehru's attachment to nonalignment indicated that India was, if not a lost cause, a losing proposition in terms of collective security. The British were exhausted. The communist victory in China and the rising anti-Western nationalism in the Middle East and Southeast Asia put Pakistan in the thick of things. At the 1951 Ceylon conference, McGhee and the other U.S. diplomats had recommended turning to Pakistan. In 1953, the Eisenhower administration acted on the recommendation.

In the late spring of that year, Secretary of State Dulles visited Karachi. As he explained to Eisenhower afterward, he was "immensely impressed by the martial and religious characteristics of the Pakistanis." Dulles predicted that Pakistan could become "a strong loyal point" for the West against communism. He advocated strengthening Washington's ties to Karachi, and Eisenhower approved.[9]

The Eisenhower administration realized that in throwing its support behind Pakistan, it would anger India. On the same tour that took him to Karachi, Dulles visited New Delhi. Dulles had yet to become the most despised man in the Third World—his "immoral" neutralism speech lay in the future—but he already possessed an unsavory reputation in India. In 1947, while India had struggled toward independence, Dulles had announced quite mistakenly that "in India Soviet communism exercises a strong influence through the interim government." The Truman administration had quickly declared that Dulles, then a delegate to the U.N., had spoken only for himself, but the egregious remark had gained wide currency in India. When Dulles became America's chief diplomat, Indians groaned. Foreign office fixture K.P.S. Menon, finding prose inadequate to describe the secretary, turned to poetry. Menon characterized Dulles as "The wind that sends your ship in circles, / The wind that neither drives out Death / Nor brings in summer."[10]

For all this, Nehru greeted Dulles cordially when the secretary arrived in May 1953. "The atmosphere was intimate and we talked with great frankness," Dulles said afterward. In a discussion that ranged the world from Korea to Kenya, Dulles explained Washington's belief that the Middle East had to be strengthened against communist aggression or subversion. At the same time, the secretary assured Nehru that the United States had no plans for any arrangement with Pakistan "which could responsibly be looked upon as unneutral" toward India. Although the prime minister almost certainly doubted this statement—at least differing on what constituted unneutrality—he chose not to press the matter.[11]

Dulles left New Delhi with a mixed impression of Nehru. In matters touching directly on Indian interests, the secretary found the prime minister thoroughly realistic. Nehru coolly weighed costs against benefits in the Kashmir quarrel. Likewise, in a boundary dispute with Nepal, his advocacy of peaceful resolution of conflicts had not deterred him from making clear that violations of Indian territory would elicit a firm response. On issues farther removed from India, however, Nehru seemed to Dulles to have a weaker grasp. Dulles described the prime minister to Eisenhower as "utterly impractical" regarding global affairs.[12]

Had Nehru impressed Dulles and Eisenhower as an international thinker, they might have reconsidered their approach to Pakistan. But he didn't, and they didn't. During the summer of 1953, the State and Defense departments pondered the optimal form and extent of U.S. military aid to Karachi; by the beginning of autumn, word of a nearing deal began to leak out. In September, the commander-in-chief of Pakistan's army, Mohammad Ayub Khan, arrived in Washington, ostensibly for medical treatment. Whatever his private physician recommended, the Pentagon prescribed armor and aircraft. Ayub shrewdly facilitated the prescription-filling by loudly avowing his country's undying hostility to communism and its willingness to stand with the United States on the ramparts of freedom. With American anticommunism in its full-moon phase, Ayub's maneuver made it easy for the administration to proceed to a deal and almost impossible to reverse course.

Ayub's manipulation of the media also limited India's options. New Delhi could not but protest a U.S. alliance with Pakistan. Nehru warned Pakistan's prime minister, Mohammed Ali, that if he tied the knot with the United States, "Pakistan enters definitely into the region of cold war." Nehru added, "That means to us that the cold war has come to the very frontiers of India. It also means that if real war comes, this also reaches the frontiers of India. This is a matter of serious consequence to us. . . . All our problems will have to be seen in a new light." In a scarcely veiled attack on the United States, Nehru declared that India would not fall into the error of treating foreign affairs simply as a test of strength: "Some people imagine that a country's policy should be what they call a "strong" policy—strong policy apparently meaning that we should go about looking as fierce and ferocious as possible, threatening everybody, telling everybody that we will punish them if they don't behave as we want them to behave. Now, that kind of thing may sound very well at a public meeting and may evoke applause, but the fact is that it represents great immaturity in political thinking or understanding." As the U.S.–Pakistani arms deal drew closer, Nehru expressed dismay that the two countries were violating the "no-war area" in Asia. "If any military aid comes to Pakistan from the United States, it is obvious that Pakistan drops out of that area. The cold war, as it is called, comes to Pakistan, and therefore, comes to India's borders." Reminding his audience of the process by which Britain had extended its control over the subcontinent in the nineteenth century, the prime minister likened the prospective U.S.–Pakistani alliance to "the history of colonial domination gradually creeping in."[13]

But India's protests only made the Pakistan deal more certain. Publicly, U.S. officials contended that the cold war had already reached the subcontinent; the Indian prime minister simply had not recognized the fact. Privately, administration leaders believed they could not risk giving the impression that they were bowing to the demands of neutralist India. Vice President Richard Nixon visited Karachi and New Delhi in December 1953 and returned convinced that for Washington to back out at this late date would damage American credibility and afford Nehru a signal victory. As a consequence, Nixon said, the United States would risk "losing most of the Asian–Arab countries to the neutralist bloc." Dulles agreed: the administration could not withdraw the offer without "disastrous" effects on U.S. relations with Pakistan. He added, "It would probably also be disastrous to our standing with the other countries of Asia, who would assume we had backed down in the face of Indian threats."[14]

Eisenhower decided to go ahead with the deal, even though he realized his decision would enrage Nehru. To soften the blow, he wrote a long letter to the prime minister, assuring him that the pact with Karachi was "in no way directed against India." Eisenhower added that if Pakistan misused American weapons—in an assault on India, for example—the United States would take "immediate action both within and without the UN to thwart such aggression." Eisenhower said he was recommending to Congress a continuation of economic and technical aid to India, and he offered military assistance as well. He expressed regret that there had occurred "such widespread and unfounded speculation on this subject," and he concluded, "Now that the facts are known, I hope that the real import of our decision will be understood."[15]

Nehru, on receiving this letter from Ambassador George Allen, Chester Bowles's replacement, adopted a surprisingly conciliatory position. He said he had "never at any moment . . . had any thought whatsoever that the United States Government, and least of all President Eisenhower, wished to do any damage to India." Even so, he could not help observing that the Americans risked destabilizing the subcontinent by arming the Pakistanis. He pointed out that although the religious passions that partition had aroused had begun to subside, they remained a danger. Extremists among India's Muslims might gloat at the newly acquired strength of their brothers in Pakistan. This could provoke a violent response among Hindus. Nehru also expressed concern that Mohammed Ali would find the weapons his undoing. Nehru considered Ali a reasonable man but worried that Pakistan's army, intoxicated by its new arms, would push Ali aside.[16]

Inwardly, Nehru was seething. "Pakistan becomes practically a colony of the United States," he said. "The United States imagine that by this policy they have completely outflanked India's so-called neutralism and will thus bring India to her knees. Whatever the future may hold, this is not going to happen." The prime minister asserted that in providing arms to Pakistan, the United States had committed "an unfriendly act" against India. He declared that U.S. policy "appears to be to give every help to Pakistan and to take a tough line with Delhi." He denounced the United States for choosing sides in the Kashmir dispute, saying, "To give military aid to one party to a conflict when armies stand on either side of the cease-fire line is obviously a breach of neutrality." As a partial response, Nehru decided to curtail programs for sending Indians to the United States and receiving Americans in return. "I dislike more and more this business of exchange of persons between America and India. The fewer persons that go from India to America or come from the United States to India, the better. . . . We have had quite enough of American superiority."[17]

THE NEUTRALIST MANIFESTO

The major portion of Nehru's response took a different form. Almost simultaneously with the announcement of Washington's pact with Karachi, two other developments complicated American relations with India. The first was the unveiling in Washington of a new policy regarding the use of nuclear weapons. In January 1954, Dulles described the defense posture that became known as "massive retaliation," by which the United States threatened to use its nuclear arsenal to prevent communist aggression. American war planners debated the merits of massive retaliation (which derived chiefly from Eisenhower's desire to balance the federal budget), but from the standpoint of international public relations, the policy proved an enormous blunder. To the hundreds of millions of people around the world who were already inclined to consider the Americans warmongers, the massive retaliation strategy confirmed their worst fears.

The announcement of the strategy afforded Nehru an opening he quickly exploited. "Peace seems far distant now," he declared. "Mankind apparently marches ahead to its doom." When an American H-bomb test provided an exclamation point to Dulles's massive retaliation speech, Nehru asserted that the purpose of the test and the accompanying publicity regarding American nuclear might was "to announce to the world and to all whom it may concern this might of the United States of America, and their readiness to blow up any people or country who came in the way of their policy." Nehru continued,

Have men's minds lost all anchorage? For this surely is the way to madness, and the great men who control our destinies are dangerous self-centered lunatics, who are so full of their conceit and pride of power that they will rather rain death and destruction all over the world than give up their petty opinions and think and act right.

It is an astonishing and shameful thing that people should put up with this madness, especially when the world seemed so near to achieving what it had desired and dreamt of for ages past. Peace and cooperation and well-being for all the peoples of the world were well within grasp. But the gods perhaps envied the lot of man and drove him mad.

Whether madness and death are the fate of man in the near future or something better, no one can say. But it is certain that the way of the atom bomb is not the way of peace or freedom. The only useful purpose it can serve is to put an end to the power-mad people in authority, to those who wish to dominate over others, to the race-proud who deny equality to others, to the men of privilege who rest on others' labour and suffering, to those who prosper when others starve and die.[18]

The United States' adoption of the massive retaliation policy gave Nehru one opportunity to contrast India's peaceful policy with the warlike stance of the United States. The second major development of the period—the Viet Minh victory over the French in Indochina—delivered another. In May 1954, French forces surrendered the fortress of Dien Bien Phu, effectively ending the eight-year Indochina war. The powers once again adjourned to Geneva to work out a permanent settlement. Washington once again sought to keep India from the negotiating table. The Americans once again succeeded—but only partially. Ignoring its lack of an invitation, India crashed the conference. Nehru sent a personal representative, V. K. Krishna Menon, who set up shop near the conference headquarters.

The Americans loathed and distrusted Menon. In this, they had company: Menon possessed a genius for antagonizing people—not least other Indians. Delhi journalist Frank Moraes captured this aspect of Menon's personality by describing him as "our Mr. Dulles." Subimal Dutt, one of Menon's governmental colleagues, put the matter delicately when he declared that Menon "did not always measure his words." Another veteran of the Indian foreign office, C. S. Jha, characterized Menon as "an outstanding world statesman but the world's worst diplomat" and added that Menon was often "overbearing, churlish and vindictive."

Nehru appreciated Menon's finer qualities, which included perhaps the sharpest mind among the prime minister's associates. "I have hardly come across a keener intelligence and brain," Nehru once commented. But Nehru also recognized Menon's deficiencies, among them a long-term dependence on the drug Luminal. On one occasion, Menon had sent Nehru a cable that so plainly demonstrated a drug-induced incoherence that the prime minister insisted Menon withdraw it. At other times, Menon accused enemies within the government of poisoning Nehru's mind against him; he threatened suicide if the prime minister did not set things right. Yet Nehru refused to fire Menon and sent him to Geneva instead.[19]

Neither Dulles nor Eisenhower could abide Menon. The secretary of state thought him "a very adroit and unscrupulous maneuverer who likes to have his finger in every pie." The president called him "a menace and a boor," who "conceives himself to be intellectually superior and rather coyly presents to cover this a cloak of excessive humility and modesty." Eisenhower added that "he is a master of twisting words and meanings of others and is governed by an ambition to prove himself the master international manipulator and politician of the age."[20]

But as much as the Americans despised Menon, they discovered that they could not do without him. The public conference sessions quickly became mired in propaganda; the real business took place in hotel rooms. Because Washington did not recognize Beijing, American officials would not meet directly with the Chinese. Menon provided a liaison. The work dragged and on a number of occasions bogged down entirely. U.S. officials never knew whether Menon was accurately reporting their comments to the Chinese; they assumed that when it suited his purposes, he lied. What the Chinese thought of the arrangement, Beijing kept to itself. Eventually, however, and in significant part thanks—very grudging thanks, from the Americans—to Menon, the opposing sides cut a deal. The Eisenhower administration refused to sign the Geneva accord, largely out of fear of domestic repercussions, but it indicated that it would consider a grave matter the accord's overturning by any party.

One of the lapses in the negotiations allowed Nehru to deliver his definitive riposte to the U.S. policy of alliances backed by the threat of massive retaliation. At a point when nothing was happening at Geneva, Zhou Enlai flew to India to consult with Nehru. The Indian prime minister sketched an alternative vision to that conjured by the Americans, specifying five principles of intercourse among nations: respect for territory and sovereignty, nonaggression, noninterference in domestic affairs, equality and mutual benefit, and peaceful coexistence. Zhou's acceptance of these principles of *panchsheel*, as they came to be called, committed, between India and China, nearly one-third of the earth's population to them. But Nehru made plain he was offering his philosophy to humanity at large. "If these principles are applied not only between various countries but also in international relations generally," he said, "they would form a solid foundation for peace and security, and the fears and apprehensions that exist today would give place to a feeling of confidence." Asserting that an "area of peace" now existed between India and China, Nehru expressed hope that "this area of peace could be spread over the rest of the world."[21]

Immediately, *panchsheel* became the touchstone of India's foreign policy. Nehru invoked the principles across a spectrum of international relations. When Zhou returned to Geneva, Nehru advocated *panchsheel* as a basis for an Indochina settlement. He warned Pakistan's Mohammed Ali that *panchsheel* would afford greater security than an alliance with the United States. At the 1955 Bandung Conference of Asian and African nations, Nehru lobbied vigorously to have the governments represented there take the *panchsheel* pledge. In the same forum, he recommended *panchsheel* as a means to end a Sino–American standoff in the Taiwan Strait.

Before long the principles themselves—fuzzy to begin with—became less important than the general mind-set they implied. By the end of 1955, Nehru was defining *panchsheel* as more or less synonymous with neutralism. "It is in no spirit of pride or arrogance that we pursue our own independent policy," he said. "We would not do otherwise unless we are false to everything India has stood for in the past and stands for today. We welcome association and friendship with all and the flow of thought and ideas of all kinds, but we reserve the right to choose our own path. That is the essence of Panchsheel."[22]

AIDERS OF THE LOST ARK

Panchsheel expressed nothing the United States could not accept, but its origins and tone implied what American leaders took as insufficient vigilance against the communist threat. They feared—rightly—that to the degree it gained widespread currency, it would erode support for collective security. It was ironic, therefore, that just as Nehru launched his campaign on behalf of panchsheel, the Eisenhower administration was considering steps to make the prime minister's life easier.

In the wake of the French defeat in Indochina, American strategists pondered the new face of Asia. More than ever, they declared, the Indian subcontinent had become "a major battleground in the cold war." American planners had previously assessed India's importance primarily in negative terms, focusing on the damage the loss of India would do to the United States and its allies. Now that the communists had captured part of Southeast Asia and endangered the rest, India's resources took on a new, positive value. India commanded the shipping lanes from the Middle East to the Far East and formed a "great land bridge" between the two regions. India possessed minerals vital to modern warfare, including fissionable isotopes necessary for nuclear weapons. India's soldiers had supported Britain through two world wars and a dozen lesser contests; they could prove crucial in a protracted conflict with the Soviet bloc.

India weighed even more heavily in the scales of international politics. Panchsheel and nonalignment exerted a powerful influence on the emerging states of the Third World; already Nehru had succeeded, with help, in forging a neutralist bloc of more than a dozen nations in the U.N. Undoubtedly, the neutralists' number would grow as the colonial empires disintegrated. In light of Nehru's appeal among the formerly colonized, it became a matter of "great importance" for the United States to reach an understanding with the Indian prime minister.

The NSC paper containing these views conceded that Nehru would not join an American alliance, and it granted that Indian nonalignment would continue to cause problems for the United States. But on balance, the paper asserted that U.S. interests would benefit from Nehru's continuance in power. Nehru offered the best hope for stability in India, and whatever his attitude toward communists abroad, he had managed to keep the Indian Communist party well under control. Further, India was more than ever functioning as an ideological counterpoise to China. The Chinese had adopted the communist path to economic development; India was following the democratic route. If the West hoped to hold Asia permanently, the

Indian government must deliver the economic goods as effectively as Beijing. Should Nehru fall, India would flounder. The communists would win by default.[23]

The importance of this paper (NSC 5409) lay in the emphasis it placed on Indian economic development as prerequisite to American security. In 1951, the Truman administration had argued that unrelieved famine in India might open the door to social and political chaos, but in promoting aid for India, Truman's people had made plain they were responding to extraordinary circumstances. By 1954, however, the highest levels of the Eisenhower administration accepted that the United States should treat India's economic development as a continuing priority.

Yet the drafters of NSC 5409 did not go so far as to specify particular programs or levels of assistance. In this respect, policy gave way to politics. For years, Republicans had charged the Democrats with profligacy in all manner of government programs, and aid to fractious neutrals like Nehru had become Exhibit A in GOP attacks. Although Eisenhower did not share the conspiratorial weltanschauung of the inveterate aid-busters, he pursued with almost mystical devotion the holy grail of a balanced budget. In respectable Republican fashion, he had run for the presidency on a platform of "trade not aid"—that is, a reliance on private commerce and investment rather than on publicly supplied capital to stake the countries of the Third World. Hardly eighteen months in office, Eisenhower could not renounce his campaign pledge, even though it grew increasingly evident that India needed more help than the financial markets were willing to provide. Consequently, Eisenhower's commitment to Indian development remained rather abstract.

Yet certain individuals in the administration were plotting nothing less than a monumental raid on the treasury. Spearheading the commandos was C. D. Jackson, Eisenhower's special assistant for cold war planning. Jackson came incongruously to this role, since no one in the administration took a harder line against communism. Long after the president and the secretary of state had given up on the "liberation" promises of the 1952 campaign, Jackson continued to plead for action to shake up the Soviet satellite belt in Eastern Europe. He heartily endorsed covert operations against troublesome leftists and made propaganda and disinformation his specialty. Thus, one might have expected Jackson to look askance at U.S. aid to a neutralist like Nehru. But he did not; rather, he promoted aid as America's secret weapon in the battle for the Third World.

Although Jackson generally had no use for liberals like Chester Bowles, Jackson's own "World Economic Plan," which called for $10 billion in aid to developing countries, made small potatoes of Bowles's $1 billion package. Jackson, on loan from Henry Luce's empire of mass-circulation slicks, understood that America's attractiveness to Third World countries had more to do with American prosperity than with the promises of the Bill of Rights. He put the matter baldly, in asserting that the World Economic Plan would demonstrate to the uncommitted nations that "the Free West offers more than the Communist East."[24]

Dulles, who also had a reputation as a hard-liner, agreed with Jackson on the importance of proving that democratic methods could outperform those of the communists. "It is going to be very difficult to stop Communism in much of the world," Dulles said, "if we cannot in some way duplicate the intensive Communist effort to raise productive standards. That is one reason why Communism has such great appeal in areas where the slogans of 'liberty,' 'freedom,' and 'personal dignity' have little appeal." Dulles explained his thinking on aid to India to the Senate Foreign Relations Committee: "We believe that India's own great effort should be supported so that its plan for economic development will succeed. We should remember that among free nations there is room for diversity of views. We should not let our wish to help the people of India to develop their own nation be swayed by temporary differences, however important. It is essential that we continue to help, if for no other reason than to save our enlightened self-interest."[25]

Dulles, however, found himself in a position like that of Dean Acheson: he was persuaded intellectually by the arguments for increased aid, yet he was unwilling to assume the political risks of publicly promoting it. "I am 100% behind your type of investment program," Dulles told Jackson, even while he added that "as far as I personally am concerned, it is just not practical for me to be a crusader for some particular program, however good it may be."[26]

Eisenhower gradually moved in the direction of committing large-scale economic aid to India and other Third World countries. The president found the success that the Soviets were achieving in their post-Stalin peace offensive troubling, and he increasingly thought the United States would have to take countermeasures. "So long as they used force and the threat of force," he told Dulles, "we had the world's natural reaction of fear to aid us in building consolidations of power and strength in order to resist Soviet advances." At first glance, the Russians' shift to nonmilitary, and especially economic, weapons seemed to play into the United States' hands. "We have always boasted that the productivity of free men in a free society would overwhelmingly excel the productivity of regimented labor." But the communists had got the jump on the United States. "While we are busy rescuing Guatemala or assisting Korea and Indo-China, they make great inroads in Burma, Afghanistan and Egypt." Eisenhower, ever the budget-balancer, still resisted massive programs like Jackson's World Economic Plan or the similar "Asian Marshall Plan" suggested by foreign-aid chief Harold Stassen. "I am by no means one of those people who believe that the United States can continue to pile up bonded indebtedness and fail to suffer dire consequences both economically and, eventually, in our basic institutions." But the aid race was beginning to look like one the United States could not afford to not afford. "If we, at such a time, cannot organize to protect and advance our own interests and those of our friends in the world, then I must say it becomes time to think of 'despairing of the Republic.' " Taking everything into account, Eisenhower decided in the spring of 1955 to send Congress a bill to create a $200 million Asian Development Fund, with a large portion earmarked for India.[27]

The measure immediately encountered resistance on Capitol Hill. Republican senator and minority leader William Knowland objected that "it would be bad if the impression got around that we reward neutralism." Republican William Jenner wanted to know why the United States should "give fifty million to India, when India is admittedly neutral in the irrepressible conflict between human dignity and human slavery." Jenner denounced the administration's "worldwide boondoggling" and said that aid to countries like India furthered a communist plot "to help us spend our way to bankruptcy."

The administration defended its request with partial success. Dulles countered charges that the United States was trying to buy neutralists by asserting, "We are not awarding gifts for policies we dislike. We are simply trying to prevent India from moving towards Communism." Eisenhower commented in similarly pragmatic fashion, "Neutralism is better than hostility. . . . We shouldn't neglect an area simply because it is neutralist." After protracted debate, the administration got its Asian development fund. The opponents succeeded, however, in slicing the program in half, to $100 million—a far cry from Bowles's billion-dollar scheme, farther still from Jackson's $10 billion plan. The big money remained safely behind the treasury's barred doors.[28]

BATTLING BANDUNG, OR NEUTRALIZING NEHRU

The debate over the Asian development fund coincided with the seminal Bandung Conference of Asian and African nations in April 1955 in Indonesia. Initially, when the Indonesian government had suggested the conference, Nehru had hesitated; he had feared it would dissolve into disputation among various local and regional rivals, especially the Arabs and their neighbors, including Israel. Rethinking the matter, however, he had decided that a gathering of nonaligned states might provide a convenient forum for countering the U.S. policy of making alliances.

The latest elaboration of the American system was the Baghdad pact, which included Iraq, Turkey, Iran, Pakistan, and Britain, with the United States an adjunct but unofficial member. Slightly older were the Southeast Asia Treaty Organization (SEATO)—which also included Pakistan—and a bilateral defense treaty between the United States and Taiwan. Along with preexisting U.S. treaties with Japan, South Korea, Australia, and New Zealand, the new arrangements appeared to complete the containment not only of the communist bloc but of India.

The Bandung Conference became part of Nehru's strategy to offset U.S. alliances by consolidating India's position with China. Until this time, the People's Republic had avoided most avoidable international conferences; by acting as China's sponsor in Bandung, Nehru would presumably score points in Beijing. A hint by British Foreign Minister Anthony Eden that an invitation to the Chinese would cause ill feelings toward India in Britain and America simply reinforced Nehru's determination to push ahead. He wrote, "For India to be told . . . that the United States and the United Kingdom will not like the inclusion of China in the Afro-Asian conference is not very helpful. In fact, it is somewhat irritating. There are many things that the United States and the United Kingdom have done which we do not like at all."

Nehru went to great lengths to ensure the success of the Bandung Conference, even reminding the Indonesians to provide enough bathrooms for the delegates. "People can do without drawing rooms," he wrote, "but they cannot do without bathrooms." Although Indonesia would host the event and Zhou and the Chinese would be present, most international observers expected Nehru to dominate the affair. His old antagonist and jailer Winston Churchill conceded Nehru's preeminence in the affair. A few weeks before the conference began, the British prime minister wished Nehru well, saying, "It seems to me that you might be able to do what no other human being could in giving India the lead, at least in the realm of thought, throughout Asia, with the freedom and dignity of the individual as the ideal rather than the Communist Party drill book."[29]

The Eisenhower administration did not oppose the Bandung Conference outright; to do so would have been counterproductive. Instead, U.S. officials sought to divest the conference of its impact. In February, the members of SEATO met at Bangkok in what amounted in part to a preemptive move against Bandung. Dulles persuaded the SEATO gathering to extend best wishes to the Bandung nations, while expressing the desire that the Indonesia meeting help ensure that "free nations would remain free." The anticommunist rhetoric of the Bangkok communiqué extended no further than this, but Dulles found it satisfactory. "Our message of greeting to the Afro–Asian conference is a good touch," the secretary wrote Eisenhower, "which, if properly played, can have an excellent propaganda value and to some extent put that conference on the spot."[30]

Administration officials also worked quietly to guarantee that the American case for collective security receive, if not equal time, at least a hearing amid the neutralist preachments of Nehru. Not surprisingly, the Pakistanis proved particularly amenable to Washington's suggestions. At Bandung, they insisted on including Soviet control of Eastern Europe under the rubric "colonialism." Krishna Menon damned this meddling by America's cat's-paw. "Pakistan made hell," he muttered afterward.[31]

In part because of American efforts, the Bandung Conference disappointed Nehru. Beyond the anticommunist activities of the Pakistanis, Zhou stole Nehru's thunder. The Chinese premier impressed all in attendance with his moderation and statesmanship. He helped resolve disputes that arose at the conference and even accepted thinly disguised criticism of the Soviet Union,

China's principal ally. He surprised many by affirming the right of all nations to choose their own economic and political systems—even capitalism. He highlighted the meeting by announcing his government's desire to settle the Taiwan Strait crisis, then on the verge of war, peacefully.

Nehru fared worse. That the Pakistanis considered the Indian prime minister and Krishna Menon rude and overbearing elicited scant surprise; but so did the Indonesians and Ceylonese. China's delegation also concurred. An Indian diplomat characterized Nehru's relationship with Zhou at the conference by commenting approvingly that the Indian prime minister took the Chinese premier "as a younger brother." Although Zhou hid his feelings at Bandung, he found the patronizing treatment insufferable. "I have met Chiang Kai-shek, I have met American generals," Zhou said, "but I have never met a more arrogant man than Mr. Nehru."[32]

Nehru tried without success to persuade the conference to embrace *panchsheel.* Instead, the delegates opted for a longer list of principles, including the right of collective defense—which directly contradicted the neutralist basis of Nehru's diplomacy. (Nehru responded by remarking that alliances were "humiliating" to smaller powers, which contributed to the ill feelings he provoked.) More than anything, Bandung demonstrated the diversity of views among Asian and African states, effectively killing Indian hopes for leadership of a coherent movement between the superpower blocs.[33]

Nehru's setback drew smiles of satisfaction in Washington. Dulles described Bandung as "a very severe reverse" for India, involving for Nehru "a great loss of prestige." The secretary deemed the final communiqué of the conference almost "a document which we ourselves could subscribe to." Even liberal Democratic congressman Adam Clayton Powell, Jr., who had showed up uninvited as the self-styled representative of America's people of color and had puzzled delegates by his penchant for passing out cigars at the slightest provocation, came away convinced that Nehru had suffered "a severe defeat."[34]

DOUBLE VISION

It was a defeat, perhaps, but not a disaster: Nehru remained a major figure on the world scene. Whether they approved or not, leaders of all the major powers paid close attention to what Nehru said and did.

During the summer of 1955, Nehru enhanced his own and India's stature by a highly publicized visit to the Soviet Union. For some time, technicians, scientists, and educators had been traveling back and forth between the two countries. During the previous eighteen months, India had signed a variety of trade and economic agreements with the Soviet bloc, and in February 1955 the Kremlin had pledged its support for the construction of a large state-of-the-art steel plant. Two months after the Bandung Conference, Nehru journeyed to Moscow, where Soviet leaders Bulganin and Khrushchev affirmed their government's concurrence with the principles of *panchsheel.* They backed India in the Kashmir dispute and urged the "liberation" of the Portuguese enclave of Goa on India's western coast.

At the end of the year, the Soviet leaders reciprocated with a three-week tour of India. Nehru himself judged the visit a "feast of friendliness." Bulganin declared that the Soviet people considered India a "like-minded ally in the struggle for peace," and millions of Indians chanted the catchphrase "*Hindi Russi bhai bhai*," or "Indians and Russians are brothers."[35]

Predictably, many U.S. observers viewed this budding détente with concern. The Eisenhower administration largely kept silent, but press commentators filled the void. *Newsweek* reported the exchange of visits in detail and asserted that if appearances told the story, Nehru was leading India directly into the Soviet camp. The magazine hoped he was too clever to be suckered entirely. *U.S. News & World Report* described India skeptically in an article bannered "Where Reds Get the Red Carpet." The *New York Times* cautioned against reading too much into the toasts and communiqués, but it could not resist commenting that Nehru's evident admiration for the Soviet Union "put a large question mark behind his professed neutrality."[36]

At one level, Eisenhower administration officials accepted Nehru's warming to Moscow as nothing unusual. Had they been in his position—facing an adversary allied to and armed by the Western superpower—they too surely would have considered an opening to the East. Moreover, recognizing Nehru's attachment to neutralism, as well as his acuity in matters touching directly on Indian interests, they had no fear he would fall into dependence on the Kremlin. He would play along with Khrushchev as long as such a strategy served his and India's purposes, but no longer.

At the same time, however, American policymakers saw trouble in recent trends. Because they recognized in Nehru India's—and America's—best insurance against radicalism in South Asia, they kept asking Congress for aid to India. Unfortunately, as the commentary in the press indicated, Nehru lost votes in the United States by traveling to Moscow and embracing Soviet leaders, if not necessarily all their objectives. In doing so, he made the administration's life more difficult than U.S. officials thought necessary.

Life in Washington threatened to get even more problematic in the spring of 1956, when the administration received reports that Nehru was contemplating the purchase of major weapons systems from Moscow, including bomber aircraft. Recently sensitized to the political dangers of East bloc military ties to neutralists by the outcry following a Soviet–Egyptian pact, the Eisenhower administration reacted at once. Dulles flew to New Delhi, where he urged Nehru to reconsider. "You can buy planes from the British," Dulles said. "You can buy planes from us. I cannot see why you should buy planes from the Russians knowing that it would make it almost impossible for the United States to carry on its efforts to assist you materially in your second five-year plan. That will be hard enough anyway, and this deal with Russia, I feel, would make it impossible." Dulles added diplomatically that he was not offering these remarks with any intention to pressure the prime minister; he simply wanted the Indian government to understand the inevitable effect in the United States of a decision to accept weapons from Moscow.[37]

Nehru had his own ideas as to what constituted pressure. But he chose to be persuaded, wishing neither to slam the door on American aid nor to carry the *Hindi-Russi-bhai-bhai* business too far. Having found the equipoise between the superpowers—the balance point at which India held attractions for and received help from both sides—the prime minister saw no reason to risk losing it. His neutralist policy was paying off in hard currency.

Events in the summer and fall of 1956, though, cast fresh doubts upon the sincerity of Nehru's neutralism. In July, Dulles announced the withdrawal of an earlier offer to fund construction of a dam at Aswan on the Nile in Egypt, partly in response to the uproar over the Soviet–Egyptian weapons pact. Just weeks before, Dulles had delivered the opinion that in the modern world, and with a few exceptions that he declined to specify, neutrality was "immoral and short-sighted." Nehru interpreted the decision against Egypt as part of an antineutralist campaign: "These people are arrogant! Arrogant!!" he said.[38]

When Egypt's Nasser responded by seizing the Suez Canal, and Britain countered with military threats, Nehru characteristically sought to prevent the crisis from widening into war. The United States pursued the same goal, although by means that did little to diminish friction between Washington and New Delhi. Dulles confronted Krishna Menon at a London conference of canal users and labeled Menon's proposals for a settlement "pure scenery." Menon accused Dulles of playing a "double game" and later commented that the American secretary had "killed" the conference.[39]

The diplomats' efforts failed, and the British joined France and Israel in an attack on Egypt. Nehru instantly condemned the operation as another manifestation of outdated and dangerous Western imperialism. Since Washington adopted the same view, to the point of threatening sanctions unless the invaders pulled back, Americans found little to fault in Nehru's actions in the matter.

Simultaneously with the Egyptian invasion, however, the Soviet Union sent troops into Hungary to suppress a nationalist revolution there. When Nehru delayed in criticizing this show of Eastern imperialism, Americans howled in protest at India's willingness to view Soviet aggression in a different light from that of the West. To some degree, events in Hungary in fact warranted a deliberate response. Confused reportage from Budapest rendered impossible precise knowledge of what was taking place. Further, Hungary appeared—to Nehru, at least—the more dangerous of the two crises in that the fighting there occurred on the front lines of the cold war. With elements of the Western press calling for U.S. support of the Hungarian freedom fighters, escalation to all-out conflict appeared ominously possible. By moving slowly, Nehru hoped to calm the situation and to keep open the possibility that India might act as mediator if necessary.

Yet calculations of Indian self-interest also figured in the prime minister's caution. Nehru did not desire to jeopardize good relations with the Soviet Union over an issue India could do little about. Additionally, because India had no personal experience of Soviet domination, he had a harder time identifying with the Hungarians than with the Egyptians—fellow neutralists and fellow victims of British oppression.

Few Americans cared to sort through the reasons for Nehru's actions; fewer still were inclined to give him any benefit of the doubt. Conservative critics had their anti-Indian prejudices confirmed. Even liberals who normally took India's part reacted with dismay. The *New Republic*, a consistent supporter of Nehru, declared sadly that "the conjunction of the Suez and Hungarian crises caught India with its double standard exposed as it never had been before."[40]

Notes

1. Sarvepalli Gopal, *Jawaharlal Nehru: A Biography* (1975–1984), vol. 2, 158.

2. Ibid., 166–67.

3. Ibid., 145–46.

4. Dulles to Eisenhower, 22 May 1953, Dwight Eisenhower papers, Eisenhower Library, Abilene, Kansas.

5. Stephen E. Ambrose, *Eisenhower: The President* (New York: Simon & Schuster, 1984), 98.

6. Gopal, *Nehru*, vol. 2, 171.

7. Ibid., 172.

8. M. S. Venkataramani, *The American Role in Pakistan, 1947–1958* (New Delhi: Radiant, 1982), 24–25.

9. Memorandum of discussion at 147th NSC meeting, 1 June 1953, Eisenhower papers.

10. Charles H. Heimsath and Surjit Mansingh, *A Diplomatic History of Modern India* (Bombay: Allied, 1971), 362 n. 1; K. P. S. Menon, *Many Worlds: An Autobiography* (London: Oxford University Press, 1965), 292.

11. Dulles to Eisenhower, 22 May 1953, Eisenhower papers.

12. Memorandum of discussion at 147th NSC meeting, 1 June 1953, Eisenhower papers.

13. Gopal, *Nehru*, vol. 2, 184–85; Heimsath and Mansingh, *Diplomatic History of Modern India*, 354–57.

14. Memorandum of discussion at 176th NSC meeting, 16 December 1953, Eisenhower papers; Dulles to Eisenhower, undated (January 1954), John Foster Dulles papers, Eisenhower Library.

15. Eisenhower to Nehru, 18 February 1954, Eisenhower papers.

16. Allen to Dulles, 24 February 1954, file 611.91, State Department records, National Archives.

17. Gopal, *Nehru*, vol. 2, 185–90.

18. Sarvepalli Gopal, ed., *Jawaharlal Nehru: An Anthology* (Delhi: Oxford University Press, 1980), 394–96.

19. Frank Moraes, *Jawaharlal Nehru: A Biography* (New York: Macmillan, 1956),

453; Subimal Dutt, *With Nehru in the Foreign Office* (Calcutta: Minerva, 1977), 241; C. S. Jha, *From Bandung to Tashkent: Glimpses of India's Foreign Policy* (Madras: Sangam, 1983), 74; Gopal, *Nehru*, vol. 2, 140–44.

20. Dulles to Eisenhower, 14 March 1955, Eisenhower papers; Eisenhower diary entry, 14 July 1955, ibid.

21. S. M. Burke, *Mainsprings of Indian and Pakistani Foreign Policies* (Minneapolis: University of Minnesota Press, 1974), 145.

22. Mahendra Singh, *Indo–U.S. Relations, 1961–64: A Political Study* (Delhi: Sidhu Ram, 1982), 10.

23. NSC 5409, 19 February 1954, NSC records, National Archives.

24. Jackson to Dulles, 3 August 1954, Dulles papers.

25. H. W. Brands, *Cold Warriors: Eisenhower's Generation and American Foreign Policy* (New York: Columbia University Press, 1988), 23; Dennis J. Merrill, "Bread and the Ballot: The United States and India's Economic Development, 1947–1961," Ph.D. diss., University of Connecticut, 1986, 190.

26. Dulles to Jackson, 24 August 1954, C. D. Jackson papers, Eisenhower Library.

27. Eisenhower to Dulles, 5 December 1955, Dulles papers.

28. Merrill, "Bread and the Ballot," 204; *Congressional Record*, 1955, 11264–65.

29. Gopal, *Nehru*, vol. 2, 232–36.

30. *New York Times*, 26 February 1955; Dulles to Eisenhower, 26 February 1955, Eisenhower papers.

31. Michael Brecher, *India and World Politics: Krishna Menon's View of the World* (New York: Praeger, 1968), 57.

32. Dutt, *With Nehru*, 98; Burke, *Mainsprings*, 91.

33. Gopal, ed., *Nehru: Anthology*, 412–13.

34. Cabinet minutes, 29 April 1955, Eisenhower papers; memorandum of conversation, 11 May 1955, ibid.

35. Ibid., 253; Burke, *Mainsprings*, 146.

36. *Newsweek*, 4 July 1955; *U.S. News & World Report*, 2 December 1955; *New York Times*, 15 December 1955.

37. Dulles to Eisenhower, 12 March 1956, Eisenhower papers.

38. Mohamed H. Heikal, *Cutting the Lion's Tail: Suez through Egyptian Eyes* (New York: Arbor House, 1987), 116.

39. *Department of State Bulletin*, 18 June 1956; Brecher, *India and World Politics*, 64; Dulles to Eisenhower, 20 August 1956, Eisenhower papers.

40. *New Republic*, 26 November 1956.

chapter 5

THE LIGHT THAT FAILED: 1956–1965

FIRST STEPS BACK

The three years ending in the autumn of 1956 marked a low point in U.S.–Indian relations, rivaled for disaffection only by the period following the Nixon administration's siding with Pakistan in the India–Pakistan war of 1971. In the middle 1950s, as again in the early 1970s, actions by Indian and U.S. policymakers raised questions on each side about the bona fides of the other. The 1954 American decision to arm Pakistan struck Indians as blatantly hostile to their country, notwithstanding Washington's professions of goodwill and its assurances against misuse of the weapons. For Americans, already concerned by Nehru's chumminess with the Chinese and the Russians, New Delhi's unneutral response to the Suez and Hungarian crises confirmed their suspicions of Indian neutralism.

Relations between the two countries at the end of 1956 could hardly get worse; they could only improve. In fact, an optimist might have detected positive cause for hope. Eisenhower's reelection made him a lame duck, as reelection does all presidents, but if it diminished the terror he held for political opponents, it also freed him from the constraints that prospective candidates inevitably face. Seventy-four years old, Eisenhower now looked to history rather than to the polls. A warrior all his life, he now sought to be remembered as a peacemaker. The time had come, he felt, for reducing tensions. Because Nehru had been preaching this message for a decade, Eisenhower not unnaturally looked to India.

On the Indian side, developments also worked in favor of relaxation. Ten years into independence, India possessed a self-confidence it had lacked earlier, and it felt less need to distance itself from the West. The second general elections were only a moderate success for the Congress party, but they pleased Nehru as a demonstration of the continuing viability of Indian democracy and the resistance of the people to sectarian demagogues. The international crisis of the latter part of 1956, while momentarily embarrassing for India, nonetheless ultimately demonstrated to much of the world the bankruptcy of colonialism as practiced by both East and West, thereby enhancing the credibility of neutralism. Finally, and perhaps decisively, India needed U.S. aid more than ever. The current five-year plan had originally predicted a balance-of-payments shortfall of a half-billion dollars; by the end of 1956, estimates had doubled. Nehru was hoping Washington would help relieve a substantial part of the deficit.

The first steps toward understanding were taken in December 1956. While the world was calming down after the dual crisis of the previous months and while Eisenhower was preparing to commence his second term, Nehru visited the United States. Wisely, the administration dispensed with the fanfare that had raised expectations before the prime minister's 1949 tour. The visit centered on personal conversations between Nehru and Eisenhower.

When either man sought to charm, few could resist. During Eisenhower's long career, scores of persons who came into contact with him commented on his open, honest demeanor; his wide, infectious grin; and his down-to-earth friendliness. Nehru once remarked that "a truly friendly man" was "one of the most remarkable things in the world." The prime minister continued, "You can tell a genuinely friendly man the moment he comes into the room, the moment he gets up to speak, the moment he comes toward you. No one can fail to respond to him." These words, though spoken before Nehru's visit with Eisenhower, fit the president perfectly and characterized the prime minister's reaction.[1]

As for Nehru, his own personal style differed distinctly from Eisenhower's. Cultivated, in the incomparable manner of a Brahmin educated at the finest English schools, Nehru possessed the knack of making his interlocutors feel as perceptive and intelligent as he. Few Americans had fewer good things to say about Nehru than did Loy Henderson, but even the U.S. ambassador, during his stint in New Delhi, had had to concede the prime minister's personal appeal. After one session with Nehru, Henderson wrote, "He made use of his great personal charm and was evidently anxious to persuade. It is easy to understand how, when the Prime Minister is in such a mood, he is so frequently able to win over so many persons. . . . In fact, as I listened to him I found myself rather regretful that I could not agree with him and say with all honesty that he was quite right and was, in my opinion, pursuing the policy most likely to preserve the peace of the world."[2]

During twelve hours of private talks in Washington and at the president's farm in Gettysburg, each man turned his magnetism to full power. The issues that separated their countries had not decreased substantially. Strain between Washington and Moscow, after a minor thaw following the Geneva summit of 1955, had again increased with the Soviet invasion of Hungary; consequently, Americans found little to commend in Nehru's cultivation of the Kremlin. China remained as contentious an issue as ever in the United States; India's ties to China constituted, if no longer an explicit demerit in American eyes, at least nothing to boast of. Eisenhower's firm public opposition to the use of force by the European imperialists against Egypt in the Suez war had momentarily raised the United States' stature in India; but Washington's immediate efforts to repair the rift in the Atlantic alliance had undone much of the good. Finally, on the critical issue of the U.S. alliance with Pakistan, nothing had changed since 1954.

Yet the talks went well. Where the two men agreed—as they did on the broad notion that countries should settle their disputes by peaceful rather than warlike means—they did so with enthusiasm. Where they disagreed—as they did on China and Pakistan—they differed politely.

Most important, each impressed the other with his sincerity. Nehru came away convinced that Eisenhower, unlike Truman and certainly unlike Dulles, genuinely sought to expand the possibilities for world peace. The prime minister conscientiously refrained from criticizing the Eisenhower administration, and before he left Washington, he made a point of commending the United States for its flexibility and willingness to adapt to changing circumstances. Eisenhower, in turn, gained a new appreciation for Nehru's policy of nonalignment. The president had never shared the uniformly negative view of neutralism prevalent among Republican conservatives, although he *had* harbored suspicions that Nehru might define neutrality in a somewhat less than neutral manner. Evidently aware of this fact, Nehru went out of his way to reassure the president. He asserted that the Hungarian uprising, by requiring the Russians to respond with force, had rung the "death knell of international communism" as an attractive ideology. He insisted that Indian neutrality did not entail indifference between right and wrong, or between democracy and despotism; on matters of morality, India had spoken out and would continue to do so. Rather, neutrality for India referred primarily to military combinations. As a poor country, India could not afford to arm sufficiently to withstand an assault from a country like the Soviet Union. Therefore, it had to rely on the weapons of peace. To join an alliance would simply make India a target in someone else's war. Besides, the president, as a military man, must realize that India would become a net burden on any alliance it joined. Since India could not defend itself, its allies would have to.[3]

With much of this argument, Eisenhower could not disagree. The president's actions during the last years of his administration would demonstrate a greater understanding of India's diplomatic predicament than American leaders had demonstrated to date. Eisenhower also gained what he considered an insight into Nehru's psyche. Commenting afterward on the recently remarked Indian double standard, Eisenhower wrote,

> As an Asian from a less-developed nation, it is possible that Mr. Nehru felt more resentment of an intangible Western condescension toward his people than he felt toward any specific act of violence that either East or West might commit. Life, after all, is cheaper in the Orient, or so it would appear; recognition as equals by the "white" race is not. Perhaps Mr. Nehru, despite his excellent Western education and flawless English, was able to identify with the Soviets at times as "fellow Asians," a point that came out continually in his hope that the West could do something to make the Soviets feel they "were not being looked down upon."

Eisenhower conceded the speculative nature of this amateur psychoanalysis; but whatever it revealed about Nehru, it reflected a growing tolerance for Indian views among top U.S. policymakers.[4]

BREAKING THE AID BARRIER

Shortly after his meeting with Nehru, Eisenhower approved a new National Security Council paper dealing with India. This paper reiterated the opinion that India occupied an essential position in U.S. strategy for keeping Asia out of communist hands. It conceded that "the Indian policy of non-alignment will on occasion bring India into opposition with U.S. programs and activities, and a strong and increasingly successful India will add weight to this opposition." Even so, the United States should promote India's development and do what it could to guarantee the success of the Indian experiment in Asian democracy.

> Over the longer run, the risks to U.S. security from a weak and vulnerable India would be greater than the risks of a stable and influential India. A weak India might well lead to the loss of South and Southeast Asia to Communism. A strong India would be a successful example of an alternative to Communism in an Asian context. . . . The outcome of the competition between Communist China and India as to which can best satisfy the aspirations of peoples for economic improvement will have a profound effect throughout Asia and Africa.

As the NSC report continued, India's success hinged at the moment on the second five-year plan. An ambitious blueprint that called for the development of a mixed capitalist–socialist economy, the plan had recently run into trouble. Increasing defense expenditures (attributable in part to the U.S. arming of Pakistan) had bloated the government's budget. Increased prices of essential imports, particularly industrial machinery, had slowed construction

1.   Prime Minister Jawaharlal Nehru meets with President Harry S. Truman in Washington in 1949. With them (*from left*) are Indira Gandhi, Bess Truman, and Ambassador Vijaya Lakshmi Pandit. *Courtesy of U.S. Department of State/Harry S. Truman Library*

2.   President Dwight D. Eisenhower greets Prime Minister Nehru at the White House in 1956. Indira Gandhi is at left; Vice President Richard Nixon is at far right. *Courtesy Dwight D. Eisenhower Library*

3.   President Lyndon B. Johnson meets with Prime Minister Indira Gandhi in Washington in 1966. With them are Rajiv Gandhi (*left*) and Sanjay Gandhi. *Courtesy Lyndon Baines Johnson Library*

4.   Prime Minister Morarji Desai and President Jimmy Carter in Washington in 1978. *Courtesy of Jimmy Carter Library*

5.   Prime Minister Rajiv Gandhi at the United Nations in 1987. *UN PHOTO 170941/John Isaac*

of factories. Unexpectedly large imports of consumer items had fostered a run on the country's dollar reserves. Food production languished. Meanwhile, population continued to grow rapidly.

Whatever the causes of the five-year plan's problems, U.S. interests dictated sending aid to underwrite the plan's success. In the words of the NSC paper, "Should India fall substantially short of the projected expansion during the crucial next five years and lose the momentum it has gained under Nehru's leadership, it is unlikely to regain this momentum during the foreseeable future." Should the plan founder, "economic and political decline would almost certainly set in, popular support for the Congress Party would diminish, dissension would grow both inside and outside the Congress Party, and unrest would ensue." Where such unrest would lead was anyone's guess. Under the circumstances, the paper concluded, the United States had no choice. It must provide the economic and technical aid necessary to push India over the top.[5]

Eisenhower accepted the NSC paper in January 1957, and its recommendations became part of established U.S. policy. In his second inaugural address, he underscored the importance of improving standards of living around the world, both for the good of those aided and for the good of the United States. "We must use our skills and knowledge and, at times, our substance," he said, "to help others rise from misery, however far the scene of suffering may be from our shores. For wherever in the world a people knows desperate want, there must appear at least a spark of hope, the hope of progress, or there will surely rise at last the flames of conflict." Following some preparatory spadework, Eisenhower sent Congress a measure for a $2 billion development loan fund. Although the three-year package targeted underdevelopment generally, India served as a prime focus and India's needs the principal rationale for the bill.[6]

By the beginning of 1957 the Democrats had recaptured control of the Congress, and although the party of Humphrey and Bowles displayed greater sympathy toward foreign aid—especially aid directed at liberals' pet projects like India—than did the Republicans, the Democratic congressional leadership insisted on putting its stamp on any foreign aid bill. Unwilling to surrender the purse strings to the executive, the Democrats in Congress allocated aid on an annual basis, rather than three years at a time; suspecting padding in the numbers and determined to demonstrate their fiduciary trustworthiness, they trimmed the request by 30 percent.

Yet the fact that both administration and Congress accepted the idea that U.S. security required American aid to countries like India—to neutralists offering no military or strategic quid pro quo, professing ideological agnosticism, practicing socialism, and sharing only a general preference for democracy over totalitarianism—marked a watershed in American relations with the Third World. Americans had not accepted neutralism as a philosophy; they still bridled at the moral equivalence between the United States and the

Soviet Union that nonalignment appeared to imply. The cold war, in the American view, had hardly ended; in some respects, it was more dangerous than ever, since the Soviets had shifted from threat and bluster to more insidious methods of economic and political cooptation. But in approving the development loan fund, both the White House and the Congress showed that they recognized that the terms of the contest with the Soviets had been transformed, and that India played an important role in this new cold war.

Critics of U.S. policy toward India could still charge, of course, that nothing had really changed, that the United States still viewed India not as a country important in itself but as a piece on the Great Power chessboard. Defenders of American foreign policy could respond (although not usually in public) that this was entirely true—and utterly unremarkable. For better or worse, American foreign policy must aim first at assuring the safety of the United States and American interests in the world. If at the same time American actions can benefit other countries, all well and good. But policymakers must concentrate on security, not philanthropy. In the latter area, the Red Cross does a better job.

Events of the second half of 1957 put the new bipartisan commitment to foreign aid to an early test. The problems vexing India's five-year plan continued to mount. Even as the government of India looked to the West for economic aid, it turned to the East for instruction in methods to raise agricultural productivity. Nehru lauded China's ability to feed itself without the high-technology, high-cost production regimes of Western states. "How has China done it?" he asked rhetorically. "China's resources in this respect are not bigger than ours. . . . Yet they are succeeding in increasing their agricultural production at a faster rate than we are. Surely, it should not be beyond our powers to do something China can do."[7]

Taking its cue from Beijing, New Delhi encouraged the formation of rural cooperatives and communally owned farms. But the notion met stern resistance from landowners and even from some members of the government, who pointed out that agricultural policy in communist countries differed in important respects from that in democratic countries. India's food minister, A. P. Jain, described the difficulties involved in implementing the cooperative plan, commenting dryly, "It requires a bit of pressure. It was Stalin and Mao who enforced it in Russia and China." Unwilling to apply such pressure, the Indian government's agricultural program fell between the two stools of free enterprise and centralized administration. Producers and traders held their crops off the market until the government's supplies cleared, creating artificial shortages, high prices, and endless complaints.[8]

The failure of the 1957 monsoon in India's northern breadbasket doubled the need for imported grain and strained all sectors of the economy. The five-year plan verged on collapse. Nehru had refrained from asking for increased foreign aid until now, hoping to demonstrate India's self-sufficiency. When the rice crop fell short, he called on the Indian people to eat wheat instead, saying that rather than depend on foreign charity, Indians should develop a taste for a varied diet. But by September 1957, he could resist the need no longer. He told an American correspondent that India would welcome U.S. assistance, suggesting a half-billion-dollar loan. He added that India's finance minister would travel to Washington within a few weeks to discuss the matter with U.S. officials.

The Eisenhower administration had monitored the Indian situation constantly and was ready for Nehru's request. Realizing that the development loan fund could not cover the emergency, the administration pressured India's foreign suppliers—especially the West Germans—to take measures to reduce India's trade deficit, and it transferred funds to India from the American Export–Import Bank. The total package, exclusive of the Europeans' contribution, came to $225 million. Although it was not even half of what Nehru requested, it represented the first installment of an ongoing program of American support.

This program grew steadily during the remainder of Eisenhower's second term. Not counting the bailout of the five-year plan, U.S. grants and loans to India rose from $90 million in 1958 to $137 million in 1959 and $194 million in 1960. The administration also signed a variety of commodity agreements, including one in May 1960 worth $1.25 billion over four years. Finally, Washington sponsored a consortium of five of India's major trading partners—Britain, West Germany, Japan, and Canada, in addition to the United States—which pledged almost $1 billion in aid through 1961.

Eisenhower capitalized on the capital-enhanced good feelings in U.S.– Indian relations with a personal visit to India at the end of 1959. As he did almost everywhere he went, the president encountered great enthusiasm among the common people. Enormous crowds spilled onto the roadways leading from the airport into New Delhi, slowing the motorcade to a halt. Nehru, annoyed at the inability of traffic and security forces to keep the route open, leaped from the car and thrashed vigorously from side to side in an effort to clear a path. Eisenhower found the scene amusing. A "lively non-violence," he noted afterward.[9]

HINDI CHINI BYE BYE

A new wrinkle in Asian affairs topped the list of topics the president and the prime minister discussed during Eisenhower's two-day visit. China and India, since their closest approach during the Bandung Conference of 1955, had begun to move apart. Like Britain during the years of the raj, India had attempted to secure the frontier regions that separated, and buffered, India from China. In 1950, India negotiated a treaty with Nepal, closely tying that country on the near side of the Himalayas to India; and during the next half-decade, Nepal remained relatively securely within India's sphere of influence. Eventually, however, the Nepalese decided that nonalignment between India and China might serve Nepal as well as nonalignment between the United States and the Soviet Union served India. In 1956, Katmandu and Beijing signed a treaty of friendship; at the same time, China inaugurated economic aid to Nepal. The next year, Zhou Enlai crossed the mountains and assured the Nepalese that they had nothing to worry about from China—from which the Indians inferred *they* might.

Tibet proved more troublesome. In a deal struck at Simla early in the century, the British government of India had recognized Chinese "suzerainty"—an intentionally vague word denoting less control than *sovereignty*— over Tibet. But through nearly four decades, during the Chinese revolution and civil war, as well as during two world wars, the Chinese government had failed to exercise even the loose control the convention had accorded it. This suited the British and the Indians well enough, but after the Chinese Communists dispatched the Nationalists, the People's Liberation Army set about "liberating" Tibet. India expressed its annoyance in a series of diplomatic notes, and in 1954, when Zhou came to New Delhi, Nehru reiterated his government's concern over China's apparent intention to swallow Tibet entire. Heightening India's worries, the parts of the border region between Tibet and India had never been adequately surveyed. The actual location of the frontier remained uncertain.

In the spirit of *panchsheel,* both China and India had sought to minimize the Tibet problem. Shown Chinese maps indicating that certain regions claimed by India lay on the Chinese side of the border, Zhou waved them aside as outdated, saying his government simply had not had time to print new ones. Nehru recognized that New Delhi could bring to bear only limited pressure on the matter, and he hoped an overall relaxation between the two countries would render a peaceful settlement possible.

On the ground, however, the problem would not disappear. In the summer of 1955 an Indian patrol came upon Chinese officials collecting grazing taxes from migrant herders on what New Delhi considered indisputably its side of the border. Not much later, Beijing reinforced its publicans with PLA troops, and glaring matches across the high border valleys became an annual summer event. In 1958 negotiations between India and China began, but they soon collapsed amid mutual recriminations. Intensified Chinese repression of nationalist and religious movements within Tibet, which increased China's military presence in the region, strained the situation further. Tibetan resistance became open revolt in 1959, and the Chinese found themselves fighting a regular war. Beijing unsuccessfully tried to close the border. Chinese troops stepped up patrols, and where they considered the frontier in doubt, they occupied first and asked questions later, if at all.

The problem came to a head following the flight of the Dalai Lama to India. Nehru had attempted to keep the border incidents quiet, to avoid endangering good relations with Beijing. With the arrival of the Buddhist leader and thousands of his followers, however, the situation burst into the open. Nehru would gladly have seen the holy man go elsewhere, but to deny refuge would have exacted too high a political and diplomatic cost. Beijing denounced India's harboring of the fugitives and even claimed that Indian agents had kidnapped the Dalai Lama. It charged that India was allowing Tibetan rebels the use of bases across the border in India. The *People's Daily* backdated Indian meddling in Chinese affairs to 1950 and asserted that India had "never pursued a clear-cut policy of non-interference."

Relations soon declined further. India discovered that the Chinese were building a road across Indian territory in the region of Aksai Chin. India's newspapers reported that a thousand PLA troops had raised the Chinese flag in the North-East Frontier Agency. A new border incident resulted in the deaths of nine Indian soldiers at the Kongka Pass in Ladakh. Provoked to the limit, Indian passions surged. One member of parliament suggested bombing the Aksai Chin road. The *Hindustan Times* declared that "the need to do something is preemptory. Mr. Nehru has warned us against brave talk and action taken in anger. Let us warn him in turn that he may not have any more opportunities to unite the country behind him, if China is allowed to go on heaping contumely and humiliation on us." A former president of the Congress party charged that Nehru's foolish idealism had brought India to a sad state of affairs. "The people were encouraged to keep shouting 'Hindi Chini bhai bhai,' when in fact aggression was taking place. The Chinese must have laughed in their sleeves at this strange and infantile exhibition of Indian sentimentality. Today the people feel humiliated and they look ridiculous."[10]

More border clashes followed, and China made a claim to forty thousand square miles of territory that New Delhi considered Indian. Nehru finally admitted the possibility that he had mistaken China's intentions. "I just do not know how the Chinese mind may think," he remarked. "I have been surprised at recent developments. . . . I have great admiration for the Chinese mind, logical and reasonable and relatively calm. But sometimes I wonder if all those old qualities have not perhaps been partly overwhelmed."[11]

Hoping to salvage something of *panchsheel* between India and China, Nehru invited Zhou to New Delhi. The Chinese premier agreed to come, although less (as events demonstrated) to seek a settlement than to buy time, which Beijing needed to assess the fallout from its simultaneously deepening rift with the Soviet Union. The two sides concurred in the appointment of a boundary commission to examine evidence regarding disputed regions. The commission met from June to December 1960. Its deliberations generated little more than paper. The Chinese evinced no desire to negotiate in good faith and were content to settle the matter by force at an opportune moment. Nehru recognized the collapse of his China policy and gloomily told the Indian parliament, "In the final analysis, it comes to this, that we must build up our strength. . . . This is not a matter which we can dispose of by a discussion."[12]

OUTPOST ON THE NEW FRONTIER

Amid these troubles between India and China, a new administration in Washington staked its claim to India as an issue in both U.S. and
world politics. As a young senator, John Kennedy had seized upon the issue of
India at just the right moment—in 1957, when America's emotional pendu-
lum was swinging in Nehru's favor. Spearheading the drive for increased U.S.
aid to help India meet the goals of its five-year plan, the Massachusetts
Democrat declared that the Russians were "trying to repeat in other parts of
Asia and Africa their takeover of China." Moscow, Kennedy said, was playing on the failure of the governments of this broad region to deliver the
masses from the cycle of stagnation. Kennedy continued,

> India stands out as one of the few countries in this non-Communist zone
> which really believes in the importance of breaking stagnation and acquiring
> habits of growth. India, like the United States, is engaged in a struggle of
> coexistence—in its case with China, which is also pursuing a planning effort
> being put under critical comparison all over the world. India, for better or
> worse, is a world power with a world audience. Its democratic future is
> delicately and dangerously poised; it would be catastrophic if its leadership
> were now humiliated in its quest for Western assistance when its cause is
> good.

Kennedy's words, spoken when India was indeed still striving for coexistence
with China, reverberated the more when New Delhi and Beijing fell out.[13]

This speech typified Kennedy's approach to foreign affairs. The administration that proclaimed a "new frontier" in American life adopted, at least in its
rhetoric, a tough-minded liberalism that the country found invigorating after
eight years of Eisenhower. Eisenhower's genius had lain in making fewer than
his share of mistakes: in avoiding war, inflation, high taxes, and the other bad
things that ruin presidential reputations. By 1960, a "new generation," as
Kennedy put it, was asking for something more. If Ike's golfing established the
ambience of his administration, football games on the White House lawn set
the tone for Kennedy's. The United States would not simply defend democracy; America would actively promote it. By demonstrating to the world
democracy's advantages over its totalitarian competitors, the Kennedy crowd
would win the cold war that the Eisenhower administration had fought only
to a draw.

In this strategy, India occupied a central position. Kennedy immediately
set about strengthening U.S.–Indian relations. A first step involved staffing
the new administration with kindred minds. He appointed Chester Bowles,
the former ambassador to New Delhi, to be undersecretary of state. Bowles
himself had had higher aims; the number-two slot at State came as a disappointment. But the position eventually served as a jumping-off point to New

Delhi, for after Bowles demonstrated his inability to become a member of the Washington team, the president reassigned him as ambassador to India.

For another key position in the State Department, Kennedy tapped Walt Rostow, an economic historian from the Massachusetts Institute of Technology. Rostow, whose specialty included studying countries that were approaching economic "takeoff," had provided the intellectual underpinnings for Kennedy's India-aid campaign. Rostow's best-known work, *The Stages of Economic Growth*, which outlined the nature of the modernization process in capitalist countries, bore a subtitle—"A Non-Communist Manifesto"—that summarized the liberal view of the relationship of economic development to the cold war. As head of State's policy planning staff, Rostow consistently pushed for aid for the Third World, especially India.

Kennedy also raided Cambridge—Harvard, this time—for his first ambassador to New Delhi. John Kenneth Galbraith's skepticism of the inevitable beneficence of the free market struck a chord in Kennedy, who once said, at a moment of particular pique with the captains of the steel industry, that while his father had always told him businessmen were sons of bitches, he hadn't believed it until now. Galbraith carried to New Delhi openness to the Indian program of mixed socialism and capitalism generally lacking in the Republicans. Like Rostow and Bowles, Galbraith enthusiastically supported increased U.S. aid to India.

During the first eighteen months of Kennedy's term, American aid constituted the principal substantive measure of American interest in India. Shortly after entering the White House, the president launched a series of initiatives building on the bipartisan backing for Third World development that had emerged during the late 1950s. At the beginning of March 1961, he announced the establishment of the Peace Corps; two weeks later, he unveiled the Alliance for Progress, a program targeting Latin America; before the end of the month, he declared the 1960s the "decade of development." Defending foreign assistance in the same terms of humanitarianism and self-interest that had formed the rationale for American aid since Truman, Kennedy asserted that the United States had "an historic opportunity" to help boost "more than half the people of the less-developed nations into self-sustained economic growth," even as he warned that "the economic collapse of those free but less-developed nations which now stand poised between sustained growth and economic chaos would be disastrous to our national security." As had the Truman and Eisenhower administrations, Kennedy's argued that India, the major noncommunist country in Asia, would serve as a sentinel on the ramparts of freedom—or a symbol of democracy's demise in the third world.[14]

During the transition from the Eisenhower to the Kennedy administrations, the international consortium for India aid, under the auspices of the World Bank, had reviewed India's third five-year plan. In April 1961, Kennedy pledged that the United States would loan $500 million to India for each of the plan's first two years, provided the other consortium members matched the U.S. contribution. The other countries came up a little short and a bit slow, but eventually the combined backing of the group guaranteed that India's new plan, which covered the first half of the 1960s, would get off to a promising start.

Nehru appreciated the American help. "Our task, great as it is," he wrote Kennedy, "has been made light by the goodwill and generous assistance that has come to us from the United States. To the people of the United States and more especially to you, Mr. President, we feel deeply grateful."[15]

CONGO CABALS

U.S. and Indian interests also converged at this time in one of the most confusing diplomatic episodes of the 1960s. As the decade began, the momentum toward independence in Africa was growing irresistible. The European colonialists (with the exception of backward Portugal) saw that continued occupation of their African empires had become a losing proposition, and with greater or less grace they began to bow out. Belgium, whose tenuous claim to world standing had rested principally on its possession of a huge domain in the basin of the Congo, decamped with singular disgrace in the summer of 1960, leaving behind almost no educated Congolese, a variety of deadly tribal and personal feuds, nearly ninety thousand worried Belgian expatriates, and a full-blown secessionist movement in the copper province of Katanga.

The Eisenhower administration had turned its attention to the Congo when the leftist prime minister, Patrice Lumumba, summoned Soviet help against his many rivals, which included the Belgians, back again, in military force, in response to pleas from the left-behinds. Hedging his bets, Lumumba also called on the United Nations, claiming aggression by Belgium. The Russians arrived first, which set Washington's contingency planners to work at top speed.

After several top-level meetings, Eisenhower decided that Lumumba had to go. He called on the CIA's covert-operations division to accomplish the feat. With much enthusiasm, the agency devised methods for killing or otherwise incapacitating the charismatic Congolese leader; their schemes involved substances ranging from exotic and untraceable toxins to more mundane high-velocity lead. But the hired killers botched the job, although Lumumba nevertheless met an untimely end at the hands of African assassins.

Kennedy's arrival coincided with Lumumba's death. Confronting what George Ball, the State Department official in charge of U.S. policy toward the Congo, described as "a frightful mess," JFK set his course by the star of the United Nations. Unfortunately, that star turned out to be a planet, moving daily. The U.N. force initially entered the Congo in an effort to persuade the Belgian troops to withdraw, while safeguarding the lives and property of those persons the Belgians had returned to protect. But the U.N. contingent had got thoroughly entangled in a three-way (counting only the major contenders) civil war. In principle, the U.N. held out for Congolese unity, despite pressure from European governments that were traveling the high road of self-determination to reach the low end of secession in Katanga—in the debatable belief that two or more successor states would prove easier to coerce than a single country.[16]

India supported the U.N. with considerably greater alacrity than it had rallied to the blue banner in Korea in 1950. The fact that the colonialists were ganging up against a fellow Third World country rendered reflection unnecessary. Commenting on the Europeans' efforts on behalf of the secessionists, Nehru declared that "the whole thing is perfectly amazing and scandalous in the extreme." In the midst of the crisis, a mysterious airplane crash in the wilds of the Congo killed the U.N. secretary-general, Dag Hammarskjöld. Many observers in Africa and Asia detected a British hand in the affair. Nehru refused to go that far, but he did consider Britain indirectly responsible, in that the policies London espoused had created the conditions leading to the accident.

By their separate routes, the United States and India arrived at the same position on the Congo—that is, support for the United Nations—and in March 1961, when Indian troops joined the U.N. operation, U.S. planes ferried them into action. Nehru expressed a view analogous to that of American leaders during the Korean war, telling Kennedy that "the future not only of the Congo but of the United Nations itself" was at stake. In the U.N. Security Council and elsewhere on the world diplomatic scene, U.S. and Indian officials coordinated their actions. Not entirely, for Nehru, Krishna Menon, and others in the Indian government sometimes suspected the Americans of double-dealing. Events occasionally justified these suspicions as Washington sought to strike a balance between its commitments to the U.N. and the sensibilities of its European allies. When the cold war intensified in late 1961 and 1962, the temptation to throw America's lot in with the anticommunist, antigovernment, anti-U.N. rebels grew strong. But Washington resisted, and for the most part, from Kennedy's inauguration until the final defeat of the secessionists in 1964, American and Indian policies in the Congo followed broadly parallel paths.[17]

ONE GOOD TURN...

In 1956, during the Suez and Hungary affairs, many commentators had noted that Western confusion regarding Egypt had allowed the Russians to suppress the revolution in Hungary more harshly than they might have otherwise. A similar conflation of crises occurred in the autumn of 1962. On 14 October American aerial reconnaissance of Cuba showed offensive missile sites under construction. Because of increasingly close ties between Moscow and Havana, facilitated by the abortive CIA effort to invade

Cuba at the Bay of Pigs in April of the preceding year, the White House immediately concluded that the Russians were probing a soft spot in U.S. defenses. During the next week, the Kennedy administration debated its possible responses; on 22 October, the president publicly charged the Soviets with violating the peace of the hemisphere. Kennedy warned Moscow to remove the missiles, and he announced an American blockade to prevent the completion or reinforcement of the installations.

In the midst of what was probably the world's closest approach to nuclear war since 1945, China moved against Indian positions along the disputed Sino–Indian border. In the first days of fighting, Chinese troops routed the Indians, easily destroying their prepared defenses and taking four thousand prisoners. Confident that despite the Kremlin's continuing interest in India the Russians would have their plate too full with the United States to give New Delhi much help, China seized the territory under dispute, then called for negotiations.

Despite India's bleak prospects, Nehru categorically rejected negotiations. "Shorn of its wrappings," he declared, ". . . this is in effect a demand for surrender." Sounding like Winston Churchill, Nehru vowed to fight to the bitter end, regardless of odds against. "China is a great and powerful country with enormous resources," he said. "But India is no weak country to be frightened by threats and military might. We shall build up our strength, both military and economic, to win this battle of Indian freedom. We shall always be willing to negotiate a peace but that can only be on condition that aggression is vacated. We can never submit or surrender to aggression."[18]

The Chinese successes led to immediate demands for the ouster of Krishna Menon, recently defense secretary and longtime advocate of warm relations with Beijing. Menon's many rivals in the Indian government had kept their knives sharp, awaiting such an opportunity; only Nehru's personal affection for the outspoken minister had allowed him to stay on. But at the end of October, Nehru conceded that Menon had outlived his usefulness and let him go—a move that did not displease Washington.

Largely as a result of Menon's poor management, Indian troops found themselves ill-equipped for the kind of fighting required of them; and when the Soviet Union, facing the prospect of general war with the United States, suppressed its misgivings about Mao and announced its backing for China, New Delhi turned to the Americans. The temptation in Washington, particularly among career officials who had suffered through the self-righteous early years of *panchsheel*, to take an I-told-you-so attitude proved nearly irresistible. But only a trace of that sentiment crept into a letter from Kennedy to Nehru at the end of October. "You have displayed an impressive degree of forebearance and patience in dealing with the Chinese," the president wrote. "You have put into practice what all great religious teachers have urged and so few of their followers have been able to do. Alas, this teaching seems to be effective only when it is shared by both sides in a dispute."[19]

Although many in the State Department had expected Nehru to call for a rescue when India encountered trouble with the communists, few in Washington had anticipated the magnitude of the request the prime minister passed along. With Chinese troops poised for a push down from the mountains onto the Indian plain, and with the Indian population in a condition of near panic (one rumor had the Chinese plotting an assault by paratroopers on New Delhi), Nehru asked for a dozen squadrons of all-weather fighters to defend Indian territory and for two squadrons of B-47 bombers to attack positions in China. Because India had no personnel competent to operate these planes, he also requested American crews. Finally, the prime minister solicited U.S. aid in constructing a radar shield for India's cities.

Washington agreed to send a significant portion of what Nehru wanted, but the American government cautioned that a major buildup would take time; and before the weapons arrived in sufficient quantity to accomplish much good, the war with China ended. On 19 November, three weeks after the Soviet Union agreed to withdraw its missiles from Cuba, and after China had amply demonstrated its ability to push India around, Zhou Enlai announced an end to the hostilities. Promising to withdraw from recently captured positions, the Chinese premier went on to say that China and India might resolve their differences regarding the location of the border by peaceful means.

The cease-fire in the Himalayas eliminated the need for the American air cover Nehru had requested, yet the potential for Chinese aggression remained. Having taken the first step toward reliance on U.S. military aid, Nehru continued in that direction. At the end of 1962, U.S. transport planes began arriving, bringing arms and equipment to supply ten divisions of mountain troops. To train Indian soldiers and generally supervise the use of American weapons, Washington sent military advisers and technicians. Before long, India—still ostensibly nonaligned—was supporting a larger U.S. military mission than Pakistan, an avowed American ally. Ambassador Galbraith, although generally favoring expanded American influence in India, thought the Pentagon was overdoing things. "This mission is so large," he commented, "that there doesn't seem to be any way of arranging conferences with the Indians short of hiring a church."[20]

...DESERVES ANOTHER?

American officials possessed sufficient tact not to demand a quid pro quo for American aid in India's hour of need, but the Indians had enough sense to realize that certain actions would increase the likelihood of receiving what they desired from Washington. The demise of Krishna Menon fortuitously removed a major obstacle to U.S.–Indian collaboration. With the possible exception of Andrei Vishinsky—the Soviet delegate to the U.N. in the early 1950s, previously chief puppeteer at the Moscow show trials of the 1930s, and a thoroughly despicable character—Americans detested Menon more than any other individual who frequented the world body. Indian officials added to American satisfaction by giving assurances, as Ambassador Galbraith noted in his diary after a meeting at the Indian foreign office, "that we could pretty well count on their restraint and U.N. support" during the confrontation with the Soviets over the Cuban missiles. Additionally, Nehru agreed to resume negotiations with Pakistan regarding Kashmir.[21]

None of these expressions of cooperativeness, however, brought what Washington really wanted, and what Nehru refused to give. By the beginning of 1963, the Kennedy administration was committing the United States ever more deeply to the defense of South Vietnam. Politically, the commitment had originated at the Geneva conference of 1954 and in the formation of SEATO shortly thereafter. But through the end of the 1950s the American pledge to defend South Vietnam against communism remained only a pledge. While an advisory group based in the country provided an American military presence, its small numbers and low visibility made a pullout possible with minimal damage to U.S. prestige. Under Kennedy, the situation changed. From 1961 through November 1963, U.S. forces increased from a few hundred individuals to more than fifteen thousand. They remained technically "advisers"; actually, many of them engaged in combat. During the last months of the Kennedy administration, the war in Vietnam was becoming America's war.

Anxious for support from credible Asian sources, Washington would have killed—diplomatically speaking—to gain Nehru's approval of America's Vietnam venture. But the Indian prime minister wanted nothing to do with it. In 1961, on Kennedy's invitation, Nehru acted as a mediator in the search for a cease-fire in Laos, where troubles like those in Vietnam had developed. In the discussions that followed, which amounted in some respects to a replay of the 1954 Geneva conference, India led the way in arranging a neutralization formula on which the great powers and Laos could agree. Kennedy expressed his thanks, saying, "I want you to know how much I appreciate your continuing efforts to create a peaceful world community."[22]

Vietnam proved another matter entirely. Having staked American prestige to the survival of a noncommunist regime in Saigon, American leaders had no interest in a negotiated settlement, which would inevitably give the communists a foot in the South Vietnamese door. The United States would talk peace, but only after Ho Chi Minh and the North Vietnamese gave up their claims to South Vietnam. This, of course, Ho would not do.

Nor did Nehru think he ought to. The Indian view of the Vietnam struggle coincided broadly with the views of the North Vietnamese. New Delhi agreed with Hanoi that the Americans had essentially taken over from the French as occupiers of Vietnam. Nehru did not deny the communist character of Ho's revolution, but as he had been telling American leaders since the 1940s, he thought the nationalist aspect of the movement more important.

On a 1961 visit by the prime minister to Washington, Kennedy and Gal braith "pressed Nehru hard," as Galbraith noted in his journal, for recommendations as to what course the United States should follow in Vietnam. Beyond suggesting pressure on South Vietnamese president Ngo Dinh Diem to clean up his administration, Nehru had little positive advice. On the negative side, he emphasized the inappropriateness of sending troops, suggesting that they would produce no better results for the United States than they had for France.[23]

TWO DEATHS

The disagreement between Washington and New Delhi regarding Vietnam had not become a major matter by November 1963 because American involvement in South Vietnam remained minor—compared with the half-decade that followed—and tentative. In addition, the Kennedy administration continued committed to friendly relations with India. If it had to disagree with Nehru's government, Washington intended to do so quietly.

The situation began to change with Kennedy's assassination at the end of November 1963. Although the new president, Lyndon Johnson, immediately vowed to carry on in the Kennedy tradition, Johnson's background and style could not have differed more from his predecessor's. Indeed, if not for the difference, Kennedy never would have asked Johnson to help him balance the Democratic ticket in 1960. A frequently crude character, a consummate political operator, and a southerner—from the state, as eastern liberals could never forget, "that killed Kennedy"—Johnson encountered hostility from many Americans who made an instant martyr of the fallen hero. Johnson's effect on U.S.–Indian relations took longer to work itself out. But with American liberals harboring *their* doubts about the new man in the Oval Office, Indians, too, could not help wondering. That Johnson came from the Jim Crow region did not reassure them.

Before they decided what to make of Johnson, the people of India suffered an infinitely more serious blow. In May 1964, a ruptured aorta killed the only prime minister India had ever known. The shock came especially hard for its surprise. Although in his mid-seventies, Nehru often seemed younger than his years. In January 1964, a slight stroke had hospitalized him temporarily, but he shook off the advice of his Soviet doctors for a slow convalescence. "Let them go to hell. If I lie down in bed for even a week, I know I will not get up." Realizing himself that the end was approaching, Nehru nonetheless pressed on in a manner to belie the fact. "I want to be able to work to the sudden end," he said. He got his wish.[24]

Nehru's passing set loose a period of mourning in India that exceeded anything since Gandhi's death in 1948. Huge crowds poured into the capital to pay their respects. So great did the commotion become that the government felt obliged to mobilize the army to restrain the millions—leading to rumors of a military coup, which were all the more believable since major questions clouded the choice of a successor. The uproar continued through the reading of Nehru's will, which specified that his ashes be spread across the countryside of India, reserving a portion for immersion in the Ganges, the river that "has been to me a symbol and a memory of the past of India, running into the present, and flowing on to the great ocean of the future."

World leaders generally regretted to see Nehru go. His complicated personality had evoked a variety of reactions, often in a single person, as Eisenhower's observations, previously noted, indicate. Britain's Hugh Gaitskell, a major figure in the Labour party, commended most of Nehru's policies but, like Zhou Enlai, found him insufferable as an individual. "He is a very arrogant man," Gaitskell wrote. "I think that is one reason why he makes such long speeches. He really thinks everyone wants to listen to them." At the same time, even persons who had nothing good to say about Nehru's policies conceded his importance to India. Pakistan's Zulfikar Ali Bhutto took a view similar to Dean Acheson, also described earlier. Bhutto once told Pakistan's national assembly that most of the troubles between India and Pakistan owed to Nehru's haughtiness, but in a private note written during the week of Nehru's death, the foreign minister offered a slightly more balanced opinion: "Although he committed aggression, alienated his neighbours, suppressed his opponents, made mock convenience of his ethics, he was Nehru the redeemer of 400 million people, a valiant fighter who led his people to freedom and, for the first time in six hundred years, gave them a place in the sun."[25]

To the diplomats of the world, Nehru's foreign policy was a known quantity. They might not like much of what he did, but they knew what to expect. They could count on Nehru to pursue a shrewd line of Indian self-interest on matters close to home: Pakistan, China, Southeast Asia. They could rely on the prime minister to seek to manipulate the rivalry between the superpowers, to play West against East to India's advantage and his own. They could look forward to a universalistic and moralistic style of lecturing that sometimes had application to the here-and-now yet often did not.

Of Nehru's successor, by unsettling contrast, they knew little. While Johnson chased Kennedy's ghost, Lal Bahadur Shastri suffered even more by comparison with his predecessor. Shastri's background lay in domestic affairs; as home minister, he had served capably and gained Nehru's trust. But he had little experience of foreign policy, and many observers considered him a timeserver who would fill the premiership until the two likeliest candidates for a permanent succession—Morarji Desai and Indira Gandhi—were ready for a test of strength. The *Times of India* aptly characterized Shastri as "a conciliator, compromiser and coordinator, above all a shy, modest, humble and unpretending man who hardly ever made an enemy during his entire career." Most students of Indian politics anticipated that Shastri would move slowly if at all in tampering with Nehru's policies. Most thought that if his tenure proved eventful, this would result more from the pressure of external developments than from anything he himself originated.[26]

AMERICA NONALIGNED

Lyndon Johnson, commemorating Nehru shortly after the prime minister's death, declared, "There could be no more fitting tribute to him than a world without war." The fine sentiment of the president's utterance unfortunately bore little relation to events of the period. Even as he spoke, Johnson carried the United States deeper into Vietnam. During the summer of 1964, his administration used a run-in between North Vietnamese and American forces in the Gulf of Tonkin to persuade the U.S. Congress to grant him wide authority to prosecute the conflict as he chose. American planes struck into North Vietnam; U.S. troops conducted larger operations in the South. Early the following year, the United States initiated a major bombing offensive. By the summer of 1965, with the dispatch of tens of thousands more of American soldiers, the war was escalating rapidly.[27]

Indian officials looked no more favorably than before on U.S. intervention in what they still considered an internal Vietnamese matter, but they had new troubles of their own to worry about. While the United States was dealing with the consequences of the partition of Vietnam that accompanied the end of French colonial rule in Indochina, India and Pakistan were attempting to settle, in similarly bloody fashion, the unresolved questions left by the British partition of the subcontinent.

The taproot of the 1965 India–Pakistan war ran to Kashmir, yet important lateral feeders branched to Washington, Beijing, and Moscow. The Pakistanis had watched the gradual warming of relations between India and the United States during the latter part of Eisenhower's administration with increasing suspicion. Their concern had increased when the Kennedy liberals made a great fuss over Nehru and what Washington endlessly called the "world's largest democracy." Their concern became alarm as the United States began shipping big quantities of arms to India in the wake of the 1962 Chinese invasion. The Pakistanis began to feel the same fears Indians had experienced eight years before, when the United States had commenced weapons aid to Pakistan. Naturally, the Pakistanis considered their grievances better founded—as indeed they were, given the exposed position of East Pakistan and the enormous Indian advantages in population and resources. President Mohammad Ayub Khan complained to Kennedy that in arming India, the United States was not only jeopardizing Pakistan's security, it was neglecting its own self-interest. For Kennedy's benefit, Ayub described what he considered the essential anti-American thrust of India's foreign policy. "This foreign policy has been based on the following factors," Ayub wrote: "(a) bending over backwards to appease communism; (b) hoist the white flag of neutralism to appease communism and get other wavering nations to join India in order to be able to create a world nuisance-value for themselves; (c) intimidate Pakistan in order to politically isolate it and economically weaken it; and (d) abuse the West, and especially the U.S.A. in season and out of season." Pakistan's president went on to say that "although India today poses as an aggrieved and oppressed party, in reality she has been constantly threatening and intimidating, in varying degrees, small neighbouring countries around her." Asserting that the shipment of U.S. military aid to India had "gravely exercised" public opinion in his country, Ayub concluded that India posed "a serious threat to our security."[28]

Pakistan could hardly have given fairer warning that it would seek shelter wherever shelter might be found. Once the most loyal of America's allies in Asia, Pakistan now started playing India's power-balancing game. It did not withdraw from its two alliances with the United States, SEATO and CENTO (the latter a remodeled Baghdad pact, with official U.S. participation), but it undertook initiatives toward both China and the Soviet Union. Early in 1963, the Pakistanis and the Chinese signed a treaty rectifying their frontiers; not coincidentally, part of the border China agreed to recognize adjoined Kashmir. This allowed Foreign Minister Bhutto to announce that if the Kashmir dispute led to war, "the international situation is such today that Pakistan would not be alone in that conflict." Lest listeners miss his point, Bhutto added, "An attack on Pakistan involves the territorial integrity and security of the largest state in Asia."[29]

For Pakistan to make amends with the Russians required greater effort and more time. While China, recently at war with India, had every reason to cultivate India's rival in the subcontinent, the Soviet Union, an Indian friend, had little incentive. This little had diminished further in 1960, when the United States launched a U-2 spy flight over Russia from Peshawar. Moscow had known of the reconnaissance missions for years, but until Soviet antiaircraft weapons knocked Francis Gary Powers's plane down in May 1960, the world had not. The Kremlin had ignored Pakistan's complicity. No longer: amid the flap the shootdown provoked, Soviet leader Khrushchev told the Pakistani chargé d'affaires that if his government repeated its mistake, Moscow's missiles would pulverize Peshawar. Not having access to the photos the U-2s had delivered to CIA headquarters in Washington, Karachi could not know that most of the missiles Khrushchev brandished so belligerently did not exist. Even had the Pakistanis known, they most likely still would have sought to lessen their exposure to Russia's wrath.

The process began with an announcement by Ayub that henceforth he would consider accepting aid from communist countries, as well as from the West. The Soviets, hoping to breach the wall the United States had created along their southern border, took the hint. In 1961, Karachi and Moscow inked a deal whereby the Soviet Union provided technical and economic assistance to Pakistan's petroleum industry. Two years later, the Kremlin floated a larger loan, supplemented by various trade and transportation agreements. During 1964, the Russian representative at the U.N. backed away from his previously staunch support for India in Kashmir. In the spring of 1965, Ayub traveled to Moscow. His talks there with Premier Alexei Kosygin started slowly. "I realized that the Soviet reputation for opening gambits in chess was not ill-founded," Ayub wrote afterward. But neither Kosygin's caution nor unseasonable cold prevented a break in the ice, and Ayub went home with a further $50 million in his pocket and the knowledge that the Soviets would not unthinkingly jump to India's side if trouble broke out in the subcontinent.[30]

Having covered its flanks, Pakistan returned its gaze to the center: Kashmir. Weighing the balance of forces between themselves and the Indians, the Pakistanis arrived at the unavoidable conclusion that time was not on their side. For the moment, control of Indian affairs rested with Shastri, a weaker figure certainly than Nehru and probably than any successor. More important, the ongoing delivery of American weapons to India indicated that if the Pakistanis did not act soon, the Indians might, with grave risk not only to Kashmir but to Pakistan proper as well.

Meanwhile, the Indians, gaining strength daily, were also acquiring larger interest in a settlement of the Kashmir question, peacefully if possible, otherwise if necessary. The talks Nehru had agreed to in exchange for U.S. aid in 1962 led nowhere, but in 1964 the prime minister tried another tack. He ordered the release of Muslim Kashmiri leader Sheikh Muhammad Abdullah, who had been arrested a decade earlier for agitating for Kashmir's independence. Nehru sent Abdullah to Pakistan to talk peace with Ayub. Abdullah managed to negotiate an agreement that Ayub and Nehru would meet face to face, but Nehru's sudden heart attack the day after the announcement of the summit also killed the initiative.

What Nehru might have accomplished, Shastri could not—at least, not without courting charges of capitulation. By the end of 1964, both sides were drawing closer to war. Given the intermingling of communal groups in Kashmir and elsewhere in the subcontinent, and the incessant incidents that resulted, neither side lacked a pretext for action. In December 1964, the Indian government decreed that in the event of a breakdown in Kashmir's legislative machinery, it would rule the region directly from New Delhi. Shortly thereafter, Shastri outlawed Kashmir's local National Conference party and established a Kashmir branch of the Indian Congress party. Not surprisingly, and correctly, the Pakistanis interpreted these actions as portending an Indian power play. Tensions increased all the more.

In April 1965, the cord snapped. For nearly two decades, the location of the border between India and Pakistan in the Rann of Kutch had been unresolved, for the good reason that this sub-sea-level salt marsh was of little use to either side, even during the part of the year when it did not lie under water. In 1965, neither India nor Pakistan possessed any greater intrinsic interest in the waste, but to each, the region seemed a good place to test the strength of the other.

The Pakistanis proved the stronger in this encounter, pushing ten miles into Indian territory. Yet Islamabad (Pakistan's new capital) declined for the moment to exploit its advantage. Upon the intercession of Britain, Ayub proposed a cease-fire. Shastri accepted, subject to the appointment of an international arbitration commission.

Rather than lance the boil and release the bad blood between the two sides, the April fighting served only to aggravate the infection. The Pakistanis had long denigrated the fighting ability of the Indians and itched to have it out with them. India, humbled by China in 1962 and now by Pakistan, sought revenge. Early in May, sporadic shooting across the truce line in Kashmir became more regular. Later in the month, Indian troops crossed the line and occupied three posts on the Pakistani side. In August, Pakistan replied by infiltrating armed "volunteers" into Indian-controlled territory. India stepped up its actions along the frontier. When Pakistan sent tanks in force against the Indians on 1 September, the second major India–Pakistan war began in earnest.

Washington observed the proceedings with ambivalence. Although the United States was still nominally tied to Pakistan via SEATO and CENTO, the Johnson administration immediately dismissed the notion that it owed anything to Pakistan in a conflict with India. Ever since the original arms deal of 1954, American leaders had consistently rejected guarantees to Pakistan in the event of trouble with India. Moreover, U.S. officials had serious reservations about the trend of Pakistan's foreign policy. The Americans had accepted Ayub's opening to Moscow. Frightened toward peace themselves by the Cuban missile crisis, the Americans had sought accommodation with Moscow, which likewise had had much of the belligerence scared out of it. Under the circumstances, Washington could hardly ask its allies to maintain a hostile front toward the Kremlin. China, however, constituted a different matter. The Kennedy and Johnson administrations went into Vietnam largely to contain the Chinese; neither Democratic president thought much of Ayub's cultivation of Beijing. Following a trip by Ayub to China early in 1965, Johnson canceled—in diplomatese, "postponed"—a scheduled visit by the Pakistani president to Washington. To appear unbiased, Johnson simultaneously pushed back an invitation to Shastri. But since the announcement came days before Ayub's planned arrival and months before Shastri's, the message was clear.

The border-crossing excursions in Kashmir during August put the U.S. embassy in New Delhi on full alert. Chester Bowles, back in India as ambassador, described the situation as "deeply worrisome" and warned the State Department that it would probably "get worse before it gets better." The day before the Pakistani invasion, the CIA predicted the attack. In noting Pakistan's use of predominantly American weapons, the agency indicated that Washington had better prepare a response.[31]

Johnson may or may not have recalled the pains the Truman administration had taken to avoid playing favorites during the first round of fighting over Kashmir. At that time, the young Texan was earning his spurs in Congress and paying little attention to foreign affairs. But Johnson's secretary of state,

Dean Rusk, an Asia specialist in the State Department during the late 1940s, remembered; and he sought to duplicate the policy. Yet as the CIA report demonstrated, this time the United States found itself involved from the start. In 1947, American neutrality between India and Pakistan had simply required staying out of the affairs of the subcontinent. In 1965, it required getting out.

At first, Rusk attempted to throw the issue to the U.N., the usual dumping ground for unresolvable problems. The day after the Pakistani invasion, the secretary of state informed Bowles that the administration would not directly pressure Islamabad to pull back but instead would work through world opinion. "Given the existing strains on our relations with both parties," Rusk wrote, "we do not believe such further actions as threats to suspend military aid . . . are likely to halt the fighting at this time."[32]

When India counterattacked, the United States found itself in much the position New Delhi had occupied during the Korean war. Fearing that the fighting in the subcontinent would spread, the Johnson administration called on both sides to halt. Washington contended that the international community might sort out the rights and wrongs of the affair once the killing stopped. On 6 September, Rusk sent a priority cable to Bowles directing the ambassador to impress the danger of the situation upon the Shastri government. "A continuation of the conflict," the secretary said, "is likely to plunge India more deeply into the cross currents of the cold war and internal Communist bloc conflicts. The Chinese Communists will be the certain winners; it is difficult to see how either India or Pakistan could benefit regardless of the outcome." Rusk concluded his appeal (which paralleled one he sent to the U.S. ambassador in Pakistan) by predicting "sheer disaster" unless the two sides heeded the U.N.'s call for a cease-fire and withdrawal behind the frontier.[33]

Although the combatants ignored this advice, the administration still hesitated to take stronger action. As White House aide Robert Komer, drafting a presidential statement, remarked to Johnson, "It will be very hard to go beyond even-handed 'grave concern' without goring someone's ox."[34]

But whole herds were getting gored already. The fighting continued to escalate, with India throwing its Russian MiG-21s into the battle, and Pakistan responding with American F-104s to reinforce the F-84s it had already committed. India mounted a drive toward Lahore, prompting Beijing to threaten to enter the war on the side of Pakistan. The U.S. National Security Agency detected heavy radio traffic out of western China, which suggested the Chinese might be serious. An official on the American desk in the Indian foreign ministry told an American visitor, "Either we fall or they fall; it's come to that."[35]

In an effort to prevent the situation from spinning completely out of control, the Johnson administration announced an embargo of American weapons, spare parts, and ammunition to both sides. The ban on parts and ammunition proved critical. Even the best-built and most carefully maintained weapons systems break down regularly. Tanks in particular require frequent repairs. Without a continuing stream of parts, sustained operations are impossible. In addition, the Pentagon had designed its aid programs to India and Pakistan in such a way as to prevent the stockpiling of more than three weeks' worth of ammunition. Sure enough, by 23 September, less than a month after the war began, Shastri and Ayub accepted a cease-fire.

Distressingly for the United States, Washington's neutrality earned it the enmity of both parties to the conflict. To Pakistan, the United States' failure to come to the aid of its ally seemed a betrayal of commitments made since the early 1950s. Papers in Pakistan denounced Americans as false friends and agents of Hindu imperialism. If alliance with the United States brought no greater thanks than this, who needed it? In Lahore and elsewhere, mobs of angry protesters attacked Americans on the streets and burned buildings housing U.S. officials.

As for the Indians, they could not forget that for more than a decade the United States had assured them that Pakistan would not use American weapons against India. If Karachi did, the Americans had said, the United States would take swift and decisive action. Yet when the attack India had long predicted took place, Washington could bring itself to do no more than slap Ayub gently on the wrist—a slap that had come only slowly and under great pressure. The Soviets had proved far better friends. Since the early 1950s, they had provided general economic and military assistance; more recently, they had begun building a factory to produce MiGs in India and had agreed to supply submarines and surface ships to the Indian navy.

The 1965 war thus proved a major diplomatic defeat for the United States and a corresponding coup for the Soviet Union. Following the cease-fire, India and Pakistan accepted Moscow's mediation. The conference that formally ended the conflict in January 1966 took place in Tashkent.

The September war fairly extinguished hopes that the improvement in U.S.–Indian relations since 1956 would become permanent. After Nehru's second visit to the United States, U.S. and Indian leaders had begun to see each other in a friendlier light, and for almost ten years the distance separating Washington and New Delhi had diminished. But the India–Pakistan war revealed that substantial differences remained, in terms of both interests and perceptions. Genuine cooperation was as far away as ever.

Notes

1. Cousins to Eisenhower, 30 August 1956, Dwight D. Eisenhower papers, Eisenhower Library, Abilene, Kansas.

2. Henderson to Acheson, 21 February 1951, *Foreign Relations 1951*, vol. 6, 2118.

3. Memoranda of conversations, 17–19 December 1956, Eisenhower papers.

4. Dwight D. Eisenhower, *The White House Years: Waging Peace, 1956–1961* (Garden City, N.Y.: Doubleday, 1965), 113–14.

5. NSC 5701, 10 January 1957, NSC records, National Achives, Washington.

6. *Public Papers of the Presidents: Dwight D. Eisenhower 1957* (Washington: U.S. Government Printing Office, 1958), 60–65.

7. Francine R. Frankel, *India's Political Economy, 1947–1977: The Gradual Revolution* (Princeton, N.J.: Princeton University Press, 1978), 141.

8. Ibid., 144.

9. Eisenhower, *Waging Peace*, 499–500.

10. S. M. Burke, *Mainsprings of Indian and Pakistani Foreign Policy* (Minneapolis: University of Minnesota Press, 1974), 159–63.

11. Sarvepalli Gopal, *Jawaharlal Nehru: A Biography*, vol. 3 (Cambridge: Harvard University Press, 1984), 97.

12. Charles H. Heimmsath and Surjit Mansingh, *A Diplomatic History of Modern India* (Bombay: Allied, 1971), 465.

13. W. W. Rostow, *Eisenhower, Kennedy, and Foreign Aid* (Austin: University of Texas Press, 1985), 6–9.

14. Ibid., 170–72.

15. Gopal, *Nehru*, vol. 3, 187–88.

16. George W. Ball, *The Past Has Another Pattern: Memoirs* (New York: Norton, 1982), 231.

17. Nehru to Kennedy, 16 April 1961, John F. Kennedy papers, Kennedy Library, Boston.

18. Gopal, *Nehru*, vol. 3, 221–26.

19. Ibid., 224.

20. John Kenneth Galbraith, *Ambassador's Journal: A Personal Account of the Kennedy Years* (Boston: Houghton Mifflin, 1969), 463.

21. Ibid., 430–31.

22. Gopal, *Nehru*, vol. 3, 187.

23. Galbraith, *Ambassador's Journal*, 246.

24. Gopal, *Nehru*, vol. 3, 266–67.

25. Ibid., 268–71.

26. Frankel, *India's Political Economy*, 242.

27. Gopal, *Nehru*, vol. 3, 271.

28. Mohammad Ayub Khan, *Friends Not Masters: A Political Autobiography* (New York: Oxford University Press, 1967), 142–43.

29. Burke, *Mainsprings*, 178.

30. Ayub Khan, *Friends Not Masters*, 169.

31. Bowles to Rusk, 14 August 1965, Lyndon B. Johnson papers, Johnson Library, Austin, Texas; CIA cable, 31 August 1965, ibid.

32. Rusk to Bowles, 2 September 1965, ibid.

33. Rusk to Bowles, 6 September 1965, ibid.

34. Komer memo, 4 September 1965, ibid.

35. CIA cable, 7 September 1965, ibid.

chapter 6

IN THE MIDST OF WARS: 1965–1971

RESETTING THE CLOCK

One observer, describing the 1965 Indian–Pakistan war, said the conflict "came at the right time for the U.S. in the way that some calamities are welcomed by debtors and bigamists." Despite the damage the war did to the U.S. position with India—and with Pakistan—the fighting afforded a certain opportunity. By 1965, Washington had got itself into an impossible situation in South Asia. Still married by alliance with Pakistan, it had been flirting for years with India; increasingly committed economically and militarily to India, it owed a debt of loyalty to Pakistan. Had the South Asian powers settled their long-standing differences amicably, American leaders might have continued their double game. But with the outbreak of war, neither would brook Washington's two-timing.[1]

Yet alienating both sides simultaneously had advantages. Johnson's neutral policy conferred credibility on the administration. "What more might we have done?" American officials could reasonably ask. To Johnson, perhaps more than to any president of recent memory, credibility counted for all. The Democratic president was leading America into the jungles of Vietnam in an effort to preserve American credibility: to demonstrate that he would honor the pledges his predecessors had given to South Vietnam. He was asking the U.S. Congress and the American people to follow him. Believe me, he would say. We must win the war; we shall win the war; we are winning the war. A newcomer to the practice of foreign policy, Johnson had to establish his credentials.

More to the point for South Asian relations, the administration had reset the clock to the era before the 1954 U.S. alliance with Pakistan by taking a neutral stance between India and Pakistan. The shattering of illusions in both New Delhi and Islamabad left neither expecting much good from Washington. Anything positive that did emerge would come as a pleasant surprise.

As during the earlier period, the United States and India decided that for all their distrust of each other, they could not get along apart. In 1951, when the Korean war had Americans flaying India for appeasement of the Chinese and Indians denouncing the United States for mindlessly drawing the world to the brink of nuclear catastrophe, a failure of the monsoon and other disruptions of India's food-supply system had forced New Delhi to come to Washington for aid. At that time, the Truman administration and Congress agreed that despite the annoyance Nehru was causing, to let mass hunger undermine Indian democracy would only delight the communists. In 1965, the monsoon again failed; once more, the Indian government turned to the United States. Lyndon Johnson had no use for those who questioned his judgment regarding Vietnam, as the Indians did. But broader thinkers reminded the president that the United States was defending Vietnam to prevent Asia from going communist; they ultimately convinced him that the United States might hold Vietnam but lose Asia if India starved.

As his vehicle for delivering U.S. aid to India, Johnson chose a program organized under the provisions of the Agricultural Trade Development and Assistance Act of 1954, better known as PL-480. Like most government programs, PL-480 served a variety of purposes and constituencies. As its name suggested, the act aimed to create new markets for American products among countries too poor to buy them otherwise. This it accomplished by arranging the "sale" of wheat, corn, and the like to countries such as India—except that Washington rebated the purchase price to the buyers. In essence, American taxpayers paid American farmers to sell crops to India. Naturally, this pleased the farmers and their representatives, a group politically formidable far beyond their numbers. Nor did it particularly alienate taxpayers at large, since the dollars involved did not amount to much when spread over the entire American tax base, and the administration could always defend the policy in humanitarian terms. Firms engaged in the transport of farm commodities favored the program, since it generated business for them; the provision specifying that at least half of all PL-480 goods travel in American bottoms appealed to ship-owners and maritime unions.

Creating as it did its own domestic lobby, the PL-480 program partially insulated itself from the vicissitudes that foreign aid often faces in Congress. During the Johnson years, this fact proved crucial. Johnson, like many driven men, suffered from an inferiority complex, from a need to continually prove himself to others. A son of the Texas hill country and a graduate of a mediocre teachers' college, he never lost his conviction that the wealthy, cultivated northeasterners of the Kennedy administration—"those Harvards," he called them—looked down on him. They would never forgive him, he thought, for stealing the place of their hero. Why did they dislike him so? "I'll tell you why," he once told aide Richard Goodwin. "Because I never went to Harvard. That's why. Because I wasn't John F. Kennedy. Because the Great Society was accomplishing more than the New Frontier." Johnson was partly right: the Kennedy liberals indeed disliked him. But he exaggerated their disdain. "I can't stand the bastard," Robert Kennedy confided to a friend, "but he's the most formidable human being I've ever met." The New York senator, a special object of White House suspicion, could not figure out Johnson's obsession with him. "Why does he keep worrying about me? I don't like him, but there's nothing I can do to him. Hell, he's the president, and I'm only a junior senator."

Johnson gradually grew to trust his secretary of state, Dean Rusk, not least because Rusk, a product of rural Georgia, shared the president's barefoot background. Yet the rest of the State Department Johnson deemed enemy territory. Among the professional foreign service, he perceived a conspiracy. Once, after reading cables bringing unwelcome information, he turned to assistant Bill Moyers. "You know what it is, Bill, don't you? It's those damn Kennedy ambassadors trying to get me and discredit me." Nor did Johnson cotton to J. William Fulbright, the prima-donnaish chairman of the Senate Foreign Relations Committee. When Fulbright turned against the administration on the Vietnam war, Johnson took the opposition personally. "That Fulbright," Johnson declared, "he never was satisfied with any president that wouldn't make him secretary of state."[2]

For these reasons, Johnson found the PL-480 program, administered through the ploddingly safe Department of Agriculture and overseen by the reliable Orville Freeman, a welcome way to accomplish his foreign-policy goals without having to work through the foreign-policy establishment. PL-480 also had the advantage for Johnson of centralizing control in the White House. In its most recent version, the act required each recipient to formulate a program putting American aid to the best use, and it decreed termination of aid "whenever the President finds that such program is not being adequately developed." Unlike other assistance programs, which often specified multiyear projects that, once approved, were difficult to terminate, PL-480 allowed short-term decisions that made it an ideal device to keep countries like India under scrutiny.

Fortunately for U.S.–Indian relations, PL-480 dovetailed with a fundamental change in the economic orientation of the Indian government. The first three five-year plans, under Nehru, had concentrated on industrial development in the public sector as the most rapid way to raise India's living standards. Nehru and his advisers, taking their cue from the development of the Soviet economy during the 1920s and 1930s, believed heavy investment in industry would spur the economy as a whole, producing growth that would trickle down to the village level. For a variety of reasons, including the unwillingness of New Delhi to adopt the brutal measures that had enforced industrialization in Russia, the strategy failed. Nehru recognized the failure, but committed to socialism, he insisted that the trouble lay in the implementation of the plans rather than in the plans themselves.

Shastri saw the issue in a clearer light. Less ideological than Nehru and less able to paper over shortcomings of the economy by force of personality and political reputation, the new prime minister recognized the need for a fix. Wisely, he couched his ideas in terms that would not alarm Nehru's followers. "Socialism is our objective," he declared. But it wasn't. Development, by whatever means, was.[3]

Shastri focused on the agricultural sector, for the good reason that the vast majority of India's people lived in farming villages and towns. Significantly, he shifted Nehru's minister of steel, Chidambaram Subramaniam, to the food and agricultural department. Subramaniam had little background in agricultural matters, but he had a reputation for results. Almost immediately, he undertook a major—if relatively quiet—revision of India's farm policy. He dismantled much of the system of government price controls in favor of the discipline and incentives of the free market, and he pressed for introduction of modern technology and techniques of the sort that had sparked agricultural revolutions in the United States and other Western countries.

Americans had long held their noses at Nehru's socialism; the Shastri shift came as a breath of air. It also played into the hands of the PL-480ers. The watchword under Orville Freeman was "self-help": efforts by recipients to guarantee that they would not perpetually remain dependent on American aid. In 1961, before the inauguration of the new Indian policy, the Indian host to a visiting member of Freeman's staff had taken his guest aback when, asked where India stored its grain reserves, he responded blithely, "In Kansas." As the Johnson administration defined the term, self-help meant India and other countries should adopt measures proven elsewhere—in the United States, for example—to have raised productivity. Subramaniam's project fit the specifications perfectly.[4]

The coincidence of these American and Indian needs and desires yielded a large harvest of aid for India. At the beginning of December 1965, the Indian government announced its new farm program; before year's end, Johnson ordered the expeditious shipment of 1.5 million tons of American wheat. Two months later, Vice President Hubert Humphrey visited New Delhi and announced a loan of $150 million. By midsummer 1966, Washington pledged an additional 3.5 million tons of grain and another $230 million in loans.

DYNASTY: PART 2

Had Shastri long continued as prime minister, the new program of American aid might have placed U.S.–Indian relations on a reasonably friendly footing. But Shastri succumbed to a heart attack in January 1966, and an individual with a far stronger personality and a more pressing sense of political mission took over.

Precisely how Indira Gandhi came to dominate the politics of a society that until recently had prescribed suttee for widows puzzled even many of her most ardent supporters. Indira's father, Nehru, once offered a partial explanation. Describing the family's ancestral homeland, Kashmir, he noted that in Kashmir, "broadly speaking, women had greater rights than in other parts of India." The fact that she shared a name, although no familial relationship, with the revered mahatma certainly did not hurt her prospects. As the only child of India's founding prime minister, Indira seemed the logical choice to those looking to extend the Nehru tradition. Before his death, Nehru had resisted pleas to name a successor; officials in a democracy, he said, do not appoint those who will follow. But just as many Americans saw in the younger Kennedys the spirit of the slain president, millions of Indians perceived in Indira the essence of her father. Upon her accession to the premiership, chants of *"Jawaharlal ki jai!"* ("Long live Jawaharlal!") intermingled with *"Indira ki jai!"*[5]

Indira, like her father, identified with her country. Granddaughter and daughter of leaders of the Congress party, she had fought the freedom struggle from her earliest years. At seven, she had followed Mahatma Gandhi's example and organized a children's spinning group, to signify rejection of dependence on Britain. During the 1930 nationalist rising, she organized the Vanar Sena (or Monkey Brigade, named from a story in the *Ramayana*) to provide support to those on the front lines. She sometimes dreamed she was Joan of Arc, rescuing her country from British oppression.

In important respects, Indira was more Indian than Nehru. Where the father had gone to England to be educated, losing some of his Indianness in the transaction, the daughter received most of her schooling in India. Moreover, although she followed the political example of her anglicized, agnostic father, she felt personally closer to her Hindi-speaking, Hindu-believing mother. Nehru's "discovery of India" had come only as an adult, as he conceded in a book of that title. Indira knew India all along.

In 1936, Nehru's wife and Indira's mother died, leaving the daughter to play hostess for the father. Her 1942 marriage to Feroze Gandhi did little to alter the arrangement. When Nehru was elected prime minister in 1947, Indira became the closest thing India had to a first lady. She accompanied Nehru to the United States in 1949 and found American culture and society as insipid as he did.

Five years before his death, Nehru began pushing Indira toward the front of Indian politics. In 1959, he let out that he wanted her to become president of the Congress party, as he and his father before had been. This move surprised party veterans, but by then no one would gainsay the premier. Indira later denied she had had any interest in the job. "I was bullied into the Congress Presidency, you know," she told an interviewer. "I didn't want it at all." Her selection did nothing good for her marriage, which had had its share of troubles already. Feroze resented her success. Indira declined to run for a second term, but she kept busy in the party. "I was in politics all the time," she said afterward. "I didn't hold any cabinet post or anything like that, but I was on the Congress Working Committees and on other committees. I watched it all. . . . I watched them all."[6]

She watched so well that by the time Nehru died, she had become a leading candidate for the succession. Another was Morarji Desai, a man of unquestioned abilities but also of an offputtingly authoritarian manner. Desai had generated such hostility among certain party leaders, in fact, that they had formed the so-called "Syndicate" principally for the purpose of blocking his ambitions. Although they succeeded, they could not prevent him from vetoing Indira Gandhi's candidacy.

Two events of Shastri's short tenure marked Indira Gandhi for greater things. As minister of information and broadcasting, she assumed responsibility for overseeing the constitutionally mandated transition from English to Hindi as India's official language. Inhabitants of the country's Tamil-speaking south resisted the move violently as the latest in a millennias-old series of efforts by the Aryans of the north to complete their conquest of the subcontinent. Demonstrating characteristic courage, Gandhi flew to Madras, near the heart of the rising. With trains derailed around her and buildings aflame, she consulted with the leaders of the rebellion and spoke with the masses. On her return to New Delhi, she lobbied vigorously and successfully for reassurances to non-Hindi speakers.

The second event occurred in August 1965, during a visit by Gandhi to Kashmir. Although she intended to take a vacation, she found herself in the middle of Pakistan's infiltration of the divided province. Military authorities on the spot advised her to return to the safety of the capital; she refused and insisted on inspecting the army's headquarters. When the commanding officers there suggested that the infiltration constituted nothing more than a probing action, she disagreed. Accurately, she asserted that Pakistan's maneuver was a preliminary to war, and she began organizing citizens' resistance committees.[7]

These actions earned Gandhi the reputation of "the only man in a Cabinet of old women," as one irreverent commentator put it, and they propelled her into the prime ministership following Shastri's sudden death at the beginning of 1966.[8]

They also marked her as a formidable person to contend with when she arrived in Washington on a state visit two months later. The Johnson administration, hoping to regain ground lost during the previous year, went out of its way to please. The president, while unaccustomed to dealing with women as political equals, displayed a charm and graciousness of which few had thought him capable. He expressed interest in Gandhi's sons (including future prime minister Rajiv) and made sure his daughters did too. He personally escorted her from the executive mansion to Blair House, where she was staying. He broke precedent by attending a cocktail party hosted by the Indian ambassador; he went so far as to remain for dinner, upstaging Vice President Humphrey in the process. Even after relations between Washington and New Delhi once again cooled, Gandhi recalled of the visit, "I enjoyed a very good reception."[9]

Of course, both parties had ulterior motives. Gandhi needed the aid the administration was providing and desired to receive more. Johnson sought Indian support for, or at least Indian nonopposition to, his policies in Vietnam. The prime minister got what she wanted, as noted above. The president thought he got what he wanted. White House aide Moyers remarked at the conclusion of the Johnson–Gandhi talks, "The bargain was essentially struck."[10]

DEEPER AND DEEPER

For a while, the bargain, such as it was, remained struck. At a moment when several of America's European allies were vociferously objecting to the American bombing of North Vietnam and the overall escalation of the war, Gandhi restrained her public remarks. No less than her father had, she considered U.S. policy toward Asia fundamentally misguided. Nehru had judged the Korean conflict essentially a civil war; Gandhi felt the same was true of Vietnam. Initially, however, she kept still.

But she could not keep silent for long. "I was accused of having turned too pro-American," she said later. India had a reputation to uphold. In October 1966, Gandhi met with her father's neutralist associates, Tito of Yugoslavia and Nasser of Egypt. She did not wish to be seen as less nonaligned than they. Nor did she desire to jeopardize India's connections with the Soviet Union, of longer standing and greater reliability than those linking India to the United States. Gandhi could hardly give what seemed silent approval of U.S. efforts to beat up the Russians' ally North Vietnam without risking damage to relations with the Kremlin. During a trip to Moscow in July 1966, she put her signature to a communiqué denouncing the "imperialists in Southeast Asia."[11]

Lyndon Johnson was a politician of the old school, a man whose hell reserved special punishment for committers of the cardinal sin of his class: failure to keep promises. Although Gandhi may not have agreed, Johnson believed he had her pledge to lay off Vietnam. He took the Moscow communiqué as a betrayal, a personal affront, and a demonstration of all that was wrong with India generally.

The president reacted by tightening to the point of strangulation the short tether on PL-480 aid to India. He doled out wheat on a month-to-month basis, which made rational planning by the Indian food ministry impossible. For four months at the end of 1966, shipments ceased entirely. Johnson did not publicly tie his action to Gandhi's stand on Vietnam; instead, he cited the need for India to expedite its agricultural reforms and for other countries to assist in alleviating India's troubles. But the message was lost on no one who cared.

Through the remainder of Johnson's time in office, Vietnam swallowed up relations with India, as it did nearly every other aspect of American foreign policy. In a manner similar to the Korean case a decade and a half earlier, the differences between Washington and New Delhi on Vietnam reflected a fundamental divergence of perceptions. The United States still believed communist aggression to be similar to the fascist aggression of the 1930s; unless stopped at once, even in out-of-the-way places like Vietnam, it would gain strength until it threatened the existence of democratic governments everywhere. While American leaders recognized the nationalist impulse behind the fighting in Vietnam, they considered the communist aspect of the North Vietnamese–Viet Cong movement more significant. Indians did not deny that the followers of Ho Chi Minh were communists, but they thought that it was nationalism that kept the conflict alive. An Indian commentator otherwise favorably disposed toward the United States remarked accurately that "most of the world believes that the Vietnamese who are fighting against the Americans are freedom fighters and are laying down their lives for the freedom of their country just as the Americans did in 1776." This individual, J. J. Singh of the India League of America, guessed that the United States might defeat the North Vietnamese and the Viet Cong on the battlefield. But he predicted a larger loss for Washington. "Even if the Americans win militarily in Vietnam, and someday the sledgehammer is likely to get the gnat, in the eyes of the world they will have become moral lepers."

Johnson, however, had given up on most of the world, including India. The president tolerated no dissent on Vietnam from a country receiving American aid. Gandhi's criticism, in fact mild compared with some other governments', made any progress toward closer relations impossible. For her part, the Indian prime minister thought she was acting with restraint in light of domestic and international pressure for an earlier and more forthright condemnation of U.S. policy. "What did India get for her patience?" she asked. American abuse, she answered, and treatment, as she later put it, as "a favorite whipping boy."[12]

MACHIAVELLI AND METTERNICH

Lyndon Johnson was a complicated individual; few of his associates felt they understood the man. But Johnson was no more complex—and considerably less devious—than his successor, Richard Nixon. Nixon knew politics. The many enemies he made on his scramble up the Republican ladder, from California congressman to vice president to president, conceded his political cleverness, although not a few considered it uncomfortably akin to dishonesty. Yet the U.S. political arena did not offer sufficient rewards for

Nixon; he aspired to fame on a grander scale. His tenure as Eisenhower's backup had introduced him to the world at large. The first vice president of the jet age, Nixon traveled the globe as no holder of the office had before. He acquired distinct views on what held the planet together and how the United States might advance its interests internationally.

Americans selected Nixon in 1968 partly on the strength of his "secret plan" to end the war in Vietnam. Once ensconced in the Oval Office, Nixon revealed that his plan involved not so much ending the war as turning it over to the Vietnamese. The United States would withdraw its troops from Indochina; at the same time, it would step up material and logistical assistance to South Vietnam. Shrewd to the point of amorality, Nixon recognized that most American opposition to the war was related to the toll the conflict was taking in American lives. By substituting Vietnamese blood for American, he could quiet dissent in the United States long enough—he hoped—to set Saigon on its feet and enable the South Vietnamese to defend themselves. And if "Vietnamization" ultimately failed—which did not seem unlikely, given South Vietnam's flounderings during the previous fifteen years—at least the program would provide cover for American withdrawal.

But for Vietnamization to have any chance of success, Nixon needed a modicum of cooperation from China and the Soviet Union, North Vietnam's principal sponsors. According to Nixon's survey of the situation, the road out of Vietnam led through Beijing and Moscow. Consequently, he sought to improve relations with the two foremost communist powers.

Nixon's navigator along this treacherous journey was Henry Kissinger. In certain respects, the national security adviser was a perfect match for Nixon. Formerly a professor of government at Harvard specializing in nineteenth-century European diplomacy, Kissinger interpreted international relations in the same cold-eyed fashion Nixon did. Like his boss, Kissinger thrived on secrecy and developed back-channel maneuvering into an art form. Like Nixon, he had a respect for power that bordered on obsession. Power, Kissinger was supposed to have said, was "the ultimate aphrodisiac." Like Nixon, he inspired enormous distrust in many who worked with and watched him.

The grand scheme of the Nixon–Kissinger era involved playing China against the Soviet Union. In the opinion of the Nixon White House (here it would be more of a mistake than usual to speak of the *administration* as if it thought with a single mind, since the people working directly under Nixon and Kissinger waged a constant guerrilla battle against those in the State Department, and vice versa), the United States was missing a great opportunity by hurling anathemas at both Beijing and Moscow. A decade after the dramatic and venomous falling out between the two contenders for ideological hegemony among the disciples of Marx and Lenin, arguments positing a monolithic communist conspiracy no longer carried conviction. Who better,

Nixon believed, to slay the monster at last than himself—a man who in his prestatesman days in Congress had contributed significantly to loosing the beast in the American political consciousness?

But the same reasoning that caused Nixon to think he could get away with undoing twenty years of anti-Chinese diplomacy made him realize he would have to handle the operation with consummate care. He could not simply announce in public a desire to normalize relations with China. To do so, while American B-52s continued to ravage North Vietnam, risked a rebuff embarrassing to the United States and discrediting to the president. Instead he must work secretly, through an intermediary on good terms with both sides. For this delicate task, Nixon chose Pakistan's Agha Yahya Khan.

The choice of Yahya could not have been more unfortunate for U.S.–Indian relations. For reasons that had nothing to do with India but everything to do with U.S. policy toward the superpowers, Nixon cast America's lot with Pakistan. The United States had taken this route before, in the Eisenhower years, but the earlier Republican administration had managed to mitigate the anti-Indian implications of its pro-Pakistan policy, largely because the troubles between India and Pakistan were momentarily quiescent. Nixon was not so lucky.

The president first raised the China issue with Yahya in the summer of 1969. In Pakistan on a swing through Asia, Nixon indicated in general terms a desire to upgrade U.S. contacts with China. During the previous several months, Chinese and Soviet troops had clashed along the Ussuri River, making an American attempt to capitalize on the Moscow–Beijing split appear more likely of success than ever. Yahya and his associates agreed, adding that the Cultural Revolution in China was subsiding. Pragmatists once more seemed to be gaining control.

At about the same time, Kissinger in Washington summoned Pakistan's ambassador, whose sister had attended Kissinger's seminar at Harvard some years before and whose brother was serving in the Pakistani embassy in Beijing. The "meticulous and discreet" ambassador, as Kissinger described him, agreed to forward Kissinger's expression of interest in establishing contact between the United States and China at the highest level. At Kissinger's insistence, he also agreed not to tell the State Department what was going on.[13]

By October of the following year, Nixon and Kissinger gained sufficient favorable feedback from China for the president to raise the issue more specifically with Yahya. Nixon said he had decided to extend diplomatic recognition to China, and he asked Yahya to act as go-between. "Of course we will do anything we can to help," the Pakistani president replied. "But you must know how difficult this will be. Old enemies do not easily become new friends. It will be slow, and you must be prepared for setbacks."[14]

Washington's feelers again elicited a positive response from Beijing. In April 1971, an American table-tennis team playing in the world championship tournament in Japan received an invitation to visit China. A spokesman for the Chinese table-tennis association declared that his country had extended the invitation "so that we can learn from each other and elevate our standards of play." He was being polite: the Americans had nothing to teach the best ping-pongers in the world. But the Chinese threw a few games, and Zhou Enlai declared that the Americans' coming had "opened a new page in the relations of the Chinese and American people."[15]

Although a variety of hints during the next months suggested more substantial moves to follow, few observers expected to see Kissinger turn up in Beijing in July 1971. Pakistan provided crucial assistance in the closely guarded Operation Marco Polo. On an ostensibly routine trip to Pakistan, the national security adviser purportedly developed the sort of digestive troubles that plague foreigners in Asia. The correspondents covering the trip, most of whom had suffered similarly, prepared to amuse themselves for a couple of days. With his cover established, Kissinger took off in the predawn hours of 9 July from a Pakistani air base aboard a Pakistan International Airlines jet, under the command of Yahya's personal pilot.

Kissinger's trip accomplished its goal: Nixon announced on 15 July that he would travel to China "to seek the normalization of relations between the two countries and to exchange views on questions of concern to the two sides."

With the announcement, Nixon scored a stunning political success. Liberals who long had advocated normalization of relations with China found themselves outflanked by one of the most notorious red-baiters of all. Democrat Mike Mansfield, the Senate majority leader, proclaimed himself "flabbergasted" but nonetheless "delighted and happy" at the president's action. Senator George McGovern, soon to capture the Democratic nomination for president, expressed hope that Nixon's trip would signal "the end of a long period of nonsense in our relations with China and the beginning of a new era of common sense." Some conservatives, for whom opposition to "Red China" had constituted a litmus test of orthodoxy since 1949, felt betrayed. Republican Senator James Buckley feared that the opening to Beijing would "inevitably strengthen the hand of those seeking accommodation with the Communist world at almost any price." Republican Congressman John Schmitz, representing the California district from which Nixon had launched his political career, asserted that the president was "surrendering to international communism." But most on the right, perhaps relieved at being unburdened of an increasingly anachronistic policy, took the view that the communist had not been born who could trick Dick Nixon. If Nixon said it was safe to talk to China, they would not complain.

The international community adopted a wait-and-see attitude regarding the American demarche. North Vietnam declared, with more hope than conviction, that it was "inconceivable" that the United States and China would negotiate an end to the Vietnamese conflict over Hanoi's head. Japan disguised its shock—and its humiliation at not receiving advance warning of a move that would have the most profound effects on the power balance in the

Far East—with a bland statement desiring that Nixon's discussions with Zhou would lead to friendlier relations in Asia generally. The Soviet Union, while hinting at "secret collusion" against the homeland of socialism, allowed that if the U.S.–Chinese talks resulted in a "more constructive" American approach to Vietnam and other sources of trouble, "there would be grounds for taking the statements about Washington's peace-loving intentions and goodwill seriously."[16]

During the summer of 1971, Nixon and Kissinger congratulated themselves on their cleverness. They were redrawing the map of the world just as they had planned. If they had incurred a few debts—to Yahya Khan, for example—they would deal with these later.

THE LAST DAYS OF UNITED PAKISTAN

Had the White House been less beguiled by its own brilliance, it might have recognized that the debts would come due soon. While Nixon and Kissinger were plotting their China spectacular, the Pakistanis were struggling to keep their country alive and whole. Since independence, little besides allegiance to Islam and hostility to India had held the bifurcated state together. The more numerous East Pakistanis had always chafed under an arrangement that gave equal parliamentary representation to the country's two halves; but as long as the army, based chiefly in the West, provided protection, demands for reform remained muted.

The 1965 war with India disrupted this accommodation. East Pakistanis had had difficulty getting worked up over Kashmir, the cause of the war, since it lay far from their homes and because annexation of the province would increase the clout of West Pakistan at the East's expense. More important, the war demonstrated the vulnerability of East Pakistan to Indian attack. Although India had refrained from carrying the war to the East, East Pakistanis attributed their salvation not to anything their own government had done but to Chinese threats of retaliation. Consequently, in the wake of the Tashkent accord, a movement for greater East Pakistani autonomy—at the minimum—gained strength. Under the leadership of Mujibur Rahman, the Awami League put forward six demands, the most significant calling for the reorganization of Pakistan's government along federal lines, provincial self-government in all areas but defense and foreign policy, and the creation of a separate militia or paramilitary force for East Pakistan.

During the succeeding months and years, Mujib and the Awami League intensified their agitation. By the beginning of 1968, Islamabad decided the dissidents were endangering state security. The Ayub government jailed Mujib and several followers for treason and incitement to secession. India, long suspected by the Pakistani government (not undeservedly) of sympathy toward secession, became implicated when the prosecution declared that the conspirators intended to import weapons from India to stage their revolt.

If Ayub had been able to count on the support of the West Pakistanis, he might have ridden out the storm in the East. Unfortunately, his political base in the West was also eroding. Although the war against India had touched a patriotic chord among West Pakistanis, who had personally witnessed the army coming to their defense, the peace proved a disappointment. As so often happens, the government had projected a more optimistic picture than the balance of forces warranted. When Ayub returned from Tashkent with nothing better than a draw, the millions who had expected the redemption of at least part of India's portion of Kashmir charged betrayal. Ayub compounded his troubles by allowing corruption to entrench itself in the government, producing a situation in which the many poor felt increasingly alienated from the few rich. Manipulated shortages of various necessities spawned a black market; in 1968, when police arrested a group of students for buying bootlegged goods, riots broke out. An assassination attempt on Ayub followed, which in turn led to the jailing of the most prominent opposition figures, including former foreign minister Bhutto.

At this point, the violence spread to East Pakistan. Clashes between dissidents and police produced a number of deaths and paralyzed Dacca. When one of the individuals who had earlier been jailed for secessionist activities died in prison under mysterious circumstances, much of the populace joined the revolt. Finally, in March 1969, with the situation completely out of hand, Ayub resigned, relinquishing control to the commander-in-chief of the army, Yahya Khan.

Yahya first declared martial law, then scheduled elections. Bad weather—a hurricane accompanied by massive flooding—delayed the polling. As many as 200,000 East Pakistanis died, while millions lost their homes. At least partly as a result of government incompetence in relieving the disaster, Mujib's Awami party accomplished nearly a clean sweep of the East's allotted seats in parliament. In the West, Bhutto's People's party claimed victory. Although Mujib commanded a majority in the parliament, Bhutto—who opposed autonomy for the East—refused to concede the premiership. Yahya attempted to forge a compromise that would keep the country together, but when negotiations failed, Mujib summoned his supporters in what they now called Bangladesh to resist the tyranny of Islamabad. Yahya responded by pouring troops from the West into the East.

In the last week of March 1971, Pakistani tanks crashed through the streets of Dacca. On the night of 25 March, soldiers arrested Mujib and opened fire on what the government branded hotbeds of treason. During the next several days, tens of thousands—perhaps 100,000—were killed. Bhutto, speaking from Karachi, applauded the show of force. "By the grace of Almighty God," he declared, "Pakistan has at last been saved."

Bhutto spoke too soon. Before being carted off to prison, Mujib raised the banner of independence for Bangladesh, and he called on his supporters to continue the struggle: "You are citizens of a free country. Today the West

Pakistan military force is engaged in a genocide in Bangla Desh. . . . They have unleashed unparalleled barbarity on the golden Bengal. . . . You should not be misled by the false propaganda of the military rulers. Our struggle is most rewarding. Certain is our victory. Allah is with us. The world public opinion is with us. Victory to Bengal!"[17]

During the weeks that followed, the world watched with horror as the Pakistani army waged war against what Islamabad still claimed were its own people. Communal fighting between Muslims and Hindus within East Pakistan heightened the carnage; by some estimates, more than a million people died.

From the standpoint of Indian national interest, Pakistan's troubles boded well. Having fought two wars already with Pakistan, India welcomed anything that might weaken its next-door antagonist. Furthermore, aside from military considerations, Pakistan posed an existential threat to India. Based explicitly on the principle of religious communalism, Pakistan contradicted the Indian emphasis on secular nationalism. A successful Pakistan, Indian leaders feared, would tend to destabilize India by dividing the loyalties of Indian Muslims. Even if the Muslims acted with the utmost circumspection, their Hindu neighbors would read fifth-column inclinations into any actions the least bit questionable.

Consequently, India was disposed to offer support to the Bangladesh separatists, even before the atrocities committed by the Pakistani army made assistance a matter of humanitarian concern. That the victims included a large proportion of Hindus increased India's willingness to help. That the fighting provoked millions to flee across the border to haven in India, where they strained the social fabric and resources available in West Bengal and especially in the city of Calcutta, clinched the argument. Even as it called publicly for a political and peaceful settlement of the dispute, New Delhi provided support to the secessionists. It allowed the formation of a Bangladesh government-in-exile in Calcutta. The Indian parliament approved a resolution declaring India's enthusiastic backing for the people of what the resolution called East Bengal. Government officials allowed guerrilla forces to train on Indian soil. India provided arms and logistical aid.

Despite India's assistance, the rebels found the going difficult. Pakistan's iron-fist policy succeeded in preventing the establishment of guerrilla bases inside East Pakistan. The army also succeeded in rendering much of the country uninhabitable. By May 1971, six weeks after the fighting commenced, some 3.5 million refugees had left for India; by the end of the summer, the number had nearly tripled.

This human wave, sweeping into a province already full to bursting, threatened to swamp the Indian government. By September, New Delhi was spending some $200 million per month to feed and house the refugees; considering the fact the entire 1965 war with Pakistan had cost India only $70 million, warnings that the government must take action before Pakistan's civil war wrecked India economically did not seem unduly alarmist.

The government of Pakistan likewise felt the need for strong measures. In several months of fighting, despite the most repressive tactics imaginable, it had failed to quash the rebellion in East Pakistan. Nor could Islamabad see any end as long as India aided and abetted the rebels. At the beginning of December, in a frantic effort to chasten India, Pakistani forces struck across the border at Indian installations in West Bengal.

This foolish move provided all the excuse New Delhi needed and it sealed Pakistan's fate. The Indian government extended diplomatic recognition to Bangladesh and ordered Indian troops to march on Dacca. Within ten days, the Indians captured—or liberated, depending on point of view—the city. Pakistan's army in the East surrendered unconditionally on 16 December, and the fighting ended.

UNNEUTRALITY

Above this regional tempest, a global storm threatened. As expected on the basis of nearly two decades of mutual good feeling, the Soviet Union sided with India against Pakistan. The Russians continued to consider India their best bet for influence in the subcontinent; they also sought to weaken Pakistan, the ally initially of Washington, now doubly damned as Beijing's protégé. The Chinese, realistic, or cynical, as ever, took Pakistan's part. Chinese communist ideology could scarcely have had less in common with Pakistan's Islamic premises or with the politics of Pakistan's reactionary generals. But China needed a South Asian counter to the Moscow–New Delhi axis, and Pakistan was nominated.

As the Bangladesh crisis took hold, India and Pakistan each looked to its great-power patron. In August 1971, Soviet foreign minister Andrei Gromyko traveled to New Delhi with a treaty of "peace, friendship and cooperation," which his Indian counterpart, Swaran Singh, promptly signed. Although the treaty included a statement affirming Moscow's respect for India's policy of nonalignment, another clause—asserting that "in the event of either being subjected to an attack or a threat thereof, the High Contracting Parties shall immediately enter into mutual consultations in order to remove such threat and to take appropriate effective measures to ensure peace and the security of their countries"—made the agreement sound very much like a mutual defense pact. The Chinese, meanwhile, condemned India for attempting to create a "puppet Bangladesh" and denounced the Soviets for "social imperialism" in getting involved. Likening Indian actions in Bangladesh to those of Japan in separating Manchuria from China in the 1930s, the Chinese *People's Daily* drew a parallel between present-day Russia and Hitler's Germany.[18]

This global context, far more than the situation in Bangladesh, conditioned the American response to the events surrounding the third India–Pakistan war. Kissinger later summarized his attitude and that of the president toward South Asia: "When the Nixon Administration took office, our policy objective on the subcontinent was, quite simply, to avoid adding another complication to our agenda." Preoccupied with diplomacy toward the Soviets and Chinese, Washington wished South Asia to keep quiet.[19]

In fact, the administration's own actions undermined this goal. The reliance on Yahya in the opening to China placed the United States heavily in hock to Islamabad, and never more than in 1971, when negotiations between Washington and Beijing were at their most delicate stage. Further, Nixon personally preferred Pakistanis to Indians. Nixon had held the Pakistanis in high regard ever since his 1953 visit to Karachi, when their "martial character" convinced him that the Eisenhower administration should go through with its plans to arm Pakistan. In 1970, Yahya had come to the United States for the twenty-fifth anniversary of the United Nations; he had detoured to Washington to speak with the president. (Gandhi, also in New York, significantly did not.) "Nobody has occupied the White House," Nixon told Yahya, "who is friendlier to Pakistan than me." On other hand, Nixon despised Gandhi, who reciprocated. Kissinger remarked that the U.S. president and the Indian prime minister were fated not to be congenial: "Her assumption of almost hereditary moral superiority and her moody silences brought out all of Nixon's latent insecurities. Her bearing toward Nixon combined a disdain for a symbol of capitalism quite fashionable in developing countries with a hint that the obnoxious things she had heard about the President from her intellectual friends could not all be untrue. Nixon's comments after meetings with her were not always printable."[20]

Nixon's preference for Pakistan first took substance in the 1970 release, as an exception to continuing restrictions on U.S. military aid to the subcontinent, of a $40 million package of weapons to Islamabad. The administration could, and did, justify the move in terms of evening the odds in South Asia. American restrictions, which allowed only the export of spare parts and nonlethal equipment, worked decidedly in India's favor, owing to India's larger industrial capacity and the deeper pockets of its Soviet ally, as compared to Pakistan's sponsor China. Between 1965 and 1970, India had consistently outspent Pakistan on defense by a factor of nearly five to one. During the same period, India had received weapons worth some $730 million from the Soviet bloc, while China had supplied Pakistan less than $135 million.[21]

Throughout 1971, Washington watched the intensifying Bangladesh crisis with concern. In February, following the elections that gave Mujib a majority in the parliament and apparently opened the path to the premiership, Kissinger sent Nixon a memo predicting trouble. Mujib and Bhutto, Kissinger said, "have failed so far to forge even the beginning of an informal consensus on the new constitution." Kissinger expected Mujib "to stick with his demands for the virtual autonomy of East Pakistan and if he does not get his way—which is very likely—to declare East Pakistan independence." This would probably provoke the government to action. Yahya, Kissinger said, "remains committed to turning his military government over to the civilian politicians, but maintains that he will not preside over the splitting of Pakistan."[22]

Although Washington stepped up its analysis of the situation, Nixon's and Kissinger's obsession with secrecy created problems in administration planning. Fearing leaks—and intent on establishing his primacy over Secretary of State William Rogers—Kissinger blacked out the State Department regarding the China initiative. Not knowing the principal reason for the president's deference to Pakistan, the department argued for a policy shift in India's favor. This simply confirmed the conviction of the White House that State, "heavily influenced by its traditional Indian bias," as Kissinger put it, could not be trusted.[23]

The onset of violence in East Pakistan in March increased pressure both within the administration and from outside for a distancing from Islamabad. The U.S. consul in Dacca cabled Washington decrying the "mass killing of unarmed civilians, the systematic elimination of the intelligentsia, and the annihilation of the Hindu population." The ambassador in New Delhi declared himself "deeply shocked at the massacre" and fearful of the consequences of "the United States' vulnerability to damaging association with a reign of military terror." The State Department, without permission from the White House, moved to curtail weapons shipments to Pakistan, as well as to decrease economic aid. In the Senate, Democrat Walter Mondale introduced legislation to ban military aid to Pakistan before "we watch the burial of another generation of babies." Democrat Frank Church of the Senate Foreign Relations Committee seconded the motion with a stinging denunciation of the entire Nixon–Kissinger approach to the subcontinent.

> We know that the Pakistan army, equipped mostly with American arms and led by U.S. trained officers, let loose a massive burst of violence on fellow Muslims. . . . Military largesse, costing the United States nearly $2 billion in arms, was perennially justified to Congress and the American people as a shield to protect the Pakistanis—and the United States—against Communist aggression. . . .
>
> Far from containing the Russian bear or the Chinese dragon, however, Pakistan has used its American-furnished military equipment first against India in 1965 and now against its own people. . . . By all standards, then, our military assistance policy has proved a failure. . . . When a policy goes sour but is not changed, the results are sordid.

Democrat Edward Kennedy visited refugee camps in India and likened the administration's handling of events in South Asia to what he considered its ineptitude in Indochina.

The face of America today in South Asia is not much different from its image over the past years in Southeast Asia. It is the image of an America that supports military repression and fuels military violence. It is the image of an America comfortably consorting with an authoritarian regime. It is the image of an America citing the revolutionary past and crowing about its commitment to self-determination, while it services military juntas that suppress change and ignore a people's aspirations. . . .

It is argued that the continuation of military aid to West Pakistan some-how gives us "leverage" to constructively influence the military's policy in East Bengal. Well, where is that leverage? Where is the leverage to stop the use of U.S. arms which produce the refugees and civilian victims that we then must help support in India? . . .

Why, if we have the leverage to influence the government of Pakistan, must our great nation assist in this shabby and shameful enterprise? It is time for Americans to ask their leaders: "Just what kind of government is it that we seek to influence—and for what purpose?"[24]

Nixon and Kissinger knew why, but they were not saying. Least of all were they telling the Indians, who had every reason to sabotage Washington's China ploy. In July 1971, on his way to Pakistan and thence across the Himalayas to Beijing, Kissinger stopped in New Delhi. In a long conversation with the permanent head of the Indian foreign office, T. N. Kaul, the American national security adviser tried to explain America's South Asian policy without really explaining anything. He defended Washington's reluctance to speak out against the actions of the Pakistani government by saying that what was occurring in East Pakistan was, "strictly speaking, not an international problem." He acknowledged that the issue was "considered on an emotional basis" in India, but he hoped the Indian government would not allow itself to be swept away by popular passions. "We are bound to disagree on some issues," Kissinger continued. "We know you have close relations with the Soviet Union. . . . That, frankly, does not bother us. We are not competing in this area with the Soviet Union." But the Russians and the Chinese *were* competing, Kissinger said, and he warned that precipitate action against Pakistan would only exacerbate the competition. If India attacked Pakistan, China might feel compelled to go to Pakistan's aid. The Soviets then would have to move against China.

"We do not want military action," Kaul countered. "If we had wanted military action we would have taken it during the first few days when it would have been easier than it is now. But that would have been against our interests and against our policies." Yet India could not ignore the conse-quences of continuing turmoil in Eask Pakistan:

We have a feeling that Yahya Khan and his advisers are deliberately trying to convert this freedom struggle into an Indo–Pak and Hindu–Muslim con-flict, by committing atrocities on the Hindus in East Pakistan in the hope that the situation will flare up. Suppose Hindu–Muslim riots spread in India; the position of 60 million Muslims in India will become untenable. It will break the very basis of our political and social structure, and Pakistan will then say: "We told you that Hindus and Muslims are two separate nations which can never live together."

When Kissinger suggested that New Delhi might calm things by preventing guerrilla attacks across the border, Kaul asserted that this was harder to accomplish than to recommend. "It is an open border without any natural obstructions or barriers. Movement to and fro has been going on across the border ever since partition."

Kissinger asked directly, "What are you going to do now? Supposing the struggle goes on for a few more months, I cannot visualize what you will achieve by military action."

Kaul responded that his government had once hoped that international pressure would force Yahya to reconsider his policies. No longer. "We have come reluctantly to the conclusion that international pressure—economic or political—is not going to influence Yahya Khan's decision." India, he reiterated, although less strongly than before, did not desire war. "We do not want to rush into a military conflict with Pakistan because we know it would be suicidal for both countries and the only gainer will be outside powers. But we have to solve this problem of refugees."[25]

After Kissinger's conversation with Kaul, Washington could not claim ignorance regarding the seriousness with which India viewed the Bangladesh situation—while India *could* fairly charge the Nixon administration with duplicity, especially when Kissinger turned up in Beijing just days later. Kaul thought the episode typical of the administration's approach to India and South Asia. He later described Nixon and Kissinger as "vindictive and spiteful, callous and cruel, conceited and domineering," not to mention "insensitive to other nations' feelings and pride."[26]

During the autumn of 1971, Nixon and Kissinger drew increasing fire for their South Asian policy. American pundits blasted the heavy-handed blundering of the White House. Following the announcement of the Soviet—Indian pact, the *New York Times* declared that the administration's "incredible" decision to continue supporting Pakistan "in spite of the ruthless Pakistan crackdown on autonomy-seeking Bengalis, and especially on Bengali Hindus" had allowed Moscow "a major foreign policy coup." The Indian government castigated Washington for abetting "genocide." Indian newspapers decried the Americans' cold-heartedness; the *Indian Express* declared, "The Nixon administration has chosen to pursue a policy of deliberate cynicism in the face of a massive human tragedy."[27]

In fact, the administration was not quite as culpable as its critics charged. The president refused to chastise Islamabad openly; Nixon said, "We are not going to engage in public pressure on the Government of West Pakistan. It would be totally counterproductive." He was probably about right. But Washington did undertake some quiet and not entirely ineffective persuasion. While administration efforts on behalf of a compromise solution and a mitigation of the use of force availed little, American urgings of clemency for Mujib helped save the Awami League leader's life.[28]

Yet the general trend of U.S. policy remained decidedly pro-Pakistan, and events in South Asia continued on their downward path. A November visit by Gandhi to America helped matters not in the slightest. In a statement on NBC television's *Meet the Press*, the prime minister explained that she hoped her coming would promote understanding of the situation in East Pakistan. Describing the "massacre, the suppression of democratic rights, the rape of women, the killing of the students of University faculty, the driving out of millions of citizens of East Bengal onto our territory," she explained that conditions were becoming intolerable. "We see it as a real threat to Indian democracy and Indian stability." In a meeting with Nixon, Gandhi expressed her country's peaceful intentions. "India has never wished the destruction of Pakistan or its permanent crippling," she said. "Above all, India seeks the restoration of stability. We want to eliminate chaos at all costs."[29]

Nixon and Kissinger did not believe her; they took India's attack on East Pakistan a short while later as confirmation of her prevaricating. The president wrote of Gandhi in his diary, "I realized how hypocritical the present Indian leaders are, with Indira Gandhi talking about India's victory wings being clipped when Shastri went to Tashkent, and her duplicitous attitude toward us when she actually had made up her mind to attack Pakistan at the time she saw me in Washington and assured me she would not. Those who resort to force, without making excuses, are bad enough—but those who resort to force while preaching to others about their use of force deserve no sympathy whatever." Kissinger, observing the conversations between the two heads of government, described it as "a classic dialogue of the deaf."

Nixon had no time for Mrs. Gandhi's condescending manner. Privately, he scoffed at her moral pretensions, which he found all the more irritating because he suspected that in pursuit of her purposes she had in fact fewer scruples than he. He considered her, indeed, a cold-blooded practitioner of power politics. . . .

Mrs. Gandhi, who was as formidable as she was condescending, had no illusions about what Nixon was up to. . . . Her dislike of Nixon, expressed in the icy formality of her manner, was perhaps compounded by the uneasy recognition that this man whom her whole upbringing caused her to disdain perceived international relations in a manner uncomfortably close to her own. It was not that she was a hypocrite, as Nixon thought; this assumed that she was aware of a gap between her actions and her values. It was rather that for her, her interest and her values were inseparable.[30]

When Indian troops crossed into East Pakistan at the beginning of December, the administration responded by canceling licenses for the small amount of arms purchases India was making in the United States. When Indian forces launched their drive on Dacca a few days later, the U.S. representative at the United Nations, George Bush, charged India with "clear-cut aggression." The State Department, at the direction of the White House, asserted that "India bears the major responsibility for the hostilities that have ensued." The administration cut off economic aid to New Delhi and introduced a resolution in the U.N. Security Council demanding withdrawal of Indian forces from East Pakistan.[31]

The White House disclaimed any intent to antagonize India. In a news conference, Kissinger said that reports that the United States had taken an anti-Indian position were "totally inaccurate." Indeed, Kissinger said, the United States "has had a love affair with India," and it was only with "enormous pain" that the administration had chosen to criticize India in the United Nations.

> We do so not because we want to support one particular point of view on the subcontinent, or because we want to forgo our friendship with what will always be one of the great countries of the world; but because we believe that if, as some of the phrases go, the right of military attack is determined by arithmetic, if political wisdom consists of saying the attacker has 500 million, and, therefore, the United States must always be on the side of the numerically stronger, then we are creating a situation where, in the foreseeable future, we will have international anarchy.[32]

Kissinger's denial that the administration was anti-Indian was simply false, as he himself privately admitted at a top-level meeting in the White House situation room on 3 December. The national security adviser came directly to the point. "I am getting hell every half-hour from the President that we are not being tough enough on India," Kissinger said. "He has just called me again. He does not believe we are carrying out his wishes. He wants to tilt in favor of Pakistan." At another conference a few days later, Kissinger reiterated the message: "We are not trying to be even-handed. There can be no doubt what the President wants. The President believes that India is the attacker. We are trying to get across the idea that India has jeopardized relations with the United States."[33]

BEAM ME UP, HENRY

Of all the Nixon administration's major foreign policy decisions, only those involving Vietnam brought upon it such violent criticism as its handling of the Bangladesh crisis. Even to that diminishing portion of the American opinionmaking elite not yet predisposed to think the worst of the

Republican president, the administration's refusal to speak out against Pakistan's undeniable atrocities in East Pakistan, and its condemnation of India for acting to end the bloodshed and the misery of the millions of refugees, seemed a clear case of power politics taking precedence over the most basic humanitarian considerations.

Afterward, the administration sought to justify its actions in the matter. Kissinger devoted one of the longest chapters in his memoirs to a detailed rebuttal. His account turned the conventional view on its head. Rather than a craven surrender of American ideals to geopolitical convenience, he wrote, the administration's backing of Islamabad represented a courageous effort to live up to commitments to Pakistan by previous administrations and, more important, a bold and successful maneuver to prevent the unraveling of the entire American alliance system. In Kissinger's view, India had far more in mind when it went into East Pakistan than the liberation of Bangladesh. Citing a source "whose reliability we never had any reason to doubt and which I do not question today"—but which he declined to identify—Kissinger asserted, "Prime Minister Gandhi was determined to reduce even West Pakistan to impotence. . . . Indian forces would proceed with the 'liberation' of the southern part of Azad Kashmir—the Pakistani part of Kashmir—and continue fighting until the Pakistani army and air force were wiped out. In other words, West Pakistan was to be dismembered and rendered defenseless." Although the administration had reconciled itself to seeing Pakistan lose Bangladesh, American credibility could not survive this total destruction of an ally by an ally of the Soviet Union. As Kissinger commented to Nixon at the time (according to Nixon's memoirs), "We can't allow a friend of ours and China's to get screwed in a conflict with a friend of Russia's."[34]

Thus, the administration converted a regional South Asian conflict into a global showdown between the superpowers. "The major problem now," Kissinger said at the height of the crisis, "is that the Russians retain their respect for us." Nixon, writing later, declared that "the Indo–Pakistan war involved stakes much higher than the future of Pakistan. . . . It involved the principle of whether big nations supported by the Soviet Union would be permitted to dismember their smaller neighbors." According to this interpretation, the United States had to take the action it did to let the Russians know that they and the Indians would not get away with their plans. "Our only card left," Kissinger said, "was to raise the risks for the Soviets to a level where Moscow would see larger interests jeopardized."

The White House accomplished this risk-raising by a move that struck much of the world as either reckless or irrelevant. The president ordered a naval task force, headed by the nuclear aircraft carrier *Enterprise*, to enter the Bay of Bengal. Ostensibly a measure to guarantee the safe evacuation of Americans from East Pakistan, the show of force was actually designed, as Kissinger himself admitted after the fact, to keep India and the Soviet Union off balance.

Were we threatening India? Were we seeking to defend East Pakistan? Had we lost our minds?

It was in fact sober calculation. We had some seventy-two hours to bring the war to a conclusion before West Pakistan would be swept into the maelstrom. It would take India that long to shift its forces and mount an assault. Once Pakistan's army and air force were destroyed, its impotence would guarantee the country's eventual disintegration.

We had to give the Soviets a warning that matters might get out of control on our side too. We had to be ready to back up the Chinese if at the last moment they came in after all, our UN initiative having failed. The Kremlin needed an excuse to accelerate the pressures it claimed it was exerting on India.

However unlikely an American military move against India, the other side could not be sure; it might not be willing to accept even the minor risk that we might act irrationally.[35]

There is a certain unreality to this approach; critics would dub it the "madman strategy." Indeed, one can argue that giving the appearance "that we might act irrationally" would provoke the other side to escalation, rather than the reverse. Nuclear deterrence rests on an assumption of rationality: they don't shoot because they know we will shoot back and destroy them. But if the Soviets come to believe the Americans have gone nuts, the Kremlin might well seize the marginal advantage that comes from firing first.

Whatever the psychostrategic implications of the Nixon administration's *Enterprise* gambit, Washington could not have chosen an action better guaranteed to alienate India. Did India really threaten West Pakistan? New Delhi categorically denied the charge. In a letter to Nixon on 15 December, Gandhi declared, "We do not want any territory of what was East Pakistan and now constitutes Bangladesh. We do not want any territory of West Pakistan." No hard evidence has ever surfaced to substantiate Kissinger's claim, which Nixon seconded in his own memoirs. Other American officials gave greater credence to Gandhi. Assistant Secretary of State Joseph Sisco told Kissinger at a meeting on 8 December that it was unlikely that the Indians intended the disintegration of Pakistan. Sisco reported that the Indian foreign minister had gone out of his way to tell the U.S. ambassador in New Delhi that India had no intention of taking any Pakistani territory. When Kissinger suggested that India might strike in Kashmir, Sisco reminded the national security adviser that Kashmir was "really disputed territory."[36]

Even if Kissinger's and Nixon's claims were true, a firm yet muted statement of the United States' resolve to defend the integrity of West Pakistan would have accomplished the same purpose as sending a gunboat—a nuclear gunboat, at that. Until 1971, suspicious Indians had sometimes felt threatened by the United States. The threat, however, had always been indirect—arms to Pakistan or a more general "neoimperialism." Now the United States was putting the pistol directly to India's head.

American leaders had previously sacrificed U.S.–Indian relations to the perceived needs of superpower diplomacy. They would do so again. But the *Enterprise* episode seared a wound, a totally unnecessary one, in the Indian consciousness. The wound would heal only slowly. The scar would never disappear.

Notes

1. Stephen P. Cohen, "South Asia and U.S. Military Policy," 101–24, in Lloyd I. Rudolph, ed., *The Regional Imperative: The Administration of U.S. Foreign Policy towards South Asian States under Presidents Johnson and Nixon* (New Delhi: Concept, 1980), 103.

2. Richard N. Goodwin, "The War Within," *New York Times Magazine*, 21 August 1988, 34ff.

3. Francine R. Frankel, *India's Political Economy, 1946–1977: The Gradual Revolution* (Princeton, N.J.: Princeton University Press, 1978), 244.

4. James Warner Bjorkman, "Public Law 480 and the Policies of Self-Help and Short-Tether: Indo-American Relations, 1965–68," 201–62, in Rudolph, ed., *Regional Imperative*, 227.

5. Dom Moraes, *Indira Gandhi* (Boston: Little, Brown, 1980), 4, 127.

6. Ibid., 113–16.

7. Ibid., 122.

8. Zareer Masani, *Indira Gandhi: A Biography* (London: Hamish Hamilton, 1975), 136.

9. Indira Gandhi, *My Truth* (New Delhi: Vision, 1980), 119.

10. Surjit Mansingh, *India's Search for Power: Indira Gandhi's Foreign Policy, 1966–1982* (New Delhi: Sage, 1984), 79.

11. Gandhi, *My Truth*, 120.

12. Selig S. Harrison, *The Widening Gulf: Asian Nationalism and American Policy* (New York: Free Press, 1978), 176–79.

13. Henry Kissinger, *White House Years* (Boston: Little, Brown, 1979), 181.

14. Richard Nixon, *RN: The Memoirs of Richard Nixon* (New York: Grosset and Dunlap, 1978), 546.

15. Lester A. Sobel, ed., *Kissinger and Detente* (New York: Facts on File, 1975), 91.

16. Ibid., 95–100.

17. Stanley Wolpert, *Roots of Confrontation in South Asia: Afghanistan, Pakistan, India and the Superpowers* (New York: Oxford University Press, 1982), 136.

18. Norman D. Palmer, *The United States and India: The Dimensions of Influence* (New York: Praeger, 1984), 48; G. W. Choudhury, *India, Pakistan, Bangladesh, and the Major Powers: The Politics of a Divided Subcontinent* (New York: Free Press, 1975), 213–14.

19. Kissinger, *White House Years*, 848.

20. Ibid., 848; Choudhoury, *India, Pakistan, Bangladesh*, 142.

21. S. M. Burke, *Mainsprings of Indian and Pakistan Foreign Policies* (Minneapolis: University of Minnesota Press, 1974), 207–8.

22. Kissinger, *White House Years*, 851.

23. Ibid., 854.

24. Ibid., 853; Wolpert, *Roots of Confrontation*, 151–54.

25. T. N. Kaul, *The Kissinger Years: Indo-American Relations* (New Delhi: Arnold-Heinemann, 1980), 37–51.

26. T. N. Kaul, *Diplomacy in Peace and War: Recollections and Reflections* (New Delhi: Vikas, 1979), 207.

27. Palmer, *United States and India*, 48–50.

28. Ibid., 50.

29. *The Years of Endeavor: Selected Speeches of Indira Gandhi: August 1969–August 1972* (New Delhi: Ministry of Information and Broadcasting, 1975), 754–61; Nixon, *RN*, 525–31.

30. Nixon, *RN*, 525–31; Kissinger, *White House Years*, 879–81.

31. Palmer, *United States and India*, 52–53; Ved Vati Chaturshreni, *Indo–U.S. Relations* (New Delhi: National, 1980), 270–71.

32. Robert Jackson, *South Asian Crisis: India, Pakistan and Bangla Desh: A Political and Historical Analysis of the 1971 War* (New York: Praeger, 1975), 207–8.

33. Ibid., 212, 228.

34. Kissinger, *White House Years*, 901; Nixon, *RN*, 527.

35. Kissinger, *White House Years*, 911–12; Nixon, *RN*, 530.

36. Gandhi to Nixon, 15 December 1971, *Years of Endeavor*, 611–13; Jackson, *South Asian Crisis*, 226.

chapter 7

SON OF DÉTENTE: 1971–1977

THREE TO TANGO

During the first half of 1972, other events distracted the Nixon administration from the negative consequences in India of its tilt to Pakistan. In May, the president visited Moscow for a summit meeting with Soviet general secretary Leonid Brezhnev. There, the U.S. and Soviet leaders exchanged signatures on ten major agreements, including a document outlining "Basic Principles of Mutual Relations" and two strategic arms accords. The basic principles document served as a blueprint for détente, the temporary (as it turned out) relaxation of tensions between the superpowers. Ironically, considering the state of U.S.–Indian relations at the time, the détente principles sounded remarkably like Nehru's *panchsheel* principles: Washington and Moscow pledged themselves to "peaceful coexistence" and to "sovereignty, equality, non-interference in internal affairs and mutual advantage."

Although symbolically important, these principles counted practically for about as little as the original version of *panchsheel,* of which not much had been heard since the Chinese invasion of India in 1962. Kissinger described them as "frosting on the cake" of détente. Nixon may never have read the entire document containing them. Secretary of State William Rogers, before arriving in Moscow, did not even know the document existed.

More to the point were the two arms control agreements, together dubbed SALT, after the Strategic Arms Limitation Talks that produced them. These agreements limited the development of offensive weapons for a five-year period, pending negotiation of a system of more permanent controls (the ill-fated SALT II), and they restricted construction of antiballistic missile (ABM) defensive installations. Equally important, the SALT agreements contained an implicit acknowledgment by the United States of nuclear parity with the Soviet Union. From the beginning of the atomic age, the United States had led the race for newer and more powerful weapons. But Washington had never managed to lose the Russians; and with his signature on the SALT accord, Nixon conceded the race could not be won.[1]

More to the point still, in terms of U.S. policy toward Asia, was the momentum the meeting with Brezhnev gave Nixon on his way to Beijing. By establishing ties with China, the Nixon administration attempted to replace the bipolar framework of international affairs with one based on a triangular scheme including the Chinese. Since his academic days, Kissinger had been fascinated by the balance-of-power approach to world politics. Kissinger had no patience with those who thought, beginning from either conservative or liberal premises, that the United States had any obligation to save humanity. He asserted instead, and Nixon agreed, that the U.S. government must premise its policy on a narrower reading of U.S. national interest. Moral precepts could guide Washington in defining that interest, but morality alone afforded an insufficiently solid footing for policy. Nixon and Kissinger adopted an agnostic posture of balancing one communist power against the other to American advantage. They did not explicitly liken their approach to the neutralism pioneered by Nehru, but they might have.

India viewed the American efforts to remodel the world with ambivalence. New Delhi could not complain at Washington's de facto embrace of *panch-sheel* with Moscow, yet Indians doubted that any good could come from meetings between U.S. and Chinese officials. Gandhi guessed that the Americans and the Chinese would attempt to combine forces against the lesser powers of Asia. "If the meetings between the American and Chinese leaders are meant to forge friendship," the Indian prime minister said, "it is welcome to us. But apprehensions are being expressed that the talks are meant to form some sort of a new power group. If so, India—although a small nation—will not be bound by any such decision which seeks to dictate terms to Asian countries."[2]

Nixon's opening to China did indeed have as a goal the dictation of terms to Asians—although at that time the target was Vietnam, not India. The Nixon administration, overestimating the degree of Soviet and Chinese influence in Vietnam (as Americans had consistently overestimated their own) hoped the communists of Moscow and Beijing would persuade the communists of Hanoi to settle for less than all of Vietnam. The Soviets tried, pressing the North Vietnamese for concessions in stalled peace talks and looking the other way when the United States stepped up its bombing of the North—to the point of essentially ignoring American hits on Soviet ships in Haiphong harbor. The Chinese likewise urged moderation upon North Vietnam. After South Vietnamese troops invaded Laos in 1971, Zhou went to Hanoi to explain that despite this widening of the war, China had no intention of intervening. Subsequently, Chairman Mao himself told Pham Van Dong, the North Vietnamese prime minister, that prudence dictated discretion—at least for the time being.

North Vietnam did its best to ignore the advice of its Soviet and Chinese sponsors. In the code that passes for communication among Marxist-Leninists, Hanoi complained that unnamed members of the socialist camp were "bogging down on the dark, muddy road of compromise," thereby departing from "the great, all-conquering revolutionary idea of the age." The United States, North Vietnam's spokesman declared, had applied "a policy of reconciliation toward certain big powers in the hope of having a free hand" in Vietnam. Those powers had fallen prey to American enticements, preferring "peaceful coexistence over proletarian internationalism."[3]

In the end, Hanoi compromised only after enduring the heaviest bombing offensive in the history of aerial warfare. The Paris peace accord of January 1973 sufficed simply to grant the United States time to withdraw from Vietnam with a modicum of dignity. No one expected the North Vietnamese to abandon their plans to reunify the country; few thought the South Vietnamese could long resist. Despite massive infusions of U.S. military aid—more than $3 billion in 1973 alone—Saigon continued to lose ground. The end came in April 1975, when the South Vietnamese capital fell to North Vietnamese troops.

AN EMBARRASSMENT OF RUPEES

Humiliating as the Vietnam experience was for the United States and ignominious as its conclusion proved to be, the liquidation of the Indochina debacle removed a primary irritant to U.S.–Indian relations. For nearly two decades, the American presence in Vietnam had served as a reminder that Western imperialism in Asia had not died. The war had afforded Indian critics of the United States ammunition both against Washington and against any tendencies on the part of the Indian government to move too close to the Americans. A solid core of principle underlay Gandhi's attacks on U.S. policy in Southeast Asia, but the prime minister understood, as had her father before, that the United States made a wonderful villain in Indian politics. After the American tilt to Pakistan in the 1971 war, New Delhi had signaled its displeasure by upgrading its diplomatic representation in Hanoi. In response to the Christmas bombing of 1972, Gandhi had expressed her shock and horror at the "savage" display of American power, and she had suggested that the United States would not have adopted such a brutal approach had the targets of the bombs possessed white skins. She was probably right; but right or not, her outrage played well in India.[4]

While the Paris accords eliminated Vietnam as a divisive issue between

Washington and New Delhi, others remained. In a December 1972 interview for *Time*, Gandhi spelled out the most important. The magazine's correspondent set up the interview with a capsule description of the prime minister, which caught something of the mixed feelings many Americans harbored toward India.

> Mrs. Gandhi, very much Nehru's daughter, displays her elitist background in everything from the way she fusses with her sari to the manner of her speech. She nevertheless has shown a remarkable compassion for the wretched poor of her country. While the world watched her prosecute the war with Pakistan a year ago with great success, her mind was on the real war she is waging in India today—the war on hunger and poverty that continues to be so pervasive in her country of 550 million people. When she talks security on the subcontinent of Asia, her words are firm and practical, but her voice is low and displays little emotion. When she talks about improving life in her country, and about how India must become self-reliant while performing that monumental task, there is genuine passion in her voice and in her aristocratic, expressive features.

In the interview, Gandhi prefaced her comments (as she often did) by averring a desire to improve relations with the United States. "I sincerely wish they were better," she said. "There should be greater friendship." Naturally, however, the burden of improvement lay upon the United States, which failed to understand that India was "a complex country with so many contradictions." The prime minister complained that "whenever we do anything, the U.S. Administration has felt it was directed against them." American leaders mistook India's relationship with the Soviet Union. "There is this constant feeling—or so we are told—that we are pro-Russian. We are certainly friends. They helped us in difficult times. But we pay for whatever we get from them. The Soviet Union does not influence policy decisions in Delhi and does not try."

The most important source of friction was Pakistan, as it had been for a quarter century. Gandhi declared that India was actively seeking to normalize relations with Islamabad. Her government had left "no stone unturned" in trying to get along with President Bhutto. A mutually profitable relationship was not beyond the realm of possibility. "It is my personal belief and the conviction of the government of India that our interests are complementary. What happens in the subcontinent is important for all of Asia." But Washington was not helping matters. As the Bangladesh rebellion and the subsequent war had demonstrated, U.S. leaders had not "faced up to the realities" of South Asia. "This didn't help Pakistan," she said. It didn't help India either, but she implied that India could take care of itself.[5]

Gandhi elaborated these themes in an article in *Foreign Affairs*. The article, written for the twenty-fifth anniversary of Indian independence, traced India's differences with the United States back to the beginning. Referring to Washington's 1954 decision to court Pakistan and to the "massive supply" of U.S. arms that secured the arrangement, Gandhi declared that "we cannot believe that the U.S. administration was unaware that these weapons could be and would be used only against India." She added, "We took considerable pains to point this out, but our protests went unheeded." What had the American people profited from their government's efforts to impose the cold war on the countries of the subcontinent? "Has the United States succeeded in containing communism?" Hardly; on the contrary, as Nixon's journey to China demonstrated, the Americans had been forced "to woo the opposite bloc—the hated Communists."

The recent conflict over Bangladesh most clearly revealed the bankruptcy of U.S. policy. "The United States openly backed Pakistan at the cost of basic human values," Gandhi wrote.

> I do not wish to analyze the U.S. role at that time or go into the misrepresentations which were circulated. But it is necessary to take note of the dispatch of the warship *Enterprise* to support a ruthless dictatorship and to intimidate a democracy, and the extraordinary similarity of the attitudes adopted by the United States and China. Imagine our feelings. The original misunderstanding with the United States had arisen because of our contacts with China, the Soviet Union and Eastern Europe. We find it difficult to understand why, when the U.S. policy toward these countries changed, the resentment against us increased.

Gandhi did not want to leave her audience with an entirely negative impression. "We do not believe in permanent estrangement. We admire the achievements of the American people." India appreciated U.S. assistance over the years, and her government valued the "sympathetic support for the cause of Bangladesh and India" expressed by many Americans, despite Washington's official opposition. "We are ready to join in any serious effort to arrive at a deeper appreciation of each other's point of view and to improve relations." But Americans would have to do some hard thinking first—"The United States has yet to resolve the inner contradiction between the tradition of the founding fathers and of Lincoln and the external image it gives of a superpower pursuing the cold logic of power politics." The United States would remain a great power; India could not aspire to such status. However, "a great power must take into account the existence not only of countries with comparable power, but of the multitude of others who are no longer willing to be pawns on a global chessboard."[6]

Gandhi might have said more if not for the factor that kept cropping up in U.S.–Indian relations and galled Indians every time it did: India's need for American assistance. The Nixon administration had suspended aid during the December war, leaving the Indian government to guess when it might be resumed. Predictably, Gandhi declared that the Americans could keep their aid, that the Indian people would rather go hungry than accept help with strings. But 1972 proved an especially trying year, and more trials appeared likely to follow. A severe drought across two-thirds of the country exacerbated the problems created by the war. A survey done for the Indian government at the beginning of 1973 characterized the previous twelve months as "very difficult" and predicted that "the task ahead is not going to be an easy one."[7]

The forecasters spoke more accurately than they knew. During the spring of 1973, widespread hunger, rising unemployment, and spiraling inflation triggered violent riots across India. Anti-government critics charged Gandhi with countenancing corruption that made the whole situation worse, and the prime minister, reelected overwhelmingly two years earlier, faced a fight for her political life. Leaders of the Jan Sangh, the second largest political party in the country (after Gandhi's Congress party), asserted that the prime minister had lost her grip. Many Indians agreed. The autumn of 1973 brought war in the Middle East, which led to a devastating increase in the price of oil. Gandhi demonstrated her solidarity with the masses by exchanging her limousine for a horsecart, but neither public relations maneuvers nor slightly more substantive measures like turning off lights in public buildings did much to alleviate the pain.

Needing help from wherever she might find it, Gandhi looked to the United States. Indian officials indicated their country's desire for friendlier relations with the United States. They suggested that they were willing to let bygones be gone. A foreign office spokesman said that Indians were "trying to put the events of 1971 behind us." Stretching the truth, he added, "There is no anger or irritation on our part."[8]

As a first step toward forgetfulness, the Indian finance ministry recommended a program for dealing with the problem of U.S. rupee holdings in India. Since the initiation of the PL-480 program, India had been depositing rupees into an American account, with the understanding that the United States would spend the money in India. From the first, it became evident that Washington would never be able to disburse the rupees as fast as they were piling up. But successive administrations had put off dealing with the issue, until by the early 1970s, American holdings were approaching the equivalent of $3 billion. American and Indian economists estimated that the accumulated interest would balloon the debt before the end of the century to a point where the United States would control as much as one-fifth of the Indian money supply.

New Delhi and Washington agreed that something had to be done about the problem. Indians objected to American control over such a large portion of the currency. To date, the U.S. government had not used the rupee debt as a hammer against India, but with the likes of Nixon and Kissinger in power,

Indians desired to decrease their exposure. (Fortunately for India, Nixon and Kissinger knew little and cared even less about international economic affairs than about South Asia.) From the American perspective, the rupee debt had become an albatross. The United States could not spend the money without seriously disrupting India's economy, which would undo the work of fifteen years of American aid. Besides, India had little the United States wanted to buy. (Had the situation been otherwise, of course, the trouble would not have arisen in the first place.) Moreover, the existence of the debt left Washington open to charges of neoimperialism. Since the debt was uncollectable, better to write it off and hope to gain some goodwill in the bargain.

Ultimately, Washington did just that—for the most part, anyway. The new U.S. ambassador in New Delhi, Daniel Patrick Moynihan, made solving the rupee problem a priority. Moynihan, a sociologist by training, had acquired prominence by advocating a policy of "benign neglect" toward the disadvantaged in the United States. The Nixon White House, perceiving Indians as exemplars of the world's disadvantaged and more than slightly inclined toward neglect in their direction, considered Moynihan just the person for the New Delhi post. The ambassador did not disappoint. Arguing for a "realistic" U.S.-Indian relationship, Moynihan supplied a syllogism for improving matters. The major premise was that the United States wished to see India's experiment in democracy succeed. The minor premise was that the United States must treat India as an equal rather than as a dependent. The conclusion was that Washington and New Delhi should liquidate the rupee problem as a first step toward creating a partnership based on equality and not on American aid.[9]

Through the summer of 1973, Moynihan and Indian officials worked to reduce and reschedule the debt. At the end of September, they reached a tentative agreement. India would pay $100 million of the $3 billion debt in dollars over a ten-year period; India would pay $900 million in rupees, which the United States agreed to spend in India; Washington would forget about the remaining $2 billion, in exchange for India's pledge to apply the money to development projects.

Veteran observers of foreign aid debates were not surprised when U.S. critics lashed the plan as another muddle-headed boondoggle. The Foreign Affairs Committee of the House of Representatives called Moynihan to Capitol Hill to explain himself; one faithful guardian of the public purse declared his intention to introduce a bill blocking what he considered a great giveaway.

But the months during which the Nixon administration became unglued over the Watergate affair provided the president's opponents much more to exercise themselves about than rupees, even billions of them. As a result, early in 1974, Congress accepted an agreement along the lines laid out the September before. In the ensuing formalities, Moynihan delivered to the Indian foreign minister the largest check ever written in India's currency: a draft for 16.64 billion rupees.[10]

THE NUCLEAR FAMILY EXTENDED

In 1951, just after Washington had agreed to rescue India from famine, Nehru had demonstrated that he could not be bought by rejecting the peace treaty with Japan. In 1974, after the United States decided to liquidate the rupee debt and ease India's crushing economic burden, Gandhi took a similar action. But where the father had contented himself with the devices of diplomacy, the daughter deployed a more powerful tool—the atomic bomb.

India's interest in atomic energy had predated independence. During World War II, the British government of India had established the Tata Institute of Fundamental Research, headed by Homi Bhabha, later director of the Indian Atomic Energy Commission. During the next decade, Indian scientists had probed the structure of the atom; in 1956, they reached a milestone in the development of atomic energy when they achieved a controlled fission reaction. If anyone in the Nehru government had plans for converting the knowledge thus gained into a deliverable weapon, no one said so. Instead, Indian officials cited the benefits that harnessing the atom might bring to the improverished masses of India and the Third World. Ambassador Pandit summarized the New Delhi line when she told the U.N. General Assembly, "Atomic energy could be of enormous importance in raising living standards to some reasonable parity with those in the West."[11]

Out of a desire to keep its ostensibly peaceful options open, India refused to adhere to various schemes for international control of atomic energy. In rejecting these plans, which included Eisenhower's 1953 Atoms for Peace proposal, New Delhi argued that it could not relinquish sovereignty in such a vital area to any international body, however well intentioned. Meanwhile, though, in consonance with India's policy of promoting peaceful resolutions of disputes, Nehru pledged not to engage in the production of atomic weapons. "India will in no event use atomic energy for destructive purposes, but only for peaceful purposes," the prime minister declared in 1957, adding, "I am confident that this would be the policy for all future governments in the country."[12]

Nehru's insistence on unilateralism in atomic affairs followed in part from the same preoccupation with independence that underpinned his nonaligned diplomacy; it also reflected a desire to keep India's powder dry. Indian officials recognized that their country could not afford to engage the superpowers in an arms race. Even the attempt would steal resources desperately needed for economic development. All the same, in a world that accorded special status to the possessors of nuclear weapons, Nehru did not wish to relegate India irrevocably to the ranks of the second-rate.

Guarding India's alternatives seemed doubly important after 1964, when China, India's recent antagonist in the Himalayan war, exploded an atom bomb. Several months earlier, the United States, the Soviet Union, and Britain had signed an agreement forbidding atmospheric testing of nuclear weapons; now the big powers were pushing for a broadly based nuclear nonproliferation pact, by which nonnuclear signatories would promise not to acquire nuclear weapons. The Chinese rejected what they interpreted as collusion by the imperialists and the Moscow revisionists. They punctuated their rejection with an atomic exclamation mark.

If China would not agree not to go nuclear, neither would India, although Indian officials refrained from rejecting nonproliferation outright. In 1965, India's representative at the U.N. listed India's conditions for adherence to a nonproliferation accord—agreement by the nuclear powers not to transfer nuclear weapons or expertise to other countries; U.N. guarantees of the security of nonnuclear states against those possessing nuclear weapons; pledges by the nuclear countries not to use nuclear weapons against those not possessing them; concrete progress toward disarmament by the nuclear states, including a freeze on production of nuclear weapons and delivery vehicles; and promises by nonnuclear countries not to acquire or manufacture nuclear weapons.

While parts of the Indian approach informed the nonproliferation treaty that came into effect in 1970 following ratification by nearly one hundred parties, New Delhi found the guarantees of the agreement insufficient to warrant India's acceptance. Indeed, because the treaty focused on forbidding the *future* acquisition of nuclear weapons, and since China already had a bomb, many Indians interpreted the treaty as favoring China against India. This increased their reluctance to ratify the accord and encouraged them to look to their own resources for India's security.

When the next year revealed the Nixon administration's opening to China, Indian wariness of nonproliferation grew further, as did New Delhi's desire to develop a riposte to Beijing's bomb. The *Enterprise* episode of 1971, which Indian officials read as a direct challenge to India's safety by the world's foremost nuclear power, heightened New Delhi's sense of being on the wrong end of nuclear diplomacy. Washington's flaunting of its military superiority over India intensified the resolve of the Indian government not to be cowed again—a reaction resembling that of the Soviet Union after the Cuban missile crisis of 1962. The Cuban affair had pushed Moscow toward the nuclear buildup that culminated in the parity acknowledged in the SALT accord; the *Enterprise* maneuver sped New Delhi along the path to membership in the nuclear club.

In May 1974, the world learned that India had joined. Although the Gandhi government averred that nothing had changed in India's approach to nuclear weapons—that the device India's scientists had just detonated was, in contrast to those of the United States, the Soviet Union, Britain, France, and China, "peaceful"—few foreign observers credited the argument. Some held that the Indians desired the explosion to serve notice on Beijing not to trifle with India any longer. Others perceived the Indian bomb as a bargaining chip for use with the Arabs, who might trade oil or other favors for assistance in building an explosive of their own. This argument collided, however, with a more plausible contrary contention that India's show of strength was meant for the edification of the Arabs' religious ally Pakistan.

Analysts of Indian politics posited a domestic cause for Gandhi's decision to take India nuclear. Despite the rupee deal and promises of further Western aid, India's economic situation continued to decline. Inflation neared 20 percent. Agricultural production was off 10 percent. A railroad strike threatened to strangle Bombay and other parts of the country; business leaders asserted that if the government did not end the walkout soon, the economy would suffer irreparable damage. A general strike staged in sympathy with the railroad workers disrupted life in all major cities. A government survey of the economy described the current period as the worst since independence.

Gandhi, assailed as never before for ineptitude in handling the crisis, launched a two-pronged counterattack. In the second week of May she jailed seven thousand of the protesting railwaymen. (Some observers thought they heard the ghost of Winston Churchill chuckling.) A few days later, she announced the detonation of India's atomic device. Whatever the external causes of the decision to go nuclear, Gandhi's action, in conjunction with strike-breaking repression of the railroad union, enhanced her domestic prestige. For the moment, she gained a respite from charges that she lacked the stuff to deal with India's troubles.

At the same time, Gandhi was barraged with foreign criticism for exploding the bomb. The government of Canada, which had provided technical and material assistance that made the Indian bomb possible, cried foul. The Canadians immediately cut off aid to India's atomic energy program and announced a review of other assistance as well. In the United States, where the Nixon administration was putting the final touches on a new aid program of its own, even commentators who had not contested New Delhi's characterization of India's bomb as peaceful expressed dismay that the Indian government had sunk hundreds of millions of dollars into atomic explosives while millions of Indians lacked food and housing. In Congress, opponents of U.S. aid policy introduced a measure to purge India from U.S. assistance rolls. Although the resolution failed, it gained 159 votes in the House of Representatives.

THE DEVIL ON THE DEEP BLUE SEA

Predictably, American criticism of India elicited renewed Indian complaints at the United States. This time, instead of recycling tired allegations of neoimperialism and proxy pressure via Pakistan, India's America-bashers adopted a new approach. Largely because of its yeoman work in widening the credibility gap, the Nixon administration found itself the victim of an unprecedented number of leaks of sensitive information. The most spectacular example of unauthorized release involved the Pentagon papers, the multivolume secret history of the Vietnam War. In second place for embarrassment was a spill touching on American relations with India. Shortly after the Nixon administration's decision to back Pakistan against India in the December war, investigative journalist Jack Anderson had obtained transcripts of conversations demonstrating conclusively that the White House, despite professions of nonpreference, had no intention of treating the two sides evenhandedly.

Nixon and Kissinger attempted to stop the leaks, but with little success. Their efforts, which took the administration outside the law, contributed materially to the president's ultimate political demise in the Watergate affair. Moreover, the attempts to stem the flow of information added to an atmosphere in which leaking became a regular form of bureaucratic warfare.

In 1973, the elected president of Chile, Salvador Allende Gossens, was overthrown and murdered in a military coup. Believable (although sometimes exaggerated) reports of U.S. complicity in the affair immediately surfaced. It was soon established that the Nixon administration, acting through the CIA, had taken measures designed to destabilize Allende's government. If American agents had not pulled the trigger of the gun that killed Allende, Washington had clearly indicated its support of those who did.

Against this background, allegations of CIA meddling in Indian affairs gained widespread credence in India. That India's Communist party responded to Kissinger's October 1974 visit with strident denunciations of the "murderer" of Allende and warnings that the United States was plotting similarly diabolical activities in India raised few eyebrows. That spokespersons for the Congress party seconded the warning and urged Indians to beware the machinations of the CIA occasioned more comment. Kissinger, now secretary of state in the Gerald Ford administration, considered the problem sufficiently serious to warrant a public response. In an extraordinary statement—which recalled to some minds Nixon's famous "I am not a crook" speech—Kissinger told a news conference that the CIA was not engaged and would not engage in efforts to undermine the government of India. Kissinger's remarks may or may not have convinced Gandhi, but as a measure of her scorn for the U.S. secretary of state, she pointedly departed New Delhi in the middle of his visit, leaving him to deal with lesser officials.[13]

While Washington sought to disabuse Indians of their CIA-as-devil theory of international relations, a more concrete—literally—source of friction appeared. At the beginning of 1974, the Pentagon announced it was considering constructing a naval base on Diego Garcia, an island in the Indian Ocean some fifteen hundred miles south of the tip of the Indian peninsula. For over a year, the United States had operated a communications facility on the British-held island, which filled a large gap between American satellite tracking stations in Australia and Africa. For an undetermined (or at least unconfirmed) but certainly longer period, American Polaris submarines had been prowling the neighborhood, from which their nuclear missiles could reach targets across a broad swath of the central Soviet Union. But the United States had not stationed surface ships in the Indian Ocean, which was why the Nixon administration, when it decided to engage in gunboat diplomacy during the December war, had to call in the *Enterprise* from the Pacific Seventh Fleet.

In the wake of the 1971 war, the Defense Department unveiled plans to establish a greater U.S. presence in the Indian Ocean. The Pentagon insisted that these plans had nothing to do with the present difficulty with India; they had been on the shelf for years but had remained there because of the Vietnam War. The Nixon administration did admit to worries about a growing Soviet presence in the area, set at fifteen to twenty vessels, and suggested that after the recently concluded Indo–Soviet treaty, the Russian force would only increase.

Events in the Middle East augmented American concerns regarding the Indian Ocean. At the beginning of 1973, Egypt hinted that it wanted to reopen and enlarge the Suez Canal, which had been closed since the Six-Day War with Israel in 1967. This would afford the Soviet Black Sea and Mediterranean fleets easy access to the Indian Ocean. The Yom Kippur War, which broke out several months later, scuttled Egypt's plans, but the Arab oil embargo it produced demonstrated the dependence of the American alliance system on Middle Eastern oil. This latest war also underlined the fragility of the distribution network that carried petroleum from Persian Gulf sources to consumers in Japan, Europe, and the United States. In November 1973, U.S. secretary of defense James Schlesinger said that the situation in the Middle East, combined with Soviet successes in gaining base rights in Yemen and Somalia, had led to an "enhanced interest" in the Indian Ocean on the part of the United States.[14]

Indian officials not unexpectedly denounced the American plans. Having felt the weight of U.S. military power when projected from the Pacific, New Delhi had no desire to allow it into India's eponymous ocean. Indian officials dismissed American arguments that the increased Soviet presence required a response, and they roundly rejected speculation that India's alliance with Russia, ratified by a November visit by Soviet party chief Brezhnev and the signing of a new trade aid pact, included provisions for servicing Soviet vessels in Indian ports. According to Gandhi, the Russians had not even asked; "They knew my views already. We do not give foreign bases."[15]

In the Indian view, the construction of a station at Diego Garcia represented a continuance of America's twenty-five-year effort to draw as much of the world as possible into the cold war. The American alliance with Pakistan had brought the Americans' conflict with the Russians across the Hindu Kush and down into the subcontinent; now the Americans were coming by sea.

New Delhi launched a propaganda campaign against the American buildup. Indian officials predicted a new arms race that would destabilize the region. Foreign Minister Swaran Singh warned of a "chain reaction" that would lead to military confrontation between the superpowers. Gandhi persuaded the Shah of Iran to join in a declaration that the Indian Ocean should remain a "zone of peace."[16]

The Soviet Union naturally supported India's efforts to keep the United States out of the area. Moscow did not wish to jeopardize détente over the issue, but the Kremlin nevertheless accounted as a "regrettable inaccuracy" a statement by President Ford that the Soviet Union possessed naval bases in the region of the Indian Ocean. Ford specified Somalia, Yemen, and Iraq as the hosts; the Kremlin countered by publishing denials from the governments of the three countries.[17]

During this period—Nixon's final days and Ford's first—the Republicans could not have persuaded Congress to endorse the Pledge of Allegiance without a fight. The extension of the U.S. military presence to a new part of the world, hardly a year after the pullout from Vietnam, provoked considerable controversy. Chester Bowles, ever the defender of India against Republican aggression, described the Diego Garcia scheme as symbolic of the kind of thinking that had led to the Indochina fiasco. Democratic congressman Lee Hamilton urged the legislature to look carefully at this unprecedented departure in foreign policy, contending it might touch off a naval arms race with the Soviets. Senator Claiborne Pell introduced legislation to ban construction of the Diego Garcia base. Oversight committees in the Senate and House of Representatives summoned Defense and State department officials to testify in the matter. A comment by the deputy secretary of defense, William Clements, that the $29 million the Pentagon was requesting would probably triple before the facility was completed did not strengthen the administration's case. No more helpful was a suggestion by Joint Chiefs of Staff chairman Thomas Moorer that the United States might someday use Diego Garcia as a launching pad for nuclear-equipped B-52s. Indians reacted to this last remark with particular outrage.

The controversy heated further when the State Department, under heavy prodding from Senators John Culver and Edward Kennedy, revealed a secret 1966 agreement with Britain, under which the British would take responsibility for relocating a thousand residents of Diego Garcia and nearby islands and establishing a base facility, in exchange for a bargain price on American Polaris missiles. This news led to a spate of articles on the uprooted islanders, as well as to embarrassment for the British government.

Opponents of the Diego Garcia base succeeded in delaying construction. In November 1975, a conference committee of the House and Senate agreed to push consideration of funding into the next year. The Defense Department, however, managed to find monies to keep the project going despite the absence of congressional approval. In July 1976, when a dispute between Kenya and Uganda prompted the Pentagon to dispatch an American reconnaissance plane to investigate, a Defense spokesman revealed that the base had become operational.

DEMOCRACY DEFERRED

Amid the protracted fuss over the expanded U.S. presence in the Indian Ocean, the resumption in early 1975 of American arms shipments to Pakistan created an additional spike of discontent between India and the United States. Swaran Singh, now defense minister, asserted that sending weapons to Pakistan, after a ten-year embargo, would "retard the process of normalization of relations in the subcontinent and may embolden Prime Minister Bhutto to take a harder line." The Indian ambassador in Washington castigated the decision in the strongest language, leading Kissinger to describe the ambassador's action as unacceptable. The Indian foreign secretary canceled a visit to the United States, eliciting a State Department response that it had intended to withdraw the invitation anyway. Gandhi declared that the American decision amounted to a "reopening of old wounds." India's President Fakhruddin Ali Ahmed, in accepting the credentials of the new U.S. ambassador, William Saxbe—who had delayed his arrival to let the worst of the storm pass—said the shipment of weapons to Pakistan "cast a shadow" across the subcontinent. Saxbe replied, in unusually pessimistic language for an arriving envoy, that the best India and the United States could expect was "grudging respect" for each other's positions.[18]

As always, Indian complaints against the United States—like American attacks on India—had to be read in the context of domestic political developments. The year 1975 was the rockiest in India's history as a republic. January began with the bombing of a political rally in Samastipur. The target appeared to be the government's minister of railways, Lalit Narayan Mishra, although two dozen other persons, including two members of parliament, sustained injuries in the blast. When Mishra, who had been bitterly denounced by opposition parties for his role in a scandal involving illegal imports, died the next day, the ruling Congress party blamed his denouncers for the death. Gandhi perceived a plot against the government—or said she did, at any rate—and likened her opponents to the Nazis during the 1930s.

If the prime minister had looked for a sympathetic backlash, she miscalculated. By-elections later in January brought a stunning defeat for the Congress party. In February, Muslims demonstrated in New Delhi against the arrest of one of their religious leaders. Police fired on the crowd, killing three and wounding fifty. The protesters fired back, injuring more than sixty police. Early in March, Jaya Prakash Narayan, a septuagenarian follower of Mohandas Gandhi—no relation to the prime minister, as Narayan's supporters incessantly reminded the foreign press—and the spearhead of the drive against governmental corruption, led a march of 100,000 persons through the streets of Delhi. At the end of the month, Indira Gandhi's old foe, Morarji Desai, began a hunger strike demanding early elections in Gujarat State, where the government had repeatedly delayed balloting after anticorruption riots. The worst drought in a century in Gujarat exacerbated the troubles.

In June, the roof began caving when India's supreme court ruled that Gandhi had gained the premiership in 1971 by deceitful and illegal means. Vowing to take her case to the people, Gandhi appealed the court's decision, which, if upheld, would also bar her from holding office for six years. Meanwhile, the Gujarat elections returned a majority for a coalition of opposition parties, whose leaders promptly announced their intention to force Gandhi from power. Following an interim court order allowing the prime minister to retain her position pending action on the appeal, the opposition called for a nationwide campaign of passive resistance until Gandhi resigned.

Facing what she called the threat of "widespread sabotage," Gandhi struck back. Through President Ahmed, she declared a state of emergency. She ordered the arrest of dozens of opposition leaders, including Narayan and Desai. By the end of July, the number of those jailed neared a thousand. Gandhi proceeded to censor the press, declaring that "in India democracy has given too much license to the people." In imposing curbs on various dissident groups, the government accused the organizations of "indulging in activities prejudicial to internal security, safety and the maintenance of order." With the principal opposition parties boycotting the parliament, Gandhi rammed through legislation ratifying her emergency powers. In August, the thoroughly intimidated legislature approved by unanimous vote a constitutional amendment to take electoral matters out of the hands of the judiciary, effectively pardoning Gandhi for what she claimed not to have done.[19]

Americans found the furor fascinating. Enthusiasts of India's experiment in democracy were shocked by the country's rapid decline into authoritarianism. Skeptics had their suspicions confirmed. Noters of parallels between the American and Indian experiences found uncanny the resemblance between Gandhi's emergency and Nixon's attempted subversion of the U.S. political system. That both leaders accepted pardons for crimes they insisted they had never committed completed the analogy—or almost completed the analogy, since Gandhi remained in office while Nixon retired to San Clemente in disgrace.[20]

The Indian emergency united the American press as few issues have. From the right, William Buckley's *National Review* lampooned, "Sieg heil, Indira!" Dripping sarcasm, the magazine wrote,

> India's generation of democracy had a certain Victorian charm, but it was always pretty much of a charade put on by the thin stratum of intellectuals which the British Raj had taught to speak English and ape parliamentary procedures. Three thousand years of monarchies, despotisms, conquests, invasions, empires, and confusion were too much for a model constitution drawn up by London barristers to overcome. So no one should be surprised, and few people *are* surprised, that democracy disappeared from India like a bubble bursting.

From the opposite end of the political spectrum, the *Nation* ran a story on India's "bribable socialism" and the "divine right of Mrs. Gandhi." The *Nation*'s correspondent likened democracy in India, as practiced by the Congress party, to "an unconvincing rope trick" and declared that "the real ruling power in India was and will continue to be money." The author described an incident in which a socialist state official in Kerala, mistaking the American writer for an agent of the CIA, offered to help pull down India's government in exchange for 300,000 rupees. The author went on to describe the cynicism surrounding the Congress party and especially the Nehru–Gandhi family. He related a conversation with B. K. Nehru, Gandhi's cousin and not coincidentally governor of Assam, in which Nehru explained his approach to imposing order on the fractious inhabitants of the state's hill country. "You can't run a government along [Mohandas] Gandhian lines," Nehru said. "I agree with Mao: power comes out the end of a gun. There are times when you have to face things, kill and be killed. We came along, moralists that we are, and said we must administer these savages. It is probably a good thing to prolong the fighting. Let these people get tired of it."[21]

Gandhi considered the damage in the United States to India's reputation and her own sufficiently serious to warrant answering the charges. Even while censorship of news-gathering and -dissemination continued, she agreed to answer questions put by the *Saturday Review*. The editors telegraphed questions to New Delhi; she cabled replies. Because of the lack of followup capability, the interview came across as a soliloquy rather than a dialogue, but it did allow the prime minister to convey her side of the emergency story.

Citing "sabotage" on the part of "supposedly responsible leaders" of the opposition, Gandhi defended her decision to respond firmly.

> The state of emergency was proclaimed because the threat of disruption was clear and imminent. When an organized attempt is made to exhort workers and farmers to withhold work and produce, when government offices are not allowed to function, when students are advised to boycott schools, when duly elected legislators are called upon to resign, when open statements are made that the prime minister will not be "recognized" and that Parliament will not be allowed to function, in spite of the clear verdict of the highest court of the land that I am legally entitled to function as prime minister, and when, finally, a call is given by a combination of five parties for countrywide civil disobedience, and, over and above all, the armed forces and police are publicly asked to disobey orders—is the situation not grave?

Gandhi declared that to have let the disruption continue would have amounted to a dereliction of duty. "I did not become prime minister in order to dismantle a structure of self-government and freedom that my father, Jawaharlal Nehru, and millions of others like him labored so painstakingly over so many years to construct." (Churchill's ghost was chuckling again, recalling his own statement that he had not become the king's first minister to preside over the liquidation of the British empire.) She dismissed as ludicrous the notion that she aimed to undermine India's democracy, but neither would she stand for its undermining by others: "I do not believe that a democratic society has the obligation to acquiesce in its own dissolution. I do not believe that a democratic society need be defenseless against those who would paralyze it. I do not believe that a democratic society cannot take strong measures to deal with its foes, from within or without."[22]

Not many Americans bought Gandhi's argument; neither did the Ford administration. Seeing no need to add to its already sizable burdens by endorsing Gandhi's autocratic acts, the White House indefinitely postponed a planned visit by the president to India.

At the same time, Washington avoided action that Gandhi could credibly cite as meddlesome. The deputy assistant secretary of state for Near Eastern and South Asian affairs, Adolph Dubs, explained the administration's position, employing the bloodless language that bureaucrats spend careers mastering. Dubs affirmed America's "longstanding interest" in India. He characterized the current state of U.S.–Indian relations as "relatively stable." Regarding the present political situation in India, the administration had made clear its "preference for democratic norms." But the United States possessed "limited influence" with the government of India. "Public polemic" to force remedies upon New Delhi would be "inappropriate."[23]

FRESH AIR

Discretion indeed was probably the better part of wisdom, but the State Department had an additional motive for keeping its mouth shut: uncertainty regarding the direction the White House would take after Ford. In Watergate's wake, a Democratic turn in the Oval Office was almost inevitable, although Jimmy Carter came near to losing the 1976 election and allowing the Republicans to continue their postwar dominance of the executive branch.

Unversed in foreign policy, Carter skillfully exploited his inexperience in the election campaign. The former governor of Georgia promised to lead the American people on a new path, away from the obsession with communism and the reflexive resort to military force that had dragged the United States into Vietnam. A Carter administration, he promised, would look at the problems of different regions and countries on their own merits rather than through the lens of the cold war. It would work for a just and equitable world order rather than one based on narrow balance-of-power considerations. It would grant the developing nations the attention they deserved instead of treating them as mere objects of manipulation.

Carter's formula seemed just the ticket for an improvement in relations with

India—except for one thing: Gandhi's continued trampling of the human rights of the Indian people. A report by Freedom House, an international human-rights advocacy group, underlined the impact of Gandhi's emergency decrees when it estimated that the number of persons in the world living under democracy had decreased by 40 percent in consequence of events in India.

As Carter's luck—which ran out soon enough—had it, developments in India saved him the trouble of determining how to deal with Gandhi. Through most of 1976, the prime minister continued to augment her authority. In April, the Indian supreme court upheld her right to jail political opponents without hearings. In June, the government extended from one year to two the period during which it could hold political prisoners before lodging charges. In September, Gandhi introduced a set of constitutional amendments granting her broad new legislative powers. In December, the measures became law.

But then, perhaps gulled by her own rhetoric about how the people supported her defense of the public order, and certainly stung by foreign criticism, Gandhi called general elections for March 1977. The opposition, which now included even Gandhi's aunt, the former ambassador to the United States, Mrs. Pandit, mounted a furious campaign. In a breathtaking upset, the dissidents toppled the acting dictator. Eight weeks after Jimmy Carter took the oath of office in Washington, Morarji Desai was sworn in as India's fourth prime minister.

Notes

1. Raymond L. Garthoff, *Detente and Confrontation: American–Soviet Relations from Nixon to Reagan* (Washington: Brookings, 1985), 289–99.

2. Sobel, *Kissinger and Detente,* 118.

3. Garthoff, *Detente and Confrontation,* 248–61.

4. *New York Times,* 4 February 1973.

5. *Time,* 11 December 1972.

6. Indira Gandhi, "India and the World," *Foreign Affairs,* October 1972.

7. *New York Times,* 23 February 1973.

8. Ibid., 25 July 1973.

9. Ibid., 11 September 1973.

10. Mansingh, *India's Search for Power,* 112–15.

11. Ashok Kapur, *India's Nuclear Option: Atomic Diplomacy and Decision Making* (New York: Praeger, 1976), 106.

12. Ibid., 99–100.

13. *New York Times,* 31 October 1974.

14. Ibid., 1 December 1973.

15. Mansingh, *India's Search for Power,* 151.

16. *New York Times,* 13 March and 6 May 1974.

17. Ibid., 1 September 1974.

18. Ibid., 6 and 27 February, 9 and 25 March 1975.

19. Ibid., 2, 3, and 5 July 1975.
20. Moraes, *Indira Gandhi*, 222.
21. *National Review*, 18 July 1975; *Nation*, 2 August 1975.
22. *Saturday Review*, 9 August 1975.
23. *Department of State Bulletin*, 18 October 1976.

chapter 8

THE GREAT GAME RESUMES: 1977–1988

DÉTENTE UNDONE

By the time Carter entered the White House, détente was fraying at the edges. The tattering resulted in no small part from the fact that neither Gerald Ford nor Jimmy Carter was Richard Nixon. Détente had never generated much enthusiasm among the conservative anticommunist types who have generally enjoyed the ability to tie American foreign policy in knots; but with Dick Nixon at the helm, most swallowed their misgivings and grudgingly kept still. Nixon's departure unsilenced them.

The campaign of 1976, which started long before that calendar year began, brought together two streams of antidétenters. Old-line conservatives—Republicans mostly, but also cold war Democrats like Senator Henry Jackson and Paul Nitze, a chief architect of the original containment policy—made up one branch. Born-again hawks—largely refugees from the leftist political wars of the Depression era who clustered around *Commentary* magazine and its master polemicist, Norman Podhoretz, and who called themselves "neoconservatives"—constituted the other. The neos and the paleos joined forces in the Committee on the Present Danger, which adopted for its mission the destruction of détente.

The Soviet Union and ally Cuba inadvertently assisted the present-dangerists by providing aid to a Marxist faction in Angola, where a replay of the Congo confusion of a decade before was taking place. Americans who expected détente to end all rivalry between capitalist and communist camps considered the Kremlin's intervention out of bounds; those aiming to kill détente seized on the situation to show that one could never trust the reds. As it happened, the Angola affair climaxed just after the fall of South Vietnam—a debacle that, although certainly not chargeable against détente, lent weight to the warnings of those who claimed that the United States could deal with the communists only from a position of strength.

Both Ford and Carter lacked the stature and background to defend détente convincingly. In its final months, the Ford administration began to distance itself from the notion and the label, announcing, "We are going to forget the word détente." Carter joined the flight. The Democratic candidate said, "Détente has given up too much to the Russians and gotten too little in return." Ford surrendered for both men just days before relinquishing office to Carter, in his valedictory State of the Union speech. Ford declared that the United States must not tolerate an unfavorable shift in the strategic balance, a statement to which no one could object. But he went on to rule out "even a situation where the American people or our allies believe the balance is shifting against us." By acknowledging the importance of perceptions, Ford granted the victory to the antidétentists, who had perfected the art of enlarging public fears. Under other circumstances, Carter might have embraced détente; under those in force in 1977, he had little chance.[1]

NONALIGNMENT REVIVED—AND REVILED

Because much of the friction in U.S.–Indian relations resulted from the grinding of the cold war, the détente period between the superpowers should have produced an analogous relaxation between Washington and New Delhi. To some degree it did, as the settlement of the rupee problem demonstrated. But the connection between the cold war and the condition of U.S.–Indian affairs was never linear, and an improvement in the former did not immediately or automatically translate into a commensurate bettering of the latter. Americans failed to realize how seriously Indians took the *Enterprise* episode; nor did most appreciate what the construction of the base at Diego Garcia implied to a people still sensitive to manifestations of Western imperialism. Indians, for their part, inflamed the relationship by continuing to charge the United States with responsibility for many of India's problems. Whatever else the CIA may have accomplished in its checkered career, it has furnished the ideal scapegoat to blame-ducking politicians in the Third World. What communism was to the McCarthyites in the United States in the 1950s, the CIA has been to nationalists and allied demagogues in Asia, Africa, and Latin America ever since. That the agency really *has* engaged in dirty tricks bears about the same relation to its epiphenomenal importance as the existence of genuine spies did to the anticommunist culture of the McCarthy era. Each verified sighting has given rise to scores that are unverifiable—but also undisprovable. Americans accept blame with as little grace as most people, and each round of America-baiting in India produced an echo in the United States. That Nixon and Gandhi personally detested each other compounded the problems of perception and interpretation.

Ironically, most of the improvement in U.S.–Indian affairs attributable to détente occurred as détente itself was dying. William Saxbe, just returned from his stint as ambassador in New Delhi, thought Indians were coming to recognize the limitations of their reliance on the Soviet Union. "I feel that the honeymoon is about over, simply because the Indians are beginning to realize they are being used," Saxbe said. "The Russians sell them tremendous amounts of military equipment at high prices and without concessionary terms. They are unable to supply India with the thing it needs most—food—in a bad crop year. Russia won't or can't take the things that India wants to sell: sugar, jute, shrimp, cashews, and heavy equipment." Saxbe conceded that old prejudices died hard. "You never read anything good about the United States in the Indian papers, and you never read anything bad about Russia." But he noted that despite Western fears, India had not granted the Soviets base rights, and although Russian naval vessels could call at Indian ports, so could American ships. Saxbe predicted a continued improvement in relations between India and the United States, especially in the area of nonpublic economic activity. "I can't help but believe that the independent Indian businessman will look to the West. There is nothing for him in Russia, nothing for him in the Iron Curtain countries or even in China. He has to look to the West, where his markets are."[2]

Partly from economic influences, partly to distinguish his government from Gandhi's, Morarji Desai sought a position for India closer to the United States. In practice, this took the form of a revival of nonalignment. Desai had campaigned against Gandhi for betraying her father's policy of equidistance between the superpowers, for puppeting Moscow's line. "Don't you see," he said, "we do whatever the Soviet Union does." In office, the new prime minister declared that India would return to its nonaligned roots. His government would practice a "proper nonalignment policy," a policy "fully nonaligned," with "no suspicion of alignment" with any nation. "We will not have any special relations with any country."[3]

Critics—and even some supporters—considered Desai naïve in international affairs. A like charge would be leveled at Carter. Yet the Indian prime minister was astute enough in matters of Indian politics to recognize that anything conceivably construable as capitulation to the Americans would do him serious damage, and he took care to balance moves in the direction of Washington with gestures toward Moscow. After announcing a visit by Carter to India, Desai traveled to the Soviet Union. At a dinner in Desai's honor, General Secretary Brezhnev reminded guests of the long history of friendship between their two countries. Desai responded in like fashion, although he appended a reaffirmation of the virtues of nonalignment.

To strengthen India's diplomatic position—and his own political position—Desai sought to improve Indian relations with Beijing. For a decade and a half, since the rupture that gave rise to the Himalayan war of 1962, India and China had shared little but mutual hostility. During Desai's first months in office, the glacier began to melt. New Delhi announced that Chinese ships would be welcome in India's ports; the Indian government proposed trade and cultural exchanges; the Indian foreign minister expressed a desire to travel to China.

In response, the Chinese government adopted a typically sinocentric and revolutionarily correct posture. Beijing admonished that if the Indian government wished to cultivate the favor of the people—including the people of India—it had better put itself on good terms with China, the protector of the world's masses. So far, the Indian government was making progress. China would examine India's overtures with care.

Desai's opening to China dovetailed with his constructiveness toward the Americans, who themselves were in the process of completing normalization toward Beijing. During the first half of 1978, Carter and Desai exchanged visits. A crowd of 300,000 greeted the U.S. president on his way into New Delhi from the airport. The throng brought to mind Eisenhower's 1959 tour and marked a definite change from any reception for American officials during the Gandhi years. After addressing an outdoor gathering of some fifty thousand, Carter spoke to a special session of the Indian parliament. The address was unmemorable but kindly and well received.

A minor flap occurred midway through the president's visit. In keeping with its general desire to limit nuclear arms, the Carter administration was pressing nonnuclear powers to adhere to the nonproliferation treaty. Congress was pressing even harder, calling for a cutoff of economic aid to countries not accepting international safeguards against the spread of nuclear weapons, including intrusive inspection. The issue proved a ticklish one in U.S.–Indian relations. Desai could not accept American dictation in the matter without jeopardizing his political future, especially since Gandhi had made the issue of nuclear sovereignty her own. But to contravene American law risked both American aid and the warming to Washington Desai desired.

Carter was willing to finesse the issue, at some political risk to himself. When India applied for a license to purchase American nuclear material, the Nuclear Regulatory Commission denied the application on grounds that India offered insufficient guarantees against diversion of the material. Carter, wishing to maintain the favorable momentum in U.S.–Indian relations and believing that the Desai government was negotiating in good faith on the matter, set aside the NRC ruling and authorized the sale as a once-only exception. At the same time, he urged Desai to come to terms quickly.

In New Delhi in January 1978, Carter was just about to begin a public speech when the issue came up with Secretary of State Cyrus Vance. Unknown to either man, the president's microphone had been turned on. What Carter meant as a confidential remark that he should send Desai a "cool, blunt letter" quickly became unconfidential.[4]

The accident produced red faces among the American entourage but little more. It did not upset Carter's meetings with Desai, nor did it derail a reciprocal visit by the prime minister to Washington in June 1978. On the latter occasion, Desai confirmed the progress that had been made in facilitating understanding between his country and the United States. Like Carter's journey to India, Desai's to the United States yielded little of substance, yet the two leaders agreed that their common fifteen months in office had witnessed a significant improvement in U.S.–Indian relations.

Gandhi, meanwhile, made the most of this improvement. The former prime minister asserted that Desai, under the label of nonalignment, was becoming a fellow traveler of the Americans, thereby inverting the argument long used by American opponents of friendly ties with India that Indian neutralism actually favored the Soviet Union. Had Desai kept his political house in order, Gandhi's charges of a double standard in foreign policy probably would have bounced off; no more often than in the United States—which is to say, rarely—have Indian elections turned on international issues. But almost as soon as the coalition that formed in opposition to Gandhi's autocratic rule brought her down, it began to disintegrate. Gandhi exploited the opening to stage a comeback, adding the charge of softness toward Washington to a variety of other complaints, the most telling involving the continued stagnation of the economy. While the government prepared to prosecute her for abuses during the period of emergency rule, she organized a new political party, the Congress–I (for Indira). The new party scored victories in state elections and returned Gandhi to parliament. When Desai responded by effecting her ejection from the legislature, a move followed by her arrest, fighting broke out between her supporters and the police.

Desai could not keep Gandhi in jail for long, and as 1979 began she pressed the attack more vigorously than ever. Lashing Desai for "weakness and incompetence"—precisely the charges conservatives in the United States were leveling against Carter—Gandhi raised a sufficient ruckus that Desai's coalition collapsed. Facing a vote of no confidence, the prime minister resigned in July.[5]

Desai's demise augured the end of the brief warming with the United States; it also set in motion what *Time* magazine's India correspondent described as "a round of political brokering that might have embarrassed a Tammany Hall ward heeler." The winning broker turned out to be Charan Singh, a seventy-six-year-old former ally of Desai and denouncer of Gandhi. As an early member of Desai's cabinet, Singh had lashed Gandhi verbally as a "fascist" and a "tyrant" and had declared that he would lash her physically as well if it lay in his power to do so. In addition to a wicked tongue, Singh possessed a consuming desire to climb the greasy pole to the top. "Every politician should have the ambition of becoming the Prime Minister," he said. Singh's ambition overcame his scruples, and when Desai slipped, Singh cut a deal with Gandhi. Congress–I's support in the parliament gave him just enough votes to grab the ring.

Those who had hoped to see India return to a semblance of democratic respectability took these developments hard. Subramaniam Swamy, a leading figure in Desai's Janata party, characterized the new prime minister as "a man possessed by his lust for office" and asserted that Singh had gone "on bended knee to eke out an ignoble axis with the discredited dictator." Jagjivan Ram, Desai's deputy prime minister, was rendered almost speechless. "The enormity of the action," Ram said, "is so ghastly that there are no adequate words to describe it." The editor of the New Delhi *Statesman* called a plague on the houses of everyone involved in the deal. "All the chief protagonists in the struggle for power are tainted men and women," the editor declared. "Their beliefs and philosophies, such as they are, are highly elastic, and few of them, if any, will refuse to sup with the devil to achieve or retain power."

Although Singh pledged to continue his opposition to "authoritarianism"— Indian shorthand for Gandhi's emergency rule—few observers expected him to make good on any such promise. Gandhi certainly did not. Asked whether Singh would govern according to her wishes, Gandhi said, "Yes, or he won't rule at all."[6]

Like Richard Nixon, whom she resembled in so many ways, Gandhi played hardball. By August, she had knocked Singh out of the box. The temporary prime minister's fall prompted the dissolution of parliament and the scheduling of new elections. In the campaign that ensued, Gandhi made the most of charges in a recent book about the CIA, published in the United States and more credible than many of the intelligence-exposé genre (Thomas Powers's *The Man Who Kept the Secrets*), to the effect that the CIA during the early 1970s had successfully planted an agent in the Indian cabinet. Since five of the fourteen members of that cabinet were taking an active part in the 1979 election campaign, the allegation provoked a furious spate of finger-pointing.

After considerable violence and slander, the Indian people spoke—and what they said was "Indira." By an overwhelming margin, Gandhi swept back into power. Immediately she demonstrated that her time in exile had changed her mind on domestic matters not a whit. She prorogued state assemblies controlled by the opposition, revived the law allowing the imprisonment without trial of political troublemakers, and filled the jails. Almost as quickly, she indicated that she would rectify Desai's errors in foreign policy, starting with his treatment of the United States.

THE AYATOLLAH'S RETURN, AND IVAN AMONG THE AFGHANS

Two sudden shifts in the winds blowing off the mountains to India's northwest facilitated Gandhi's desire to steer away from Washington. In January 1979, the Shah of Iran fled his capital. Twenty-six years earlier, he had done the same thing, only to regain his throne days later with the help of the CIA. This time, he had no such luck. Anti-Shah forces carried all before them. On 1 February, Ayatollah Ruhollah Khomeini, the exiled leader of

Iran's Islamic fundamentalist opposition—and a bitter critic of the United States, the "great Satan" of the West and the power behind the Shah—returned in triumph from Paris.

The revolution in Iran forced a rethinking of the United States' Asia policy analogous to that provoked by the communist revolution in China three decades before. Like China, Iran had gone from being a defender of Western interests to being a principal challenger of those interests. Furthermore, just as the communist victory in China had carried frightening ideological implications for countries nearby, so the ayatollah's triumph in Iran portended a tidal wave of Islamic fundamentalism that might overturn other pro-Western regimes in the Muslim world.

While the Carter administration was figuring out how to raise the dikes against this disaster—a question sharpened by the seizure of the American embassy in Tehran in November and the taking of more than seventy American hostages—equally ominous developments unfolded just to Iran's east, in Afghanistan. To those familiar with the history of the region, the Soviet invasion of Afghanistan should not have come as a great surprise. For more than a century, Afghanistan had marked the boundary between the Russian and British empires; during much of that time, British and Indian troops had fought a series of small but brutal wars in Afghanistan to keep the country out of Moscow's control. After 1945, Afghanistan had enjoyed a precarious neutrality between the Soviet and American alliance systems. In the mid-1950s, John Foster Dulles had considered sending military aid to Kabul, but when the Afghans declined to join the Baghdad pact and the Pakistanis objected, the Eisenhower administration had confined itself to economic aid.

Just as Pakistan feared India, Afghanistan feared Pakistan. And while Washington armed the Pakistanis, Moscow sent weapons to the Afghans. Afghanistan never dropped its official adherence to neutralism, but by the latter half of the 1970s, the Russians enjoyed a cozy relationship with the Afghan government of Prime Minister and President General Mohammad Daoud Khan. Daoud, however, had enemies, various of whom tried to overthrow him. In April 1978, they succeeded—slaughtering the entire Daoud family and those of Daoud's principal assistants for emphasis. Fortunately for Moscow, the new men in Kabul, Nur Mohammad Taraki and Hafizullah Amin, were not opposed to cooperation with communists. Indeed, although neither knew much Russian, they spoke modern Marxist, promising land to peasants, relief for debtors, shelter for homeless, and elimination of all "rotten customs" from Afghan law.[7]

Yet those "rotten customs" included many cherished by devout Muslims. Taking courage from the success of followers of the prophet in Iran, Afghan Muslims mounted an insurgency against the Taraki government. Amid the fighting, the American ambassador was kidnapped and murdered. In September 1979, Taraki himself went down, although his death was directly attributable not to the rebels but to Amin, who sought power for himself.

Ever flexible in its choice of collaborators, the Kremlin congratulated "Comrade Hafizullah Amin" on his "election" and expressed hope that relations between the Soviet Union and Afghanistan would continue on the basis of "friendship, good neighborliness, and cooperation."

When Amin failed to stem the insurgency, Moscow decided to lend direct assistance. On 25 December, a massive airlift began, pouring Soviet troops into Afghanistan; tanks and ground support followed in short order. Although Moscow claimed that Amin had requested the intervention, he became one of the first casualties. His replacement, Babrak Karmal, soon discovered that Amin was not what he had seemed. Rather, he was an "oppressor and dictator," a "murderer," a "bloodthirsty agent of American imperialism," and a "charlatan of history"—whatever that was. *Pravda* reported the verdict as 1980 began: "Overthrown by a wave of popular indignation, the treacherous scoundrel was tried and shot."[8]

DEAR ZIA

The Taraki–Amin coup, which installed an avowedly Marxist government in Kabul, had elicited relatively little reaction from Washington. In the aftermath of Vietnam, the Carter administration had made a point of not letting itself get carried away by mere fact of the leftist character of a foreign government. Besides, Afghanistan was far away, and it was insulated from sensitive regions like the Persian Gulf by a U.S. ally, Iran. But the collapse of the Shah's government and the rise of Khomeini forced Washington to pay greater attention to Afghanistan, and the Soviet invasion in December 1979 provoked a sharp reaction. With awkward honesty, Carter conceded that he had underestimated the malevolence of the Russians. The president withdrew the SALT II treaty from Senate consideration; he embargoed grain exports to the Soviet Union; he canceled American participation in the 1980 Olympic games in Moscow; and, wrapping himself in the mantle of his cold war predecessors, he announced what came to be called the "Carter doctrine": a declaration that "an attempt by any outside force to gain control of the Persian Gulf region will be regarded as an assault on the vital interests of the United States of America, and such an assault will be repelled by any means necessary, including military force." To put teeth into this threat, he ordered the creation of a Rapid Deployment Force, with supplies cached on Diego Garcia.[9]

The Soviet invasion of Afghanistan also revived American interest in Pakistan. Until now Carter had not attempted to conceal his distaste for the current ruler in Islamabad, Mohammed Zia ul-Haq, who had seized power in a military coup in 1977. Carter, who took human rights more seriously than any American president since Wilson, disliked Zia's generally dictatorial ways; he considered Zia especially odious after the Pakistani strongman executed his predecessor, Z. A. Bhutto—not in the heat of the takeover but a full two years later. Washington also distrusted Zia on the nuclear weapons score. Claiming a need to defend itself against India's bomb, Islamabad refused to pay even lip service to nuclear nonproliferation. While Carter waived the American ban on aid to noncomplying India, the president suspended assistance to Pakistan. A seizure of the American embassy in Islamabad, triggered by rumors of American involvement in an attack on the Grand Mosque in Mecca, and coming just days after the storming of the embassy in Tehran, added to tension all around. The Pakistani government lifted the siege in relatively brief time, but much of the strain persisted.

Moscow's move into Afghanistan changed Washington's attitude. Overnight, the Carter administration ceased harping on Zia's deficiencies in the realm of civil liberties and appreciated him for the staunch anticommunist he indisputably was. Carter called Zia on the telephone to say all was forgotten. A short while later, he offered Pakistan $400 million in military aid. When Zia sniffed at the offer as "peanuts," the president sent National Security Adviser Zbigniew Brzezinski and Deputy Secretary of State Warren Christopher to Pakistan. There Brzezinski, a hard-liner whose stock in the administration rose with each threatening step the Soviets took, played the determined cold warrior, picking up an assault rifle and aiming it in the direction of Kabul and Moscow. But Zia realized that events were moving in his direction, and he refused to accept Washington's initial bid for cooperation. He did, however, agree to travel to the United States, where Carter declared himself "personally honored" by the visit. The American president, submerging all shame in a desire to bring Zia aboard, went on to say the Pakistani leader's "knowledge of the sensitivities and ideals of America make him particularly dear to us."[10]

"Dear" was right. Over the course of the next several years, Zia received billions of dollars of American economic and military assistance. To some degree, history was repeating itself. As in 1954, the United States chose to support Pakistan in the hope the Pakistanis would help contain the Soviets. This time a new twist was added, for Pakistan became the funnel through which Washington supplied aid to the Afghan resistance, the *mujahideen*. Recognizing his country's importance to the United States, Zia set his price high. He got it: not only American weapons and money but American acquiescence in Pakistan's continued pursuit of nuclear weapons.

THE REVISED STANDARD VERSION

That India was put off by Carter's cultivation of Pakistan startled no one. That Gandhi, as suspicious of Washington as ever, denounced it was equally predictable. And that her denunciation provoked an anti-Indian backlash in the United States was fully in line with precedent.

Many Americans likened the Soviet assault on Afghanistan to the Kremlin's invasion of Hungary in 1956, and when Gandhi responded as slowly as her father had they revived earlier claims that India used one standard for measuring the transgressions of the West and another for the sins of the Soviets. While Indian officials condemned the resumption of American military aid to Pakistan, they refused to join the majority of the international community in labeling the Russians aggressors in Afghanistan. Gandhi blandly urged the withdrawal of all foreign troops from the South Asia region, but she insisted that quiet diplomacy rather than public name-calling afforded the greatest hope of accomplishing this result. For the record, New Delhi accepted the Russians' claim that in entering Afghanistan, they were simply responding to an invitation from the Afghan government.

Western observers noted that, as usual, finely calculated considerations of personal and national self-interest lay behind Gandhi's actions. A writer in *Forbes* magazine suggested that by following Moscow's line, New Delhi hoped to keep the large and vocal Indian Communist party under control. A foreign diplomat quoted in *U.S. News & World Report* contended that Gandhi once again was using the Soviet Union as a strategic counterweight to Pakistan. "Gandhi clearly worries about superpower competition moving closer to India, and would like to see the Soviets out of Afghanistan on that score," this unnamed source asserted. "But it's just as obvious she isn't nearly as concerned about the actual presence of Russian troops there as she is about potential American or Chinese military aid to Pakistan." To offset the aid to Islamabad, Gandhi in May 1980 agreed to a new weapons deal with Moscow, which provided for the sale on highly concessionary terms of $1.6 billion in East bloc arms.[11]

India's drift toward Moscow encouraged further American leaning toward Pakistan. The replacement of Jimmy Carter by Ronald Reagan changed Washington's international policies less than Republicans liked to think; by Carter's last year in office, the Democratic president had essentially adopted the present-dangerists' agenda. Regarding South Asia, Reagan quickly picked up where Carter left off. Shortly after entering the White House, Reagan announced a large new package of assistance for Islamabad: a five-year program totaling $3.2 billion. The centerpiece of the arrangement was a forty-plane group of F-16s, among the most advanced aircraft in the world.

The F-16s in particular triggered a fresh round of criticism from India. As usual, Indians complained that Pakistan had no intention of using its American weaponry against communists; Islamabad would target India instead. "Those planes will not be going on deep penetration raids in the Soviet Union or Afghanistan," a close adviser to Gandhi predicted. "They will be pointed toward India." The prime minister herself described the F-16s as "a generation ahead of anything operating with other air forces of the area" and declared, "We are against the collection of highly sophisticated arms in the region." She said she worried that the American shipments were "creating a situation where everybody is drifting toward war."[12]

The fact that these charges were doubtless correct did not deter Gandhi's government from adding baseless allegations to its indictment of the United States. New Delhi refused to accept the assignment of longtime foreign service officer George Griffin to the American embassy, on grounds that he was a CIA operative. U.S. officials blamed Soviet disinformation specialists for originating the ruckus; one observer characterized it as "a masterful campaign." Washington tit-tatted by rejecting an Indian envoy.[13]

Double standards flourished in this atmosphere of distrust. Reagan's ambassador to the United States, Jeane Kirkpatrick, closed a brief visit to New Delhi by pronouncing U.S.–Indian relations "estranged." Kirkpatrick had made her reputation and gained her job by positing a crucial distinction between "authoritarian" regimes and "totalitarian" ones. The former, she claimed, might in time be persuaded to reform; the latter were irredeemable. Indians were not alone in having difficulty seeing the difference, especially when the authoritarian camp conveniently included most of the governments the United States favored at the moment, while the totalitarian group comprised those on the unfavored list. That the Reagan administration did not apply the formula to China occasioned additional snide comment. The "authoritarian" labeling of Pakistan, a country whose government only a decade earlier had engaged in genocide against its own people, particularly annoyed Indians, who were more convinced than ever of U.S. hypocrisy.[14]

The Reagan administration further antagonized Indians by an unprecedented effort to apply conservative capitalist theories of economic development to India. Convinced that free enterprise held the solution to most of humanity's ills, Reagan frowned on India's socialistic policies. The White House attempted to export its supply-side gospel, contending that if Gandhi granted greater incentives to private entrepreneurs and made India more attractive to foreign investors the country would grow its way out of the need for aid from abroad. Washington supplemented exhortation with extortion: it withheld support from a proposal by the International Monetary Fund to lend India $5.7 billion. Although the IMF went forward with the plan over the Reagan administration's objection, Indians interpreted the affair with about as much charity as the United States showed them. Previously, Washington had tried to punish India for not toeing its line in foreign matters; now it was claiming the right to dictate India's internal policies. As Nehru had said in 1956, "There is no end to their arrogance!"[15]

In the face of this provocation, Gandhi demonstrated what for her was remarkable restraint. (Her reasons would become clear presently.) She patiently pointed out that Americans, as often before, were reading Indian history in terms of their own. She explained that the conditions under which the United States had industrialized in the nineteenth century differed crucially from those India confronted in the twentieth. "You must remember the circumstances here—that we had several delayed revolutions at the same time," she told an American interviewer. "You had your Industrial Revolution; as a result of that came political consciousness. Then you had equal rights and human rights, rights of labor and so on. And very much later came the rights of women. But we have got this all together and in some ways the other way around. I mean, we started with political consciousness and the consciousness of rights and privileges without the wherewithal to meet the demands. The workers said we want this and the peasants said we want this, and we just had nothing to give them." She added, "It is difficult for the affluent countries to understand the pressures we have from our own people." Methods that might work in an advanced country like the United States would fail in India: "We are told by the U.S., for instance, that we should depend more on private commercial borrowing, but that is just not possible. There are limits to it. And where there are gaps, the state has to step in."[16]

The Soviets, of course, had no philosophical problems with India's emphasis on government intervention in the economy. Beyond the $1.6 billion arms deal announced in 1980, Moscow continued to provide vital support to Indian development. The Russians supplied some fifteen million barrels of crude oil to India under a barter agreement that saved the Indian government scarce hard currency. They continued to sponsor construction of steel mills and electrical generating facilities. Trade between the two countries totaled more than $2 billion annually.

Unsentimental though Gandhi was, she and her associates appreciated the fact that Moscow had been a reliable partner for almost thirty years—far more reliable, certainly, than Washington. One Indian official put the matter simply: "The Soviet Union has been a good friend of our country in times of crisis both abroad and at home."[17]

Yet the Indian government recognized the limits of friendship. "Look, the big powers are all out for their own interests," Gandhi told an American correspondent. "We are not under an illusion that anybody is going out of his way to help us." By the first months of 1982, she was beginning to perceive the limits of her tilt to the Soviet Union. Although New Delhi continued to refrain from public denunciation of the Russian presence in Afghanistan, the war there occasioned considerable worry. It provided Pakistan the justification Islamabad needed to acquire the latest U.S. military equipment. The plight of Afghan Muslims stirred passions among Muslims in India, whose 12 percent of the population often supplied the swing vote in close electoral contests. With most of the world firmly on record as condemning the Soviet invasion of Afghanistan, India perceived the risks of international isolation, especially from the nonaligned world, whose good opinion New Delhi courted. Finally, India's economic planners were agitating for access to kinds of technology that Moscow could not supply.[18]

Consequently, Gandhi gradually broadened her diplomatic base. She supplemented India's Soviet weapons with a deal to purchase $1.3 billion worth of French Mirage jets. She resumed talks with China and hosted a visit by Foreign Minister Huang Hua to New Delhi, at the end of which the two sides pledged to work to restore normal relations. She lowered her guard against Pakistan far enough to allow the signing of a five-year agreement establishing a joint commission to facilitate improved ties between the two countries. And she began to reach out to the United States.

During the summer of 1982, Gandhi journeyed to Washington—the first time she had seen the United States since just before the December war of 1971. "We think we should be friends and want to do everything we can for friendship," she said, while adding significantly, "Of course, we cannot jettison our basic policies." The prime minister naturally denied that her trip to America signified a turning away from Moscow: "I do not think there has been any cooling of relations. Our policy has always been based on certain principles and what we consider our national interest. So it cannot swing from side to side. We believe that we should have friendship with all countries and that friendship with one country or group of countries should not come in the way of friendship with all the others." Questioned about India's position on Afghanistan, Gandhi said, "We have made our stand very clear. We are opposed to a foreign presence, whether in the shape of troops or any other type of interference." India had expressed its dislike of the Russian occupation, "but we did not join in the condemnation because we felt that it would not improve the situation. We have said from the beginning that there has to be a political solution in Afghanistan, a negotiated settlement."[19]

Gandhi's American trip turned out well. The prime minister declared that her objective had been to "clear up misconceptions" that clouded the U.S.–Indian relationship and said that her discussions with President Reagan had proved "very good." The two leaders promised to work to enhance economic, cultural, and scientific cooperation between their countries. They resolved to rectify difficulties regarding India's nuclear program. At the administration's initiative, Congress enacted a bill opening the way for the sale of $1 billion of American weapons to India.[20]

During the next several months, the United States and India built upon this propitious foundation. Despite the publication of a book by American author Seymour Hersh (*The Price of Power*) charging that former prime minister Morarji Desai had been on the CIA's payroll during the Johnson and Nixon years—a charge the eighty-seven-year-old Desai vigorously contested, to the point of gaining a court order requiring booksellers to include a statement that they had no reason to believe Hersh's allegation—Washington and New Delhi drew closer together. (That Hersh's claim involved a political enemy of Gandhi, rather than an ally, doubtless made matters easier than they might otherwise have been.) Negotiations proceeded on further sales of American weapons. When Secretary of State George Shultz traveled to India in July 1983 to endorse a major contract, he also announced that the United States was prepared to supply India with sophisticated nuclear reactor components.

DYNASTY: PART 3

To some degree Gandhi's efforts to improve India's standing in the world reflected concern over increasing troubles at home. From the middle of 1982 until the end of 1984, India was rocked by political and communal violence that at times approached civil war. Fighting focused on two areas, Assam in the northeast and Punjab in the northwest, although it was not confined to them.

The troubles in Assam essentially continued those initiated in 1947 with the partition of the subcontinent and exacerbated by the creation of Bangladesh in 1971. Hindu residents of Assam were having a hard time getting along with Muslim migrants from Bangladesh, confirming the fears Gandhi had expressed to the Nixon administration before the December war. Tensions reached the snapping point at the beginning of 1983, when Hindu Assamese staged a protest to prevent the immigrants from voting in state elections. The demonstration quickly took a violent turn. One candidate was assassinated; a bomb wounded more than a dozen people at a campaign rally. Hoping to quell the disturbances before they escalated, Gandhi poured in army troops and police. But seventy thousand of the former and twenty thousand of the latter failed to stanch the bloodletting. By mid-February 1983, the death toll reached the hundreds; following a Hindu massacre of Muslims in the area of Bhagduba Habi at the end of the month, the body count reached four figures.

While the fighting continued in Assam, even more serious trouble erupted on the other side of the country in Punjab. There, Sikh nationalists had mounted a campaign for the creation of an independent homeland. Members of the above-ground portion of the Sikh movement undertook various forms of protest, including a blockade of roads, in which twenty persons were killed when police forcibly removed the protesters. At the same time, the Sikh underground launched a terrorist offensive. In April, a Sikh youth gunned down a top-level police officer outside the Golden Temple in Amritsar, killing a child in the process. In February 1984, Sikh riflemen battled police from inside the Golden Temple, prompting New Delhi (which several months before had suspended local government in Punjab) to issue an order to law enforcement officials to shoot rioters on sight. At the beginning of April, terrorists killed a member of parliament; in May, they murdered the editor of a leading Hindu newspaper. In June, radical separatists holed up in the Golden Temple. After a protracted standoff, army troops stormed the temple, adding hundreds—some said thousands—to the death figure.

The killing and capture of several Sikh leaders did little to calm the situation. Indeed, the violence spread, as Sikhs throughout India demonstrated their outrage at the desecration of their holiest shrine. A leading army commander was assassinated in Bihar, after which six hundred Sikh troops mutinied and fought a fierce skirmish with loyalists. Some Sikh members of the Indian government resigned in protest—or out of fear at what might happen to them if they didn't. In July, Sikh hijackers ordered an Indian Airlines jet to Pakistan, where they eventually released the crew and the 255 passengers but received asylum from President Zia—who reminded New Delhi that India had not seen fit to sign an extradition treaty with Islamabad.

Expectedly, the United States came in for blame in all this. At the beginning of July, six weeks after a visit by Vice President George Bush—formerly head of the CIA—one hundred demonstrators marched on the American embassy in New Delhi charging that American machinations lay behind the Sikh rebellion.

The violence reached a climax in October, when Sikh members of Gandhi's personal bodyguard assassinated the prime minister at her home. News of this killing touched off a wave of communal mayhem unmatched since 1947. Throughout the country, mobs of Hindus assaulted Sikh communities. Five hundred persons were killed in New Delhi alone; the bloodshed was all the more visible as dignitaries from around the world gathered to pay their final respects to Gandhi. In a grim replay of thirty-seven years earlier, trains arrived from the countryside bearing the bodies of those hacked and beaten to death as they attempted to flee to the relative safety of the capital.

From the standpoint of Indian politics, the pressing question of the hour was: After Gandhi, who? The immediate answer, reflecting both the needs of the moment and the four-decade domination of Indian political life by the Nehru family, was: Gandhi—Rajiv Gandhi, the slain prime minister's son and the grandson of Nehru.

Rajiv embarked on a political career in much the same fashion as the standard-bearer of America's most famous modern dynasty, John Kennedy. Just as young Jack had been pushed by his father into politics following the untimely death of a favored brother, so Rajiv had been plucked from peace and obscurity as an Indian Airlines pilot when mother Indira's first hope for immortality, Sanjay, died in a 1980 plane crash. Although subsequently groomed by Indira and promoted to prominence in Indian politics, Rajiv remained an enigma at the time of her death. Considering the anarchic state of Indian society at the time—after a lull, as Sikhs hunkered down against the storm of Hindu outrage, the terrorist activity recommenced—few observers looked to India's future with anything approaching confidence.

Fortunately for Rajiv, despite the chaos that reigned across the Indian countryside, Indira departed the scene with India's foreign affairs in unusually good order. Secretary of State Shultz competed with Soviet prime minister Nikolai Tikhonov to offer condolences at the funeral. Chinese premier Zhao Ziyang extended best wishes and spoke his country's continued desire for improved relations. Even President Zia declared Pakistan's readiness to provide Rajiv full support in fostering an atmosphere of subcontinental trust.

Demonstrating their desire for stability and continuity amid the domestic disintegration, the Indian masses ratified Rajiv's accession in December 1984.

On his coattails, the Congress party rolled up winning margins not witnessed since the days of Rajiv's grandfather.

THE MAHATMA LIVES

Like his mother, Rajiv benefited from mistaken identity at times; persons who were aware only that he came from some important family placed him in the lineage of Mohandas Gandhi. Two generations after his murder, the mahatma had become the closest thing India had to a patron saint. Consequently, it was with intense concern that Indians viewed a highly publicized effort by Western moviemakers to capture the life of the great soul on film.

Gandhi, directed by Britain's Richard Attenborough, opened to tremendous acclaim in the United States. It triumphed at the Academy Awards, winning prizes for best picture, best director, best actor (Ben Kingsley as Gandhi), and best cinematography. Politically, however, the film provoked as much controversy as its namesake had forty years before. Liberal friends of India saw and heard the apostle of nonviolence speaking from beyond the grave. "Let there be no doubt," former ambassador John Kenneth Galbraith wrote, "this is a wonderful achievement. . . . The Gandhi story is told, if not in all its length and complexity, at least with an honest commitment to important detail, subtlety and contradiction." Even journals that had registered skepticism toward the real mahatma found the silver screen's version compelling. Newsweek ran a cover story on the film; the magazine's reviewer recommended the picture as "fresh, electric and moving . . . a popular movie in the best sense. It deals with a subject of great importance and it does so with a mixture of high intelligence and immediate emotional impact. It orchestrates the events of a life that changed history."[21]

Critics, on the other hand, objected that the Gandhi Ben Kingsley portrayed bore little resemblance to the flesh-and-blood individual. Richard Grenier, film reviewer for the neoconservative Commentary, the journal epitomizing the certitude and self-righteousness that lay beneath the revival of the cold war in the United States, went to the greatest lengths to challenge the movie, its hero, and the approach to international affairs he represented. The movie did indeed tread lightly on certain topics that its New Delhi backers might find objectionable (although many in India thought Attenborough had let the British off too easily). But Grenier went out of his way to be nasty. He described the picture as "a pure pacifist film and a pious fraud from one end to the other," as "a large, pious, historical morality tale centered on a saintly, sanitized Mahatma Gandhi cleansed of anything too embarrassingly Hindu" and as a "paid political advertisement for the government of India." (New Delhi had in fact underwritten part of the cost of production.) Selecting his evidence as carefully as Katherine Mayo had done six decades earlier in writing Mother India, Grenier dwelt on Gandhi's strange and sometimes distasteful—to Americans, at any rate—habits, particularly his daily administration of enemas and his general concern with excretory functions. (Nor could Grenier resist retelling the irrelevant story that Krishna Menon until his death made a practice of drinking his own urine.) As for Gandhi's philosophy and understanding of the world, Grenier trashed them thoroughly. "Throughout his entire life," Grenier wrote, "Gandhi displayed the most spectacular inability to understand or even really take in people unlike himself." Grenier detailed what he called Gandhi's "monstrous behavior" toward his own family; he castigated Gandhi for alleged insensitivity to the plight of peoples of color in countries other than India; and he ridiculed what he considered the mahatma's indifference to the reality of the fascist threat during World War II. "Here then is your leader, O followers of Gandhi: a man who thought Hitler's heart would be melted by an appeal to forget race, color, and creed, and who was sure the Japanese would be hurt if they sensed themselves unwanted."[22]

Like the Mayo book, Grenier's article on Gandhi provoked a storm of protest. *Commentary* received letters denouncing Grenier's "scurrilous" and "disgraceful" treatment of the mahatma and his "venomous outpourings against Hinduism." One correspondent asserted that "he insults the faith of half-a-billion people. His warped grasp of Hinduism is reminiscent of Adolf Hitler's musings on Judaism." An Indian living in Canada wrote that he read Grenier's piece with "disbelief, shock, and dismay." Grenier, the writer continued, had "misrepresented, maligned, and abused a great man, a great religion, and a magnificent civilization." Grenier's article also inspired counterarticles and a running debate on television and radio talk shows.[23]

Perhaps the furor the movie aroused prompted some in the United States to learn more about the historical Gandhi and the movement he led; certainly it demonstrated that millions of Americans still dealt in stereotypes regarding India, whether of the Richard Attenborough–Ben Kingsley or the Katherine Mayo–Richard Grenier variety. For sixty years, India had periodically captured America's attention, but the reality of the country and its people remained as elusive as ever.

BHOPAL DIES

The shouting over *Gandhi* had hardly faded when another event—this a great tragedy—demonstrated that India's perceptions of the United States suffered from the same tendency to oversimplification. At the end of 1984, in the central Indian city of Bhopal, a deadly gas (methyl isocyanate) leaked from an American-owned chemical plant and spread through heavily populated neighborhoods. Within a short time, more than 2,500 persons died (the toll eventually rose to 3,500), many in the most horrible fashion, and some 200,000 suffered permanent damage to eyes, brains, kidneys, livers, and reproductive systems.

The Bhopal disaster, the worst industrial accident in history, produced an explosion of outrage across India. When Warren Anderson, the chairman of the operating Union Carbide corporation, flew to Bhopal to survey the damage and offer relief support, local officials arrested him on charges of criminal negligence. The arrest was widely applauded. "Guilty in Bhopal" screamed one headline; another, likening the disaster to a nuclear holocaust, dubbed the affair "Bhoposhima."[24]

In the Indian parliament, Union Carbide became a symbol of American dollar imperialism. Critics made much of the fact that the multinational corporation also produced methyl isocyanate at a factory in the United States but that the manufacturing process there had more stringent safeguards against leaks. "Union Carbide is a multinational company," one exercised legislator pronounced, "and as you know, all the multinational companies have the same attitude—a double standard for working in developed countries and developing countries." Members alternated between images of nuclear war and Nazi death camps. A "chemical holocaust" was how one speaker described the scene; he demanded that the American company be held to strict accountability. "Genocide" was alleged, and all parties urged tough treatment for Anderson, the "big boss of Union Carbide." One M.P. summarized a prevalent view when he declared that "by arresting him, a warning has been given to these multinationals that they will not be allowed to go scotfree if they participate in the death and destruction of our people in this country."[25]

Class action and other suits were brought against Union Carbide; claims totaled in the billions. Adjudication clogged Indian courts for years. Indian officials asserted that the disaster had resulted from Carbide's negligence; the company claimed sabotage by a disgruntled Indian employee. At one point, the Bhopal district court became so frustrated at Carbide's delaying tactics that it issued a warrant for Anderson's arrest on charges of homicide. In February 1989, a settlement was finally reached. The Indian supreme court agreed to drop criminal charges against Anderson and Union Carbide in exchange for a payment by the corporation of $470 million in damages.

But the decision did not erase the bitterness. A representative of a victims' group stated that the Indian government had capitulated to American capitalism. "This settlement is a victory of Union Carbide," he said.[26]

THE EVIL EMPIRE STRIKES BACK

A few months after the Bhopal disaster, the most important event in international affairs of the mid-1980s occurred. Following Leonid Brezhnev's death in 1982, primacy in the Kremlin briefly passed to a pair of successors before coming to rest in 1985 with the youthful—by Moscow's standards—Mikhail Gorbachev. Almost at once, Gorbachev began turning Soviet society upside down. His calls for *glasnost* (openness) and *perestroika* (restructuring) jolted bureaucrats out of their stupor and led to fundamental changes in Russian life.

Gorbachev then turned to the world at large. Foreigners accustomed to the geological pace of diplomacy under Brezhnev found this man, who made decisions fast and acted on them faster, more than a little disconcerting. Further, in sharp contrast to the gray, rumpled party bosses who had preceded him, Gorbachev knew how to manipulate the Western media. Smooth yet opinionated, facile in debate without appearing slippery—and accompanied by a wife who rewrote the briefing book on Soviet first ladies—he generated what headline writers called "Gorbomania" wherever he visited in the democratic countries.

In the process, Gorbachev destroyed the basis for much of the foreign policy of the Reagan administration. During his initial term in office, the Republican president had delighted in denouncing what he called the "evil empire." As long as Brezhnev, Chernenko, and Andropov (the last once chief of the dread KGB) directed Moscow's affairs, Reagan could make the charge stick, at least in the minds of most American voters. But the emergence of Gorbachev forced the president to find a different script. Not only did the new captain of the Kremlin give every indication of moving toward the sorts of domestic reforms Americans had demanded for years, he adopted an external policy designed to appeal to America's European allies. He accepted Washington's proposals for the removal of intermediate-range nuclear missiles stationed in Europe. He called for deep cuts in strategic nuclear forces. He announced the unilateral demobilization of 500,000 troops and the removal of 10,000 tanks and 800 airplanes from the central European theater.

Most portentously for South Asian affairs, Gorbachev withdrew Soviet troops from Afghanistan. The Russian evacuation, pledged in April 1988 at a conference of representatives of the Soviet Union, Afghanistan, Pakistan, and the United States and completed in early 1989, opened the way to a general easing of tension in the region. Pakistan, realizing that its days of carte blanche with the Americans were drawing to an end, sought friendlier ties with India. The death of Zia in a plane crash—thought but not proved to be sabotage—led to the election of Bhutto's daughter Benazir and facilitated the trend; in December 1988, Rajiv Gandhi traveled to Islamabad to exchange good wishes with Pakistan's new prime minister. At about the same time, Gandhi visited China, to which no Indian head of government had journeyed since his grandfather had called on Mao Zedong in 1954 in the salad days of *panchsheel*. "Between us we represent a third of humanity," Gandhi told his hosts in Beijing's Great Hall of the People, "and there is much we can do together."[27]

What "much" entailed remained to be seen—not only in relations between India and China but in relations between India and the United States. As recently as January 1988, Reagan had exempted Pakistan from congressional strictures on aid to countries not committed to nuclear nonproliferation. The decision had created the usual annoyance in India. By the middle of 1989, Pakistan mattered less to the United States, and if the past was any guide, this augured well for the U.S.-Indian relationship.

The final year of the 1980s brought a new leader to each country. In January George Bush replaced Reagan, to no one's surprise. In November Gandhi's Congress party somewhat less expectedly fell victim to corruption charges and other complaints, resulting in the accession of V. P. Singh as prime minister. Meanwhile glasnost jumped Soviet borders in Eastern Europe, signaling an imminent end to the cold war. Prospects for converting the cold peace between India and the United States into something warmer and more constructive were as hopeful as they had ever been.

Notes

1. Raymond L. Garthoff, *Detente and Confrontation: American–Soviet Relations from Nixon to Reagan* (Washington: Brookings, 1985), 548–51, 564.

2. *U.S. News & World Report,* 24 January 1977.

3. K. P. Misra, ed., *Janata's Foreign Policy* (New Delhi: Vikas, 1979), 28–30.

4. Zbigniew Brzezinski, *Power and Principle: Memoirs of the National Security Adviser, 1977–1981* (New York: Farrar, Straus & Giroux, 1983), 133.

5. *New York Times,* 17 May 1979.

6. *Time,* 6 August 1979.

7. Wolpert, *Roots of Confrontation,* 166–67.

8. Adam B. Ulam, *Dangerous Relations: The Soviet Union in World Politics, 1970–1982* (New York: Oxford University Press, 1983), 256–57.

9. *Public Papers of the Presidents of the United States: Jimmy Carter, 1980–81* (Washington: U.S. Government Printing Office, 1981), vol. 1, 197.

10. Smith, *Morality, Reason, and Power,* 232.

11. *Forbes,* 12 March 1984; *U.S. News & World Report,* 16 June 1980.

12. *U.S. News & World Report,* 21 December 1981.

13. Ibid.

14. Ibid.; *New York Times,* 27 August 1981.

15. Heikal, *Cutting the Lion's Tail,* 116.

16. *Forbes,* 12 March 1984; *Time,* 2 August 1982.

17. *U.S. News & World Report,* 2 August 1982.

18. *U.S. News & World Report,* 15 February 1982.

19. *Time,* 2 August 1982.

20. *New York Times,* 31 July 1982.

21. Lloyd I. Rudolph, "The *Gandhi* Controversy in America," in Robert M. Crunden, ed., *Traffic of Ideas Between India and America* (Delhi: Chanakya, 1985), 153–54.

22. *Commentary,* March and June 1983.

23. Ibid., July 1983.

24. *Indian Express,* 18 and 19 April 1985.

25. *Lok Sabha Debates,* 8th series, vol. 1, no. 5 (21 January 1985), cols. 221ff.

26. *New York Times,* 15 February 1989.

27. *Economist,* 24 December 1988.

CONCLUSION

AMBIENCE COUNTS

At one level, U.S.–Indian relations have been unexceptionable during the four decades since Indian independence. The two countries have not warred against each other. They have never broken diplomatic ties. Economic disputes have been slight. Such difficulties as have developed over the years have usually been in the realm of atmospherics rather than of bedrock interests, and they have reflected little more than differences that might develop between any two strong-minded parties. Considering the significantly greater troubles that have marked American relations with the other major countries with which it has not been allied, namely the Soviet Union and China, this is not a bad record.

Yet the relationship has yielded considerably less fruit than it might have. Talleyrand (and Palmerston, and a variety of others) remarked that countries do not have friends, only interests. A country whose government takes such an attitude will certainly have few of the former; it will also hazard the latter. The argument from narrow interest underestimates the creative possibilities of diplomacy. States are not individuals, and friendship between countries is not the same as friendship between persons. But neither are states billiard balls. Their affairs are managed by people who bring to their tasks the idiosyncracies and follies that afflict all members of the human race. When the countries in question are mass democracies, whose leaders answer to constituents numbering in the tens and hundreds of millions, the human factor is much magnified. It mattered greatly that Indians distrusted the U.S. government and thought Americans unable to appreciate India's point of view. A high-level Indian defense official once lectured an American visitor:

The whole military problem of India is your fault: if in 1953 you hadn't armed Pakistan there would have been no problem. Now see what has happened. You shouldn't help them. Pakistan is like a prostitute that gives herself to everyone. It is easy to be unchaste, but difficult to be chaste, like India, which has no plans to invade Pakistan, to occupy it. Our non-alignment is based on sincere motives, a genuine love for peace. It is because we are essentially a Hindu society. But they are guided by hatred of us, and here you are supporting them. Why?

American officials knew why—because Pakistan cooperated with America's global plans, while India did not—yet Washington's explanations hardly registered in New Delhi or among the Indian people at large. The explanations certainly did not convince.[1]

Misunderstanding and failure of appreciation plagued both countries. Indians judged Americans guilty of betraying the principles of the Atlantic Charter; Americans accused the Congress party of attempted sabotage of the Allied war effort in 1942; Nehru believed the United States an obstacle to the advancement of human civilization; Americans despised Krishna Menon and reckoned him a front man for the Chinese Communists; Lyndon Johnson could not tolerate India's criticism of his handling of the war in Vietnam; Nixon and Indira Gandhi detested each other and saw in each other each's own worst traits; Indians deemed Washington complicit in genocide in Bangladesh; Americans charged New Delhi with countenancing the same crime in Afghanistan and with employing a double standard in evaluating the actions of East and West; Indians thought Americans applied a double standard of industrial safety that resulted in the deaths of thousands at Bhopal.

The emotions that clouded the conduct of affairs between the United States and India did not lead to a collapse of relations. The purposes that bound the countries together—the United States' desire to promote India as a strategic and ideological counterweight to Communist China, and India's hope for U.S. aid to offset excessive dependence on the Soviet Union, to cite two prominent objectives—prevented complete alienation. As much as each country annoyed the other, neither could afford to write the other off.

But the irritations that pervaded the relationship prevented each from achieving more than its minimal aims. Both countries desired the expansion of the area of democracy. Both sought the lessening of threats to peace. Both looked to economic development as a means of diminishing tensions within countries and across borders. That the United States pursued these goals through alliances and by a capitalistic form of domestic organization, while India preferred the path of nonalignment and a larger economic role for the state, did not require that persons in each country read sinister designs into the actions of the other. But the temptation existed, and too often individuals on both sides succumbed.

Why were tolerance and goodwill in such short supply? The dearth resulted partly from the general fear that characterized the age. After two cataclysmic wars in hardly a generation, humanity had reason to be fearful that another would follow; after the invention of atomic weapons, it had cause to worry that the next war would be the last. Americans, by underestimating the difficulties the communist countries faced at home, doubtless overestimated the danger communism posed to the United States and to the world Americans desired. But the danger did exist, as witnessed by communists' success in capturing control of Eastern Europe, of China, of North Korea, and eventually of Vietnam. And Americans had it on good authority—the communists themselves—that the communists considered liberal capitalism irreconcilable with the teachings of Marx and Lenin and the practices of Stalin and Mao. Fear often begets distrust; in the era of the cold war, it certainly did. And distrust reproduces itself. Secretary of War Henry Stimson once remarked, "The chief lesson I have learned in a long life is that the only way to make a man trustworthy is to trust him; and the surest way to make him untrustworthy is to distrust him and show your distrust." Stimson's warning applied with full force to the U.S.–Indian relationship. Americans interpreted Indian actions through the veil of their fear of the Soviet Union and China. Fearing, they distrusted. Distrusting, they helped make India untrustworthy, in American eyes, by encouraging actions on India's part that seemed calculated to frustrate U.S. objectives. The circle closed as India's own fears—of Pakistan, of continuing Western intervention in Asia, of American trigger-happiness, of national disintegration in the face of continuing social strain—led Indians to distrust the United States. Indian distrust inclined Washington to actions, like the arming of Pakistan, that made the United States appear untrustworthy to Indians.[2]

The democratic character of the polities of the United States and India exacerbated the distrust. Elected officials and aspirants in both countries could not resist blaming foreigners for their own failings. Indians did not go quite as far as the revolutionary Iranians who in the 1980s identified the United States as the Great Satan, but Indians did discover in Americans convenient scapegoats for much of the evil that befell India. Facts of the matter lent themselves to exaggeration. The United States shipped weapons to Pakistan; therefore, as the Indian official cited above claimed, India's "whole military problem" was the United States' fault. The U.S. Congress was less forthcoming with assistance to India than with help for allies pledged to the American cause in the cold war; therefore, the United States was punishing India for its independence. American agents subverted governments in certain Third World countries; therefore, the CIA was behind civil unrest in India. Because India loomed less large on the United States' horizon than the United States did on India's, American critics charged India with proportionally fewer crimes; but many Americans had no doubt that Indian leaders, behind a facade of neutrality, were giving aid and comfort to the enemies of democracy. If Krishna Menon had not existed, American opponents of the U.N. would have had to invent him. In fact, they did to a considerable degree: the Menon they attacked often bore only a passing resemblance to the real article. Faulting foreign devils is politics' oldest device. Demagogues and less culpable characters in both the United States and India kept the device in active use.

That each country considered itself an exemplar to the world complicated matters further. American manifest destinarianism, though perhaps less virulent than in the nineteenth century, survived into the postwar era. As fully as ever, Americans believed their model of political development better than those of all competitors. Indians were not quite so prone to proselytizing, but they—Nehru especially—were convinced the planet would be a more peaceful place the more Asia and Africa followed India's nonaligned lead. Neither the United States nor India took kindly to the competing claims of the other.

Finally, the cultural and historical divide between Americans and Indians made genuine understanding nearly impossible. Americans looked at India and saw a country that in superficial respects resembled their own. India gained independence after a struggle with Britain; Indians practiced a form of government derived from British precedents; educated Indians spoke English. But most Americans missed the deeper India, the India whose roots as a civilization lay in an era when the United States had not been dreamed of by the peoples who would colonize it. Having won their own battle with imperialism two centuries before, and thoroughly Western themselves, Americans failed to understand India's sensitivity to anything that smacked of continuing colonialism or Western aggrandizement. Having weak neighbors, and having ruled religious communalism out of political bounds, Americans could not appreciate India's preoccupation with Pakistan as both a strategic and an existential threat. Having paid the cost of misjudging the world in the 1930s, Americans found incomprehensible India's imperviousness to the lessons of Munich and the arguments for collective security.

Indians should have had an easier time understanding Americans. There was less American history to unravel, fewer dark recesses to explore. But they did hardly better. Indians observed a discrepancy between American principle and practice—during the independence struggle of the 1940s, in the 1971 war—and accounted it as hypocrisy symptomatic of the whole U.S. approach to international affairs. Indians experienced American culture and judged it shallow and crass. Indians perceived in American actions in Vietnam and elsewhere an unseemly urge to neoimperialism. In such interpretations, Indians were not entirely wrong. Yet they were partly wrong, and their error did significant harm. Americans *are* hypocritical at times, but scarcely more than other people in other circumstances, and no more hypocritical than Indians themselves on occasion. American culture *can* be shallow and crass—but it also possesses an energy and an idealism that have helped make the United

States the most dynamic social and cultural organism of the twentieth century. The United States might have been guilty of neoimperialism in Vietnam, but the problem was less with motivation than judgment. To attempt to defend South Vietnam was not ignoble; to persist far beyond the point of diminishing returns—for Americans and Vietnamese both—was imprudent and destructive.

Because no disasters have befallen U.S.–Indian relations, none can be charged to the mutual failure of comprehension and the atmosphere of distrust it engendered. Such improvements as a more favorable ambience might have produced lay at the margins of the relationship—but they were hardly marginal in significance. Greater American understanding of Indians' worries regarding Pakistan, for instance, would have made Washington tread more gently in aiding India's rival. A cautious American policy would not have resolved the underlying conflict in the subcontinent, but it might have rendered war less likely. Nixon's deployment of the *Enterprise* in 1971 was an especially egregious trampling of Indian sensibilities; had the president and Kissinger not insisted on cutting the State Department out of the decisionmaking process, they might have understood that this needless action would set relations with India back a decade. A less provocative gesture would, at the minimum, have made it more difficult for New Delhi to ignore the nuclear nonproliferation treaty.

A recognition by Indian leaders of the constraints under which the United States, for all its global power, operated would have made New Delhi slower to take offense at American actions. America's recurrent tilt to Pakistan owed not to enmity toward India, but to a belief that the United States needed Pakistan's help in achieving its goals vis-à-vis the Soviet Union and China. Yet Indians interpreted America's rejection personally, as people do. Less haughtiness on Nehru's part toward American society and culture, even without any material shift in his policy, would have gone far toward encouraging the cooperation from which both sides would have benefited. As confirmed a skeptic as Loy Henderson conceded Nehru's overwhelming charm; with half an effort, the prime minister could have had Americans eating out of his hand—and perhaps more Indians eating more regularly. Had Indian office-seekers refrained from campaigning against the Pentagon and the CIA, the overall tone of the relationship would have improved markedly.

Especially in affairs between two open, democratic societies like the United States and India, tone and ambience matter. What is said in one country is heard in the other. Hearers have feelings—and votes. Voters follow their emotions as often as their interests. If elected leaders do not always heed voters' desires, they rarely rise above voters' prejudices.

That the divisive emotions and prejudices that have separated the United States from India, rather than the mutual interests that might have brought them together, have characterized the relationship ought to be a source of disappointment. Yet it need not be cause for discouragement, for people—the sources and objects of the feelings and misconceptions—can learn from experience, if they will.

Notes

1. Stephen P. Cohen, "Image and Perception in India–Pakistan Relations," in M. S. Rajan and Shivaji Ganguly, eds., *Great Power Relations, World Order and the Third World* (New Delhi: Vikas, 1981), 286–87.

2. Stimson in Reinhold Neibuhr, *The Structure of Nations and Empires* (New York: Scribner's, 1959), 264.

CHRONOLOGY

1947   March–June: Truman Doctrine and Marshall Plan announced. August: India and Pakistan gain independence; Kashmir fighting begins.

1948   January: Gandhi assassinated. July: Berlin blockade.

1949   March: Cease-fire called in Kashmir. April: Atlantic alliance created. October: Communist victory in China; Nehru visits the United States.

1950   January: India becomes a republic. Korean War begins in June; China intervenes in November.

1951   July: India's first five-year plan announced. August: India rejects Japan treaty.

1952   January: First Indian general election on basis of universal adult suffrage.

1953   Stalin dies in March; Soviet "peace offensive" commences in April. July: Korean War armistice declared.

1954   February: U.S.–Pakistani arms deal. May–July: Geneva conference. Zhou visits India in June; Nehru visits China in October. September: SEATO formed.

1955   February: Baghdad Pact signed. April: Bandung conference of Asian and African nations. July: Geneva four-power summit. Nehru visits Soviet Union in June; Khrushchev and Bulganin visit India in November.

1956   January: India's second five-year plan announced. July–November: Suez and Hungarian crises. December: Nehru–Eisenhower talks.

1958   March–August: United States makes major commitment to Indian development.

1959   April: Dalai Lama flees Tibet for India. December: Eisenhower visits New Delhi.

1960	April: Zhou visits India. December: Nehru–Eisenhower talks at the United Nations.
1961	December: India occupies Goa.
1962	October: Cuban missile crisis. October–November: Himalayan War.
1963	August: Partial nuclear test ban signed. November: Kennedy assassinated.
1964	May: Nehru dies.
1965	February–December: United States escalates war in Vietnam. August–September: India–Pakistan War.
1966	Indira Gandhi succeeds Shastri in January, visits United States in March.
1969	July: Nixon visits India.
1971	December: India–Pakistan War; Bangladesh created.
1972	April: Nixon visits China.
1973	February: Last U.S. troops leave Vietnam.
1974	May: India expands nuclear capacity.
1975	June: Gandhi declares state of emergency.
1977	March: Gandhi loses prime ministership to Desai.
1978	January: Carter visits India.
1979	January: Iranian revolution. December: Soviet invasion of Afghanistan.
1980	January: Indira Gandhi returns to premiership.
1981	June: Gandhi and China's Huang Hua meet in New Delhi.
1982	July: Gandhi–Reagan summit. September: Uprising in Punjab.
1983	February–September: Violence in Assam and Punjab.
1984	June: Indian army occupies Golden Temple. October: Indira Gandhi assassinated. December: Rajiv Gandhi elected; Bhopal disaster.
1985	March: Gorbachev comes to power in Soviet Union.
1988	April: Soviets pledge to withdraw from Afghanistan. Pakistan's Zia killed in airplane crash in August; Benazir Bhutto elected Pakistani prime minister in November, meets with Rajiv Gandhi.
1989	January: George Bush becomes President. February: Soviet troops evacuate Afghanistan. November–December: Contress Party rejected; V. P. Singh succeeds Gandhi.

SUGGESTIONS FOR FURTHER READING

Those interested in more information on U.S.–Indian relations should begin with one or a few of several general studies, most of which place the relations in a regional context. W. Norman Brown, *The United States and India, Pakistan, Bangladesh* (Cambridge, Mass.: Harvard University Press, 1972 ed.) is a classic, although it has less to do with the United States than the title implies. More succinct, and written with great vigor, is Stanley Wolpert, *Roots of Confrontation in South Asia: Afghanistan, Pakistan, India, and the Superpowers* (New York: Oxford University Press, 1982). William J. Barnds, *India, Pakistan, and the Great Powers* (New York: Praeger, 1972), a Council on Foreign Relations book, provides the view of the U.S. establishment. G. W. Choudhury, *India, Pakistan, Bangladesh, and the Major Powers: Politics of a Divided Subcontinent* (New York: Free Press, 1975), gives a solid accounting of events through the early 1970s. Norman D. Palmer, *The United States and India: The Dimensions of Influence* (New York: Praeger, 1984), covers ground closer to the present, updating his earlier *South Asia and United States Policy* (Boston: Houghton Mifflin, 1966). Selig S. Harrison, *The Widening Gulf: Asian Nationalism and American Policy* (New York: Free Press, 1978), sets U.S.–Indian relations against the broader backdrop of American dealings with Asia. Also deserving special note are Charles H. Heimsath and Surjit Mansingh, *A Diplomatic History of Modern India* (Bombay: Allied, 1971), an indispensable survey of Indian external affairs; and S. M. Burke, *Mainsprings of Indian and Pakistani Foreign Policies* (Minneapolis: University of Minnesota Press, 1974), an insightful comparison of the fractious neighbors. Another broad-gauged overview is A. Appadorai and M. S. Rajan, *India's Foreign Policy and Relations* (New Delhi: South Asian Publishers, 1985). Two annual publications of use are Shri Ram Sharma, *Indian Foreign Policy: An Annual Survey* (New Delhi: Sterling, 1971–); and Satish Kumar, ed., *Yearbook on India's Foreign Policy* (New Delhi: Sage, 1985–).

More specialized are Robert Jackson, *South Asian Crisis: India, Pakistan and Bangla Desh: A Political and Historical Analysis of the 1971 War* (New York: Praeger, 1975), particularly valuable for including as appendixes the leaked documents that proved so embarrassing to the Nixon administration; Ashok Kapur, *India's Nuclear Option:*

Atomic Diplomacy and Decision Making (New York: Praeger, 1976); L. P. Singh, *India's Foreign Policy: The Shastri Period* (New Delhi: Uppal, 1980); Larry W. Bowman and Ian Clark, eds., *The Indian Ocean in Global Politics* (Boulder, Colo.: Westview, 1981); Shashi Tharoor, *Reasons of State: Political Development and India's Foreign Policy under Indira Gandhi 1966–1977* (New Delhi: Vikas, 1982); Surjit Mansingh, *India's Search for Power: Indira Gandhi's Foreign Policy 1966–1982* (New Delhi: Sage, 1984); Mahendra Singh, *Indo–U.S. Relations, 1961–64: A Political Study* (Delhi: Sidhu Ram, 1982); and Robert J. McMahon, "Choosing Sides in South Asia," in Thomas G. Paterson, ed., *Kennedy's Quest for Victory: American Foreign Policy, 1961–1963* (New York: Oxford University Press, 1989), 198–222. Notable for their coverage of events from an Indian perspective are T. V. Kunhi Krishnan, *The Unfriendly Friends: India and America* (New Delhi: Indian Book Company, 1974); Baldev Raj Nayar, *American Geopolitics and India* (New Delhi: Manohar, 1976); S. C. Tewari, *Indo–U.S. Relations, 1947–1976* (New Delhi: Radiant, 1977); Ved Vati Chaturshreni, *Indo–U.S. Relations* (New Delhi: National, 1980); and P. K. Goswami, *Ups and Downs of Indo–U.S. Relations* (Calcutta: Firma, 1983).

For the period leading to Iranian independence, the most incisive works are Gary R. Hess, *America Encounters India, 1941–1947* (Baltimore: Johns Hopkins, 1971); two by M. S. Venkataramani and B. K. Shrivastava: *Quit India: The American Response to the 1942 Struggle* (New Delhi: Vikas, 1979), and *Roosevelt, Gandhi, Churchill: America and the Last Phase of India's Freedom Struggle* (New Delhi: Radiant, 1983); Diwakar Prasad Singh, *American Attitude towards the Indian Nationalist Movement* (New Delhi: Munshiram Manoharlal, 1974); and A. Guy Hope, *America and Swaraj: The U.S. Role in Indian Independence* (Washington: Public Affairs, 1968).

Cultural and intellectual connections between India and the United States form the subject matter of Robert M. Crunden, Manoj Joshi, and R. V. R. Chandrasekhar Rao, eds., *New Perspectives on America and South Asia* (Delhi: Chanakya, 1984); Robert M. Crunden, ed., *Traffic of Ideas Between India and America* (Delhi: Chanakya, 1985); and R. K. Gupta, *The Great Encounter: A Study of Indo–American Literature and Cultural Relations* (New Delhi: Abhinav, 1986). The last is especially illuminating for the nineteenth century. Joan M. Jensen, *Passage from India: Asian Indian Immigrants in North America* (New Haven: Yale University Press, 1988), examines the experiences of those who forged a human connection between the subcontinent and America. Harold Isaacs, *Scratches on Our Minds: American Images of China and India* (New York: John Day, 1958), investigates American perceptions.

On the Indian economy the essential survey is Francine R. Frankel, *India's Political Economy, 1947–1977: The Gradual Revolution* (Princeton, N.J.: Princeton University Press, 1978). P. J. Eldridge, *The Politics of Foreign Aid in India* (Delhi: Vikas, 1969), is dry but contains statistics on foreign assistance during the 1950s and 1960s not readily available elsewhere. W. W. Rostow, *Eisenhower, Kennedy, and Foreign Aid* (Austin: University of Texas Press, 1985), traces the development of American aid policy in two presidential administrations, placing special emphasis on assistance to India. Dennis J. Merrill, "Bread and the Ballot: The United States and India's Economic Development, 1947–1961," Ph.D. diss., University of Connecticut, 1986, covers the same topic during an overlapping period. Robert L. Paarlberg, *Food Trade and Foreign Policy: India, the Soviet Union, and the United States* (Ithaca, N.Y.: Cornell University Press, 1985), elucidates India's links to both superpowers.

U.S.–Indian relations have inspired countless conferences, often attended by both scholars and diplomats. Not infrequently, the sponsors of the conferences have gathered delivered papers and comments into volumes for publication. In other instances, editors have simply solicited articles and chapters from various individuals without bothering about getting together. Either way, the student of U.S.–Indian affairs gains the benefit of several points of view within a single set of covers. Among the best of such collections are B. R. Nanda, ed., *Indian Foreign Policy: The Nehru Years* (Delhi: Vikas, 1976); Bimal Prasad, ed., *India's Foreign Policy: Studies in Continuity and Change* (New Delhi: Vikas, 1979); John W. Mellor, ed., *India: A Rising Middle Power* (Boulder, Colo.: Westview, 1979); M. S. Rajan and Shivaji Ganguly, eds., *Great Power Relations, World Order and the Third World* (New Delhi: Vikas, 1981); Lawrence Ziring, ed., *The Subcontinent in World Politics: India, Its Neighbors, and the Great Powers* (New York: Praeger, 1982 ed.); Zalmay Khalilzad et al., *Security in Southern Asia* (New York: St. Martin's, 1984); K. P. Misra, ed., *Janata's Foreign Policy* (New Delhi: Vikas, 1979); and especially Lloyd I. Rudolph, Susanne Hoeber Rudolph, et al., *The Regional Imperative: The Administration of U.S. Foreign Policy Towards South Asian States Under Presidents Johnson and Nixon* (New Delhi: Concept, 1980).

Pertinent in tangential fashion are M. S. Venkataramani, *The American Role in Pakistan, 1947–1958* (New Delhi: Radiant, 1982); Robert H. Donalson, *Soviet Policy toward India: Ideology and Strategy* (Cambridge, Mass.: Harvard University Press, 1974); Latif Ahmed Sherwani, *Pakistan, China and America* (Karachi: Council for Pakistan Studies, 1980), a Pakistani view; and Yaacov Y. I. Vertzberger, *Misperceptions in Foreign Policymaking: The Sino–Indian Conflict, 1959–1962* (Boulder, Colo.: Westview Press, 1984).

Memoirs are irreplaceable, as long as the reader dodges the sparks from the grinding axes. The most detailed on the American side are Henry Kissinger, *White House Years* (Boston: Little, Brown, 1979); Richard Nixon, *RN: The Memoirs of Richard Nixon* (New York: Grosset and Dunlap, 1978); Chester Bowles, *Promises to Keep: My Years in Public Life, 1941–1969* (New York: Harper and Row); and John Kenneth Galbraith, *Ambassador's Journal: A Personal Account of the Kennedy Years* (Boston: Houghton Mifflin, 1969). Of less importance for matters touching India but worth a look for what they do contain are Dean Acheson, *Present at the Creation: My Years at the State Department* (New York: Norton, 1969); George McGhee, *Envoy to the Middle World: Adventures in Diplomacy* (New York: Harper and Row, 1983); Zbigniew Brzezinski, *Power and Principle: Memoirs of the National Security Adviser 1977–1981* (New York: Farrar, Straus & Giroux, 1983); Jimmy Carter, *Keeping Faith: Memoirs of a President* (New York: Bantam, 1982); Harry S. Truman, *Memoirs: Years of Trial and Hope* (Garden City, N.Y.: Doubleday, 1956); Dwight D. Eisenhower, *The White House Years* (Garden City, N.Y.: Doubleday, 1963–65); and George W. Ball, *The Past Has Another Pattern: Memoirs* (New York: Norton, 1982).

Indian first-person tellings include Indira Gandhi, *My Truth* (New Delhi: Vision, 1981); T. N. Kaul, *Diplomacy in Peace and War: Recollections and Reflections* (New Delhi: Vikas, 1979), and *The Kissinger Years; Indo–American Relations* (New Delhi: Arnold-Heinemann, 1980); Vijaya Lakshmi Pandit, *The Scope of Happiness: A Personal Memoir* (New York: Crown, 1979); K.P.S. Menon, *Many Worlds: An Autobiography* (London: Oxford University, 1965); K. M. Panikkar, *In Two Chinas: Memoirs of a Diplomat* (London: Allen and Unwin, 1955); Subimal Dutt, *With Nehru in the Foreign*

Office (Calcutta: Minerva, 1977); C. S. Jha, *From Bandung to Tashkent: Glimpses of India's Foreign Policy* (Madras: Sangam, 1983); and B. N. Mullik, *My Years with Nehru: The Chinese Betrayal* (Bombay: Allied, 1971).

Biographies of U.S. officials typically do not accord India much space. Lives of Indian leaders, by contrast, often pay close attention to relations with the United States. The most thorough and insightful biography of Nehru is Sarvepalli Gopal's three-volume authorized version, *Jawaharlal Nehru: A Biography* (Cambridge, Mass.: Harvard, 1975–84). Closer to the breathing man himself, with the attendant advantages and drawbacks, are Frank Moraes, *Jawaharlal Nehru: A Biography* (New York: Macmillan, 1956); and Michael Brecher, *Nehru: A Political Biography* (London: Oxford University Press, 1959). Moraes's is the insider's account; Brecher's is analytical. Zareer Masani, *Indira Gandhi: A Biography* (London: Hamish Hamilton, 1975); and Dom Moraes, *Indira Gandhi* (Boston: Little, Brown, 1980) deal with the heiress; the latter is more complete. Michael Brecher, *India and World Politics: Krishna Menon's View of the World* (New York: Praeger, 1968), gives the brilliant but difficult Menon a chance to speak his mind.

The basic collection of published U.S. documents is the State Department's *Foreign Relations of the United States* series (Washington: Government Printing Office), whose recent volumes include increasing numbers of items originating outside the State Department. Regarding India and South Asia, the series currently includes material dated through 1957. The *Public Papers of the Presidents* series (Washington: Government Printing Office) has White House statements, presidential remarks at press conferences, messages to Congress, and the like.

The Indian government has published numerous speeches of prime ministers, including *Jawaharlal Nehru's Speeches,* (New Delhi: Ministry of Information and Broadcasting, 1961–); and *Selected Speeches of Indira Gandhi* (New Delhi: Ministry of Information and Broadcasting, 1975–). Sarvepalli Gopal, ed., *Jawaharlal Nehru: An Anthology* (Delhi: Oxford University Press, 1980), extends beyond the years of Nehru's premiership. There exist several other collections of Nehru's writings; among the most useful is G. Parthasarathi, ed., *Jawaharlal Nehru: Letters to Chief Ministers, 1947–1964* (Oxford: Oxford University Press, 1985). Handy also is A. Appadorai, ed., *Select Documents on Indian Foreign Policy and Relations* (Delhi: Oxford University Press, 1982–). The indefatigable R. K. Jain has compiled several variously titled volumes of speeches, executive agreements, treaties, and communiqués dealing with India's relations with other countries.

Whatever it might do to the reader, the listing of titles here scarcely exhausts the literature. Hardy and ambitious souls should consult the notes and bibliographies found in the majority of the books cited, starting with the general surveys and working to the particular.

INDEX

ABOUT THE AUTHOR

H. W. Brands is an associate professor of history at Texas A & M University. He is the author of *Cold Warriors: Eisenhower's Generation and American Foreign Policy* and *The Specter of Neutralism: The United States and the Emergence of the Third World, 1947–1960*.